FORTRAN IV

IRWIN-DORSEY
INFORMATION PROCESSING SERIES

EDITOR   ROBERT B. FETTER   *Yale University*

FORTRAN IV

FRITZ A. McCAMERON
Director of Continuing Education
Louisiana State University

 Revised Edition • 1974

RICHARD D. IRWIN, INC. *Homewood, Illinois 60430*
Irwin-Dorsey International *Arundel, Sussex BN18 9AB*
Irwin-Dorsey Limited *Georgetown, Ontario L7G 4B3*

Revised Edition

First Printing, May 1974
Second Printing, June 1975
Third Printing, January 1976

ISBN 0-256-01582-1
Library of Congress Catalog Card No. 73–93357
Printed in the United States of America

Preface

FORTRAN IV is the most recently developed, widely used version of the FORTRAN language. Incorporating improved techniques of data input-output and logical control, version IV brings additional versatility to an already proven computer language.

WATFOR and WATFIV compilers, developed by computer scientists at Waterloo University have vastly enhanced the use of FORTRAN by permitting very fast in-core translation and execution of programs. This makes the FORTRAN language very attractive as an instructional tool, because most classroom problems can be compiled and executed very rapidly. This text presents FORTRAN IV as used with the WATFIV compiler.

Almost all FORTRAN IV instructional material is written for the scientist or engineer, a natural condition inasmuch as the language was created for use in these areas. At the same time, however, the language is also widely used in business administration and teaching. Its simplicity makes FORTRAN IV popular when an introduction to computers is desired, and many business firms use FORTRAN in data processing as well as in a problem-solving environment.

This book's purpose is twofold. First, it provides a basic introduction to FORTRAN IV in business administration and, through the terminology and examples used, makes the nature of the language comprehensible to the business student. Second, it suggests the business use to which a computer may be put.

This book is designed for use as a text in any business course in which FORTRAN IV is taught. It may be used alone in a one-hour course, or in a three-hour course in which the FORTRAN IV instruction constitutes a part of the material covered. It may be used with students at any level in college, although the higher numbered problems in each chapter may prove rather difficult for a beginning student.

This revised edition permits students to write executable programs sooner than did the first edition. Because students seem to learn much more about programming once they begin actual compilation and execution, the first material cycle is aimed at the earliest possible preparation of meaningful programs. Then, material slighted in this coverage is added to the student's store of knowledge.

This edition also gives additional emphasis to FORTRAN IV as a data-processing language. Statement headings are covered in greater detail than in the first edition. A discussion of list-directed processing with a section on object-time formatting has been added. Because direct-access file processing is coming to play such an important part in data processing, this subject is treated at length. Techniques of data sorting, record merging, and sequence checking are emphasized.

The text assumes the student to have no previous knowledge of electronic computers. Therefore, Chapter 1 contains a brief description of computers, and an explanation of a computer program.

Chapter 2 defines the nature of FORTRAN IV data. A firm understanding of computer-sensible data and related organizational requirements, which are rather different from the structure found in other types of data manipulation, is essential to a mastery of the language.

Basic Input, Output, and Control commands are covered in Chapter 3. This permits simple programs to be executed at this point, familiarizing the student with such matters as getting a program compiled, debugging, and the like.

The Arithmetic Assignment Statement is covered in Chapter 4 and basic conditional statements in Chapter 5. These lie at the very heart of FORTRAN IV. The mastery of the text material through this chapter equips one to program any computer-suitable problem, even though certain sophisticated processing techniques have not yet been introduced.

Chapter 6 treats advanced input-output topics. These include FØR-

MAT specifications not treated in Chapter 3, list-directed processing, and direct-access processing.

The DØ statement is discussed in Chapter 7. This command, while it does not add to the sum of the computer capabilities already covered, facilitates greatly the construction of looping routines. As such, the DØ statement is a great convenience in programming many business problems.

The nature of data arrays and array processing, so essential to the orderly manipulation of many kinds of data, is covered in Chapter 8. These topics are treated at some length because they are foreign to many business students, and because they hold a promise of new, efficient processing methods.

Chapter 9 introduces functions and subroutines. These are not basic to the FORTRAN language, and their study may be omitted if necessary. Effective programming does require that these techniques be used when very long programs are created, however, and a real understanding of FORTRAN must include their mastery.

This book is dedicated to my wife, Jeannine, and my daughter, Mary Hartley, who are responsible for all the worthwhile things I do.

April 1974   FRITZ A. MCCAMERON

Contents

1 Using the Computer with FORTRAN IV

The electronic computer is one of man's most significant inventions, and the ability to use a computer properly is a vital skill in modern business. Proper computer utilization requires a knowledge of programming. However, before one may hope to master programming, he must know something of the instrument he would command. Thus, a brief introduction to the electronic computer is in order before its use can be investigated.

INTRODUCTION TO ELECTRONIC COMPUTERS

The electronic computer may be considered first in the light of its similarity to other calculating devices. All such devices are designed to manipulate data of a quantitative nature. They accept data, make calculations, and emit results. A desk calculator is a good example of a typical calculating machine, and most now use electronic circuits similar to larger computers.

The electronic computer differs in several major respects from its smaller counterpart, however. The major difference is found in the method of control.

A small electronic calculator, like its mechanical and electrical predecessor, is controlled by an operator who initiates action by pressing

1

keys. While calculations may be made very quickly, overall machine effectiveness is limited by the speed and accuracy of the operator.

On the other hand, the electronic computer is equipped with an electronic storage, or "memory," large enough to contain very complicated processing instructions. These instructions are transmitted to the computer in advance of actual processing. Then, when processing is desired, control is transferred to the machine itself, which operates automatically at a very high speed.

The computer's ability to retain long, complex sets of instructions and execute them automatically has been extended to the control of many components, which may be located near the main computer or at some remote station. A major characteristic of the modern electronic computer is its growth from a single calculator into a data processing system.

Basic Computer Components

While electronic computers vary greatly in their operating characteristics, all such instruments have the same basic components. The modern electronic computer may be considered abstractly as it is depicted in Figure 1–1. Here the instrument is seen to consist of some input device, a storage or memory unit, an arithmetic unit, a control unit, and some device for emitting results.

Once again, it may be noted that simple calculators also have these components. In a typical desk calculator, the keyboard serves as the input unit through which both data and operational commands are en-

FIGURE 1–1
Basic Computer Components

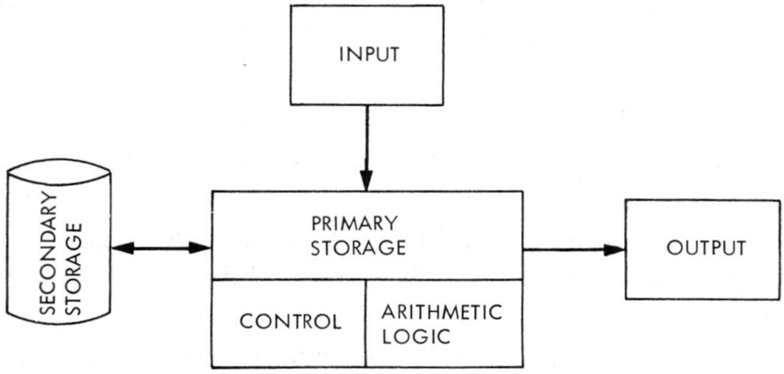

tered. The machine's memory unit is usually a set of wheels similar to an automobile odometer, or simple electronic circuitry. Machine control is effected through action keys and appropriate construction, and the output unit is usually a simple tape printer, counter wheels, or display lights.

Each of these components is much more complex in the electronic computer. Many components can be obtained in different forms at the user's option. Some of the more typical ones are described below.

Input. The input unit is used to enter the set of instructions, or program, and data to be used by the computer.

The unit may be as simple as an electric typewriter wired to the computer. Matter typed on the typewriter is transferred to the computer's memory unit in this instance. Many computers use this instrument as a low-volume input unit.

One of the most popular input units presently used is the punched card reader. Information punched in cards is transferred by the reader to the computer's memory. The punched card as an input medium will be discussed in detail in a subsequent chapter, and its use will be assumed throughout the text.

Another very popular input unit is the high-speed magnetic tape reader. This device is much faster than the punched card reader, and the tape serves as a more compact data storage medium than punched cards. Thus, it is commonly used when great masses of data are to be processed.

The relative speed and size advantages enjoyed by magnetic tape may be seen in the following comparison with punched cards. A punched card measures slightly more than seven inches by three inches and may contain as many as 80 characters of data. High-speed card readers can read something like 80,000 characters per minute from punched cards. On the other hand, one inch of magnetic tape may contain more than 1,000 characters and the tape reader may read more than 100,000 characters per *second*.

Modern computers also use many other input units. One, an optical scanner, can read man-sensible data such as regular printing. Other input units may be located far from the computer proper and may be used as computer input units (on-line) or as independent devices (off-line). Indeed, with the advent of touch-tone telephones, the common telephone has become one of the most useful computer input units available.

A single computer may have very many input units attached to it. Thus, it may serve as a data center with input units of various types located anywhere in the world.

Storage. The computer's storage unit serves two major purposes. It contains the set of instructions, or program, currently being executed by the computer. It also contains the data being manipulated—as they are read by some input unit or calculated by the machine itself.

The computer's storage, which may be imagined as a set of very many pockets, exists in the form of electronic devices. Each pocket can contain a single item, such as an instruction or an amount. The programmer can instruct the computer to store a certain bit of data at a particular memory location, and he can also instruct the machine to retrieve the data.

Actually, many modern computers contain two types of data storage units. One, called the primary memory, is designed to contain the program being executed and its necessary data. This memory usually has a storage capacity not exceeding 1,000,000 characters. Data may be entered or retrieved in a few nanoseconds (billionths of a second).

The other memory unit ordinarily has much larger capacity, and access to it is much slower. It is commonly capable of storing millions of characters of data which can be stored or retrieved in a few milliseconds (thousandths of a second) or microseconds (millionths of a second).

The large memory (called a secondary unit) is used to store great masses of data to which high-speed access is not important. For example, many firms use this unit for the storage of information pertaining to inventories, accounts receivable, or other operating data. Once called for, information can be retrieved in a few seconds. Thus, access is "slow" only when compared with the retrieval time of the primary memory.

The memory of modern computers is nonvolatile; that is, stored information will not automatically be erased by the passage of time or by reading it out or shutting off the machine. Data stored in memory are erased only by storing new information in the same location.

Control. The computer has a control unit capable of causing the execution of commands in the program. Each command is brought into the control unit and analyzed, and the computer is directed accordingly.

Commands are ordinarily executed in the sequence in which they are written and stored in memory; when necessary, however, this routine may be interrupted and the program may "branch" to some command not next in sequence. When all commands in a program have been executed, the computer may be made to stop or to return and repeat execution.

Arithmetic-Logic.   The arithmetic-logic unit lies at the very heart of the electronic computer. Data can be brought here and manipulated arithmetically. An electronic computer can add, subtract, multiply, and divide. These are its only arithmetic capabilities, but these can be done very quickly and may be repeated as many times as necessary. The computer can also determine whether two items are alike or not. This capability forms the heart of the computer's "decision-making" power.

Output.   Answers stored in the computer's memory are not available to its user. They must be communicated before they are comprehensible other than to the computer itself. For this reason, the computer's output unit is of great importance.

The output unit may be as simple as an electric typewriter, which might also serve as an input device. Greater masses of data will be written out on high-speed printers or magnetic tape units, however. An output unit of increasing popularity is the television screen. When this is used, contents of the computer's memory are displayed on the screen without being written in a permanent form.

A Computer Program

All computers have the ability to do a relatively few things. Basically, they can accept data (called reading), perform arithmetic, test data for type and magnitude, and write. These activities can be performed in different ways, and so a list of computer activities may contain about 50 discrete operations. For each operation there is an instruction.

A set of instructions is designed to cause desired computer operations. This set of instructions is known as a *program*. The program must be submitted to the computer before execution begins, for the machine's speed would be lost if it were forced to wait for operator control. Therefore, the full set of instructions is prepared in advance by the *programmer*. Only then is he ready to have his problem solved through the execution of his program.

Using the Computer

The process of using the computer can best be understood by a review of Figure 1–2. Here, the following sequence of activities may be seen:

FIGURE 1–2
Using the Computer

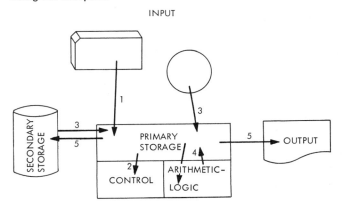

1. The program is entered through some input device. This assumes that the program has already been created by its programmer and reduced to a machine-sensible form, as by punching into cards.
2. When the entire program is stored in the computer's memory, execution begins. This involves transfer of each instruction to the control unit in its turn, at which time the computer is caused to perform the appropriate operation.
3. Under control of the program, data may be read from an input device. This may be the same unit used for reading the program, or some other instrument. Some programs may not require the reading of data but may contain all required information as parts of instructions. In this event, of course, this step would be omitted.
4. Data stored in the computer's memory may be subjected to arithmetic manipulation or logical evaluation. This involves transferring data from memory to the arithmetic unit and the return of the modified data to storage if necessary. This occurs under the control of the computer's program.
5. Finally, data may be output by writing on one of the computer's output units or transmission to secondary storage.

THE FORTRAN IV LANGUAGE

As computers evolved over the past two decades, programming languages were found to have two major defects. First, all programming schemes involved the use of complex numerical codes. The codes were difficult to remember, and programs tended to become quite long because each instruction governed a fairly small step in the computer's operational process. A second defect arose from the requirement that the programmer assign all used computer memory segments.

Furthermore, the programming scheme of each computer was different. This made it most difficult for one to master the programming requirements of several computers, and impossible to create a set of instructions that would control more than one machine.

To correct these programming defects, a language was devised that was machine independent in the sense that a program could be written for execution by many different computers. The language also eliminated numerical codes and direct memory assignment and permitted the combination of several small machine oriented commands into one instruction. This language was called FORTRAN, coined from the words FORmula TRANslation. FORTRAN IV is the most recent version of the language available.

FORTRAN was originally devised as a scientifically oriented language and is still used mainly in the sciences. As it exploits all a computer's capabilities, it is currently being used in business administration data processing as well as in scientific computation.

Using FORTRAN

As mentioned above, FORTRAN IV is the most recent version of the FORTRAN language, and it contains several extensions of the basic model. However, FORTRAN IV is used in the same way as earlier levels of the language. The following explanation applies to all FORTRAN versions.

Actually, commands written in the FORTRAN language cannot be used as such to control a computer. A FORTRAN program must first be translated into the computer's own operational codes, called its machine language. After this process, which is called *compilation,* the computer may execute its machine language program.

The FORTRAN program (called the *source program*) is compiled into the machine language or *object program* by the computer itself. Thus, the computer is used as a tool in converting the FORTRAN commands into a usable set of instructions.

A third set of commands is encountered in the compilation process— the translator program. This governs the conversion of the source program into its object counterpart. In the process, it causes the computer to check for programming errors and provides the programmer with information, called *diagnostics,* concerning the validity of his instructions.

Thus, the process of using FORTRAN is as depicted in Figure 1–3 (unless WATFOR or WATFIV is used, as explained below). First, the translator program is entered into the computer's memory. It then controls compilation. The source program is entered and translated into the object program.

FIGURE 1–3
Compiling a FORTRAN Program

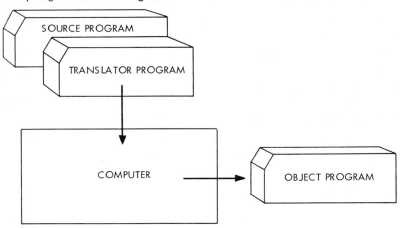

Some computers have primary memories large enough to contain both the translator and object programs. In this event, the object program is not written out unless it is to be used later; instead, it is compiled and used immediately.

Translation into machine language may be effected very rapidly, and the computer user need not even be aware of its occurrence. Therefore, one quickly comes to think of the FORTRAN program as *the* computer program and ceases to be concerned with the process of translation.

WATFOR and WATFIV Compilers

Several years ago, computer scientists at Waterloo University of Canada created a very compact, efficient FORTRAN translator. It was named WATFOR, coined from the term WATerloo FORtran. This translator permitted programs written in an early form of FORTRAN to be translated into object form for execution very quickly, without the necessity of writing the program out of primary storage and subsequent re-entry. It was called an "in-core" compiler, because the WATFOR translator and the object program were maintained in the computer's memory, or core storage, throughout the latter's compilation and execution. This greatly accelerated the speed with which short programs were handled by the computer, and was very widely used.

With the wide acceptance of FORTRAN IV, Waterloo University computer scientists have created a new compiler. This is named WATFIV, taken from the phrase WATerloo Fortran IV. It serves FORTRAN IV translation as its predecessor did basic FORTRAN and FORTRAN II, causing in-core compilation for rapid processing. Many computer centers now use the WATFIV compiler.

All problems and programs in this text can be processed by this very useful translator, and all programs can also be translated by the WATFOR compiler, except those so indicated in Chapters 6 and 8. However, whether compilation occurs by use of FORTRAN IV, WATFOR, or WATFIV translators, the FORTRAN coding language is virtually the same. Any minor differences are noted at appropriate places in the text. Therefore, all subsequent references will be made to FORTRAN, and unless modified, this implies FORTRAN IV as acceptable to FORTRAN IV, WATFOR, and WATFIV compilers.

Writing a FORTRAN IV Program

Programming is the process of causing a computer to serve in the solution of a problem. It is similar to any other activity where tools must be used properly. First, one must be familiar with the nature and use of his tools—in this instance, the computer and its programming language. Next, he must have a thorough understanding of his objectives. This text's purpose is to provide an introduction to the tools embodied in the FORTRAN IV language.

FORTRAN IV Statements. The FORTRAN IV language consists of computer commands called *statements.* These are illustrated in Figure 1–4. Statements are of five general types:

1. Input. These, called *read statements,* cause the computer to accept data from an external source. Data are read from *records;* these may be recorded on punched cards, magnetic tape, or any other appropriate medium.

2. Arithmetic. The arithmetic statement is the computer's computational command. It may take on many different forms and may command a very complex computation.
3. Output. A computer must communicate the results of its calculations. This is caused by output commands, commonly called writing instructions, which can transmit information from the computer to a printer, a television screen, or some other device.
4. Control. FORTRAN includes several control commands. These are used to cause the computer to stop, or to make logical decisions, or to act in some way other than following the normal, sequential process.
5. Finally, the language includes specification statements, which provide the compiler with information about the nature of the data to be processed, in addition to supplying data on computer storage utilization.

These types of commands are mutually exclusive. It is not possible to perform arithmetic while reading data, nor may writing occur during computation. Control statements are also of such a nature that they cannot be executed while reading, computation, or writing is being carried on.

Illustration of a FORTRAN IV Program.   To illustrate the nature of a FORTRAN IV program, assume that interest amounts are to be computed for a group of notes receivable. The principal amount of each note has been punched into a card, with its life expressed in days. An identification number is also included in the record. The interest rate on all notes is 6%.

The resulting FORTRAN program may be seen in Figure 1–4. Line identification numbers are shown in positions 73–75 on the far right as 010, 020, 030, etc.

Essentially, this program commands the computer in much the same way as a clerk might be instructed when interest is to be calculated. On line 030 of the program is found the instruction

$$10 \qquad READ(5,1,END=20)N\emptyset,PRIN,TIME$$

This commands the computer to read an input record from input unit 5 according to design (called FØRMAT) 1 and look for three items of data on it. The three items of data are identified by name as NØ (the identification number), PRIN (principal), and TIME (the note's life).

FØRMAT 1, the statement immediately above the READ command,

FIGURE 1-4
Computing Interest

IBM

FORTRAN CODING FORM

X28-7327-6 U/M 050
Printed in U.S.A.

| PROGRAM | FIGURE 1-4 | | | | PAGE | OF |
| PROGRAMMER | McCAMERON | DATE | | | CARD ELECTRO NUMBER* | |

| PUNCHING INSTRUCTIONS | GRAPHIC | | | | | |
| | PUNCH | | | | | |

FORTRAN STATEMENT

C/COMMENT	STATEMENT NUMBER	CONT	FORTRAN STATEMENT	IDENTIFICATION SEQUENCE
C			EXAMPLE ØF A FØRTRAN PRØGRAM	010
	1		FØRMAT(I4, F7.2, F3.0)	020
	10		READ(5, 1, END=20)NØ, PRIN, TIME	030
			XINT = PRIN * .06 * TIME / 365.	040
			WRITE(6, 2)NØ, PRIN, XINT	050
	2		FØRMAT(5X, I5, 5X, F9.2, 5X, F7.2)	060
			GØ TØ 10	070
	20		STØP	080
			END	090

indicates that the first data item may be found in the first four positions of the input record, the second item in the following seven positions, and the third in the next three places. Thus, the READ and FØRMAT statements work together and control input.

The input unit designated may be whatever is used in the particular computer center. Therefore, the appropriate assignment varies according to the computer being used. In this example, input unit 5, the standard IBM and WATFIV card reader designation, is cited.

The READ instruction also contains the clause END=20. This means that, if no more input records are available when the computer attempts to execute the READ command, it is to go to statement 20 for its next instruction. This is a *conditional* control clause—when input records are available the computer is directed to one set of instructions, but it is sent to another when they are not.

The FORTRAN IV statement on the line 040 is an arithmetic command. It is of the form

$$XINT=PRIN*.06*TIME/365.$$

and instructs the computer to calculate interest by the standard equation, Interest equals Principal times Rate times Time. The product is called XINT.

Statements on lines 050 and 060, working together, control output. They appear as follows:

WRITE(6,2)NØ,PRIN,XINT
2   FØRMAT(5X,I5,5X,F9.2,5X,F7.2)

The statement on line 050 instructs the computer to write out the note's identification number, NØ, and the principal amount, PRIN, as well as the amount of interest calculated, XINT. This is linked by the computer with the sixth instruction, indicating the appearance, or format, of the output. Output unit 6 is used for writing.

The command on line 070,

GØ TØ 10

is a control instruction. It tells the computer to go to statement 10 next.

Statement 10 is the READ command; thus, the computer is commanded to repeat the process of reading, computing, and writing. The program will continue to be executed until no more input records are available.

When this happens, the END=20 will sense that the computer cannot read another record, and will transfer the program to statement 20 for the computer's next instruction. This is the command

20   ST∅P

Accordingly, the computer is released from the control of this program and available for any other program awaiting execution.

Lastly, the command END is not a command the computer executes as part of the program. It simply indicates the end of the FORTRAN IV language.

Using the FORTRAN Coding Form

A FORTRAN IV program consists of a series of statements. The program is written, or coded, on a special form. It is then punched into cards, an action transforming the program into a machine-sensible form for entry into the computer.

To insure that the statements are punched correctly, the proper use of the coding form is important. Figure 1–4 illustrates a coding form in common use. This should be inspected before attempting actual coding.

In Figure 1–4, the body of the form may be seen to consist of several lines. Each FORTRAN IV statement is written on a different line. This is essential because each statement will be punched into a different card. Thus, each line on the coding form is the equivalent of a punched card. Figure 1–5 illustrates a standard IBM card containing the fourth statement of the program from Figure 1–4.

FIGURE 1–5
A FORTRAN IV Statement

Each horizontal line of the coding form is divided into small spaces by small vertical marks on the line. Each space may contain one character.

Larger vertical marks on the line divide the coding form further into writing areas. Each writing area has a special purpose and is discussed below.

Positions 1–5.   The first five positions on the coding form are reserved for statement numbers. Statements themselves must never be written in these positions or punched in these columns on cards. If no statement number is used, the positions are left blank.

The first position serves another purpose as well. A "C" in this column indicates that the remainder of the line contains a "comment" statement. This is not a true FORTRAN statement but is merely a comment that will be printed with the program. The comment may occupy any positions through column 72. It permits the programmer to make brief comments about his program. The first line of Figure 1–4 contains such a comment.

Position 6.   Statements are sometimes so long that they exceed the writing positions available on a single line. When this occurs, the statement is continued on the next line and some character other than zero is written in column six of that line. Thus, column six is used only when statements are continued to more than one line. The number of lines to which statements may be continued varies from computer to computer.

Positions 7–72.   The actual statement is written in these positions. As mentioned above, each character—letter, numeral, or other symbol—occupies a separate position. Long statements may be continued to more than one line by use of the continuation column.

Positions 73–80.   Line identification numbers may be written here if desired, or any other identifying information may be included. These are not a part of the program, but merely serve to code the statements for reference purposes. A standard way of identifying statements is by numbers such as 010, 020, 030, etc., representing the lines one, two, and three. The trailing zero position makes easy the insertion of additional statements in order, as 011, 012, and the like.

Writing the FORTRAN IV Statement

In coding the FORTRAN IV statement, certain writing requirements must be observed.

Statement Numbers.   A FORTRAN IV statement need not be assigned a number unless some other statement refers to it. In Figure 1–4, both the FØRMAT statements were assigned statement numbers because they were referenced by either the READ or WRITE statement. The READ statement was also assigned a number because the GØ TØ statement referred to it, as was the STØP command because of its reference in the END=conditional. As might be expected, all statement numbers must be different.

The general rules governing statement numbers are:

1. The statement number may appear in any of the positions 1–5. It need not be left-justified.
2. Statement numbers may be used with all statements. Each number must be unique.
3. Statement numbers must be unsigned, unpunctuated integers. Unless a particular computer imposes some other restraint, they must be not more than five characters long or of maximum size 99999.
4. Statement numbers need not be consecutive, nor must they be used sequentially.

Writing Style.   Statements are always printed in capital letters. Care must be taken in printing certain characters because of their similarity to others. Therefore, the following characters are printed in the indicated manner:

Letter	Numeral
I	I or 1
Ø	0
Ƶ	2

It is most important that the letter "I" be printed with serifs head and foot to distinguish it from the numeral one which may be written as "1." Likewise, the letter "Ø" must always have a slash through it to differentiate it from the numeral 0.[1] The letter "Ƶ" is also slashed, making it easy to distinguish from the numeral "2."

Of course, all characters must be printed as clearly as possible. Other symbols that may be mistaken for one another are the letter S and the numeral 5, the letter C for the left-hand parenthesis, and the slash for the right-hand parenthesis.

Spacing.   With minor exceptions, which are pointed out at the appropriate time, spacing within a statement is not required. For instance,

---

[1] Some computer centers reverse this convention, and slash the numeral rather than the letter. In practice, the rule of the particular center should prevail.

GØ TØ 10 may be written as GØTØ10, and XINT = PRIN * TIME / 365. * .06 may be written as XINT=PRIN*TIME/365.*.06, or any combination of spaces may be used. However, spacing does greatly improve the statement's readability.

Order of Execution.   Ordinarily, statements are executed in the order in which they are written on the coding sheet, just as one reads English. When it is necessary to interrupt this order, a special control statement must be used. In Figure 1–4, for example, the program proceeds to line 070, where the order must be changed. At that point the instruction GØ TØ 10 is encountered, causing the program to transfer to statement 10 which happens to lie above. Likewise, the END=conditional causes a jump to statement 20, written several instructions below.

CHAPTER SUMMARY

The basic purpose of this text is to provide an understanding of FORTRAN IV. However, this may only be done if the reader is aware of the nature of the electronic computer, described as a device having one or more input units, a memory unit, an arithmetic-logic unit, a control unit, and some output ability.

While this could also describe the common desk calculator, the major difference between an electronic computer and its electromechanical counterpart is found in the computer's very large memory and internal control capability. It is controlled by an internally stored set of instructions called a program.

The basic nature of a computer program is quite simple. Programs consist of a group of different instructions used at the proper time to achieve the desired results. Learning to program, then, is actually a dual undertaking. First, one must master the fairly simple characteristics of computer instructions. Second, the very difficult task of determining when to use a particular instruction must be given attention. This is never really completed, and it contains the challenging and creative aspects of computer utilization.

The FORTRAN IV language was devised in an attempt to create a programming method capable of exploiting the computer's abilities, yet easy to learn and use. It achieves these ends handsomely and provides a language similar to that of ordinary algebraic manipulation.

The balance of the text explores the nature of FORTRAN IV, and the illustrations and problems suggest ways of using the language in a business environment.

QUESTIONS

1. How does an electronic computer differ from an electronic calculator?
2. What are the two major types of computer data storage?
3. What are the functions of the computer's input units?
4. What are the basic types of FORTRAN statements?
5. What is WATFOR? WATFIV?
6. What is the difference between a source program and an object program?
7. What is a FORTRAN statement number?
8. Why are statement numbers used?
9. Must each FORTRAN statement have a number? Which statements must be numbered?
10. What may be written in space one of the FORTRAN coding sheet?
11. What may be written in spaces 1–5 of the FORTRAN coding sheet?
12. What may be written in space six of the FORTRAN coding sheet?
13. In what spaces may FORTRAN statements be written?
14. Must spaces be left between the components of a FORTRAN statement?
15. In writing FORTRAN statements, how is the letter O differentiated from the numeral 0? The letter I from the numeral 1? The letter Z from the numeral 2?

EXERCISES

1. Assuming the logic of the following statements to be sound, indicate the error or errors (if any) in each:

```
C           EXERCISE 1-1
2           FORMAT (F3.2, F3.0)
25    READ1, SALE, TAX
           GRØSS=sale + tax
           WRITE(6,2) GRØSS
2          FORMAT( F5.2)
           GØTØ25
END
```

2. Assuming the logic of the following statements to be sound, indicate any errors in the use of statement numbers:

STATEMENT NUMBER		FORTRAN STATEMENT
50		FORMAT(F7.2,F5.2)
10		READ(5,15)GROSS,DISC
12.5		XNET = GROSS - DISC
12X		WRITE(6,10)XNET
100		FORMAT(F7.2)
10		GO TO 25
		END

2 The Nature of FORTRAN Data

In the main, computers solve problems by accepting data from some external source, performing necessary processing steps, and emitting answers. Computers recognize three types of data. They are:

1. Numeric. This class includes quantitative data, represented by the numerals 0 through 9 and an arithmetic sign. The character set includes the decimal in certain instances.
2. Alphabetic. This type consists of data represented by the letters A through Z and the space.
3. Alphanumeric. The alphanumeric group includes data symbolized by alphabetic or numeric characters. In addition, certain special symbols such as parentheses, the comma, and the dollar sign are recognized.

These three types of data are shown in Figure 2–1 as they appear when punched in card form suggestive of the coding systems used by other electronic devices. To the left is shown the alphabetic character set; in the center the numeric; and on the right certain special characters. All are included in the alphanumeric system.

Most data processed by FORTRAN programs are numeric in nature; alphabetic or alphanumeric data items are more rarely found. Therefore, unless otherwise instructed, all data referred to in this text may be assumed to be numeric.

FIGURE 2–1
Three Types of FORTRAN Data

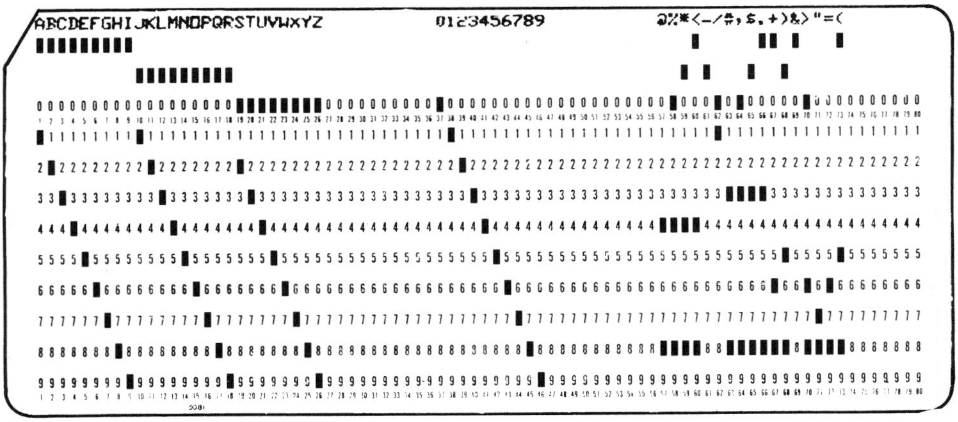

This concentration on numeric data, arising from the fact that FORTRAN was devised for use in a scientific environment, by no means makes the language unusable in business data processing. As a matter of fact, much of the data processed in business is numeric in nature and FORTRAN can handle the small amount of alphabetic and alphanumeric data manipulation required.

The FORTRAN language embraces a very elaborate numeric structure consisting of two systems: integer and real. Briefly, the integer system includes only whole numbers, while the real system includes all real numbers. These numeric systems are discussed below. Alphanumeric data systems are considered later in the chapter.

THE INTEGER SYSTEM

As its name implies, this number system admits only whole numbers, and its character set is restricted to the numerals 0–9 and the plus and minus sign. It is also called the "fixed-point" system.

Values may be either positive or negative. If positive, the number is ordinarily left unsigned; negative values are indicated by a minus sign as their leftmost character.

Computers vary in the magnitude of the numbers they can process. For example, the IBM 360 and 370 series can handle an integer of up to 10 positions, the largest number being 2147483647 ($2^{23}-1$), and the same limit is found in WATFIV. This may be either positive or negative.

Statement numbers and other FORTRAN control values must be integers. Data may also be in integer mode, although the inability to handle decimal fractions precludes the form's use in many instances.

Examples of valid integers are:

$$1975$$
$$123456$$
$$-208$$

The following integers are invalid:

1,000	(Includes nonnumeric symbol)
1.234	(Decimal not allowed)
1234.	(Decimal not allowed)
123—	(Minus sign in wrong place)

THE REAL SYSTEM

The real or "floating-point" numeric system gets its name from its ability to recognize all real numbers, including those containing decimal fractions. It provides a more versatile means of data representation than does the integer method. For this reason, it is frequently used when values are to be manipulated arithmetically.

Real Number Characteristics

Values in the real number system must contain some indication of their decimal place. This is usually done by using a decimal point. The letter "E" or "D" may be used to denote an exponent and the decimal point may be omitted, although this is seldom used in business processing. Thus, floating-point numbers are easily recognized by the presence of a decimal point or by the use of an exponent.

The Character Set. The floating-point system includes in its character set the numbers 0–9, arithmetic signs, and the decimal. As mentioned above, in some cases the letter E or D may also be used.

Size Restrictions. The size of a floating-point number must be viewed in two ways. The first refers to the number of digital positions, or *significant digits,* the value contains. The second refers to the number's magnitude.

The maximum number of significant digits a valid floating-point number may have depends on the computer used. The IBM 360 and 370 computer series, and WATFIV, will accept up to seven significant digits in a single precision operation and up to 16 positions in double precision.[1] This means that in single precision, a number may have no more than seven significant places. Therefore, in single precision, the largest number that may be written in *standard* form is 9,999,999. Double precision, allowing 16 places, is capable of showing more significant digits in larger (and smaller) numbers, but its capacity is still limited.

The E Notation. The *magnitude* of a value may exceed the capacity of its significant digital positions, however. When this happens, the value is written as mantissa and exponent. For example the value 1,000,-000,000, containing too many significant digits for regular representation in single-precision form, may be written as 10^9.

It is not possible to record computer-sensible numbers that show the exponent above the mantissa. Therefore, a form of writing is used where the mantissa is written in the regular way and is followed by the letter "E" and then the exponent. Therefore, 10^9 would be written for the computer as 1.0E9.

Use of the exponent permits the representation of very large or very small values. In the IBM 360–370 and WATFIV systems, the value may vary from 10^{-78} to 10^{75}.

No more than seven significant digits may be written, excluding the exponent. Therefore, if the value 12345678912345 were to be written, it would be shown as 1234568.E7. This, in turn, would be read as 12345680000000. While the location of the decimal has been retained, the value of the least significant digital positions is lost.

When the E notation is used, the mantissa may or may not contain a decimal. If the decimal is not shown, it is assumed to lie to the right of the mantissa. Thus, the values 12345.E6 and 12345E6 are the same. Written decimals are treated in standard fashion; for example, the value 1.2345E4 is the same as 12345. A sign may be shown to the left of the mantissa; negative values must have a minus sign; and unsigned values are assumed to be positive.

The exponent must always be preceded by the letter E. It must be an

---

[1] Single and double precision refers to the computer's construction and its systems programs. Double precision simply allows more significant digits to be carried in memory and computation than single precision does. Single precision will be assumed throughout this text unless double precision is expressly specified.

integer constant and may be signed or unsigned. If unsigned, the exponent is assumed to be positive. A sign, if used, must appear immediately after the letter E and before the integer representing the exponent's magnitude.

A positive exponent indicates how many places to the right of the written decimal the true decimal is assumed to lie, while a negative exponent determines the number of places to the left. For example, 12345.67E4 would be read as 123456700., while 12345.67E—4 would be read as 1.234567. The sign of the exponent has nothing to do with the sign of the mantissa, which determines whether the value is positive or negative.

Double Precision Values.   Double precision numbers permit more significant digits to be carried in a value than is possible when single precision values are used. The exact number of places carried in the double precision form varies from one computer to another, but it is ordinarily about twice the number of places carried in single precision.

Double precision values may contain a maximum of 16 significant positions in 360–370 FORTRAN and WATFIV. Significant digits in the number must be followed without intervening space by an exponent notation of the nature "D±ee," in which "D" specifies the value as being double precision and "ee" indicates the proper location of the decimal place. If the sign of the exponent is positive, the decimal must be moved to the right the number of places specified by "ee;" if negative, "ee" indicates the number of places to the left the decimal should be moved. The notation "ee" must always be some integer constant.

The exponent may be shortened under certain circumstances. If the exponent is positive, its sign may be omitted. Further, the leading zero may be omitted if the value of the exponent is less than 10.

Examples of Floating-Point Values

Floating-point values falling within the range of single precision representation appear as follows:

1234567.

1234.

.1234

12.34

123456.7

—123456.7

—.1234567

Each number, even a whole number, includes a decimal point. Also, the minus sign, when used, occupies the leftmost position; positive values are usually unsigned. No punctuation other than the decimal is permitted. Seven *digital* positions are permitted; the sign and decimal are not counted as significant positions.

The following are invalid as real single precision values:

1234	(Does not contain a decimal)
—1234	(Minus sign not correctly located)
$12.34	(Contains an invalid character)
1,234.	(Contains an invalid character)
123456789.	(Too many positions)

Examples of valid E-notation values follow:

Value in E Notation	Should Be Read as
12345.E3	+12345000.
.12345E3	+123.45
—.12345E+3	—123.45
—12345.E—4	—1.2345
.12345E—4	+.000012345
—.12345E6	—123450.
12345E—5	+.12345
—1234567.E—10	—.0001234567

Some examples of double precision values are shown below:

Example No.	Double Precision Value	Should Be Read as
1.	.123456789123D+14	+12345678912300.
2.	.123456789123D3	+123 .456789123
3.	.123D—3	+ .000123
4.	—.123D2	—12.3
5.	—.123D—2	—.00123

In Example 1, the exponent of a positive number is written out in full. Example 2 shows a similar exponent, written in shortened form. In Example 3 a negative exponent is depicted, making clear the difference between a negative value and a negative exponent. This distinction may be seen in Examples 4 and 5 also. It may be noted that the exponent in double precision and E notation is basically the same.

Most values are of such a nature that they may be adequately represented by computers with either single or double precision capability, and so the E notation is not frequently employed. It is available for the representation of extremely large or small values, however, and may be useful in computations such as are found in statistics.

METHODS OF NUMERIC VALUE REPRESENTATION

There are two ways to represent both integer and floating-point values. A quantity may be symbolized by a data name or it may be itself present. The first is called a variable; the second, a constant.

Variables

When the magnitude of a value may change, it is referred to by name rather than by amount. Thus, the value is known as a *variable*.

Several variables were mentioned in the illustration of a program in Chapter 1, which for convenience is repeated in Figure 2–2. For example, in the FORTRAN statement

10   READ(5,1,END=20)NØ,PRIN,TIME

NØ, PRIN, and TIME are variables. Presumably, more than one input record is being processed, and while these data items will assume one set of values with one input, they will quite probably represent some other set of values with another input record. Thus, the amounts of principal and time must be symbolized by assigning names rather than by specifying certain values. As will be seen in Chapter 3, all values read in from records must be called for by name rather than by setting some amount.

Again, in Figure 2–2 the statement

XINT=PRIN*TIME/365.*.06

cites the variables PRIN and TIME, and also introduces a new variable, XINT. This computational command is considered in Chapter 4 where it is shown that XINT is the name of the "receiving area" for computation and must always be specified as a variable.

Distinguishing between Floating-Point and Integer Variables. Both integer and floating-point values may be represented by variable names. Therefore, some means must be had for indicating to the computer whether the variable is in integer or floating-point mode. This distinction is usually made by the first character in the name. If the variable name begins with any letter A through H or Ø through Ƶ, it is under-

FIGURE 2-2
Example of a FORTRAN IV Program

IBM

FORTRAN CODING FORM

X28-7327-4 U/M 050
Printed in U.S.A.

| PROGRAM | FIGURE 2-2 | | GRAPHIC | | PAGE | OF |
| PROGRAMMER | M.C. CAMERON | DATE | PUNCHING INSTRUCTIONS | PUNCH | CARD ELECTRO NUMBER* | |

STATEMENT NUMBER	CONT.	FORTRAN STATEMENT	IDENTIFICATION SEQUENCE
C		EXAMPLE OF A FORTRAN PROGRAM	010
1		FORMAT(I4, F7.2, F3.0)	020
10		READ(5, 1, END=20)NO, PRIN, TIME	030
		XINT = PRIN * .06 * TIME / 365.	040
		WRITE(6, 2)NO, PRIN, XINT	050
2		FORMAT(5X, I5, 5X, F9.2, 5X, F7.2)	060
		GO TO 10	070
20		STOP	080
		END	090

stood to be a floating-point item. Should the name begin with I through N, it is known to be an integer. This rule may be abridged by a "type statement" discussed below.

In the program example in Figure 2–2, PRIN is used to represent principal, TIME is used to represent the life of the note, and XINT is the amount computed as interest. These all represent floating-point values. NØ, representing the identification number, is an integer variable.

Naming Variables. To this point, variable names have been used without considering the rules governing their formation. These rules are set out below and must be observed:

1. A variable name may contain from 1 to 6 characters.
2. The first character *must* be a letter, and the remaining five characters, if used, may be either letters or numbers.
3. The name may contain *only* letters and numbers.
4. Floating-point variables must be assigned some name starting with one of the letters A through H or Ø through Ƶ unless a modifying type statement is used.
5. Integer variables are assigned a name starting with some letter I through N unless a modifying type statement is used.
6. Names differing in any one character are considered totally different.

Examples of Variable Names. A few examples of floating-point variable names are given below:

A	X4	ACCT
XBAR	STD	DEBIT

On the other hand, for the reasons indicated, the following are not acceptable floating-point variable names:

MEAN	(Does not begin with an appropriate letter)
1A	(Does not begin with a letter)
ACCØUNT	(Too long)
A B	(The intervening space is an invalid character)
A.B	(Invalid character)
I22	(Does not begin with an appropriate letter)

Integers might be assigned names such as the following:

K	NØ	INDEX
KA	M14	ITEM

The data names listed below are not valid integer variable names:

4K	(Does not begin with a letter)
ITEM-X	(Invalid character)
PK	(Does not begin with an appropriate letter)

When possible, it is desirable to assign variable names suggestive of the nature of the represented data. This makes the program more readable and makes it somewhat easier to remember the purpose of particular instructions when they are reviewed later.

This is done in the example in Figure 2–2. PRIN is used to represent principal, and TIME is used to represent the life of the note. The interest is computed as XINT. This might have been called INT, but the value calculated most likely contains a decimal fraction and may not be represented by the name of an integer variable. Therefore, the name is modified to floating-point form.

It is possible to modify the requirement that real variable names must begin with one of the letters A through H or $\emptyset$ through $\mathbb{Z}$ and that integer names must begin with some letter I through N. This is accomplished through the use of a *specification statement.*

Specification Statements. These are special statements that indicate the nature of data being processed where this would not be done properly by the variable's name alone. Because its function is to describe a variable, the specification statement must always precede the first use of the variable in the program.

FORTRAN contains several specification statements, which will be introduced throughout the text as appropriate. Two, called "type statements," must be considered at this point because they modify the rules controlling data-name assignments. These are the REAL and INTEGER statements discussed below.

Using Type Statements to Specify Variable Mode. Two type statements are available for controlling the mode of a single precision variable. They are

$$\text{INTEGER } a_1, a_2, \ldots, a_n$$
$$\text{REAL } i_1, i_2, \ldots, i_n$$

where "a" is any floating-point variable name and "i" is any integer variable name. If more than one data name is specified, commas must be used as separators.

As an example of these two type statements, assume that data names A and X are to be used to represent integer values and the data name

INT is to represent a floating-point value. The following type statements would be used to declare the appropriate mode:

INTEGER A, X
REAL INT

These type statements are very useful in converting data names suggestive of an item's nature to the appropriate mode. For example, assume that the variable UNITS is to represent the number of units of some item sold but that for output purposes it is required as an integer value. The type statement INTEGER UNITS would convert this item to integer mode and it would be so treated throughout the program.

Double Precision Variables. A double precision value is always considered to be of floating-point mode. Double precision variables must be identified in some manner, however, and so a specification statement is used to declare the data-item's form.

The DØUBLE PRECISIØN Statement. The specification statement designating variables to be of double precision form is as follows:

DØUBLE PRECISIØN $a_1, a_2, \ldots, a_n$

As in the specification statements above, *"a"* represents a variable name.

One or more variables may be specified as being double precision in a single DØUBLE PRECISIØN statement. When more than one variable is included in the list, commas are required as separators.

Examples of DØUBLE PRECISIØN statements are shown below:

DØUBLE PRECISIØN A, IBEX, Y
DØUBLE PRECISIØN ITEM

It may be recalled that by definition, the double precision variable is of floating-point mode. Therefore, once identified in the specification statement, the double precision data name may begin with any letter.

Like all specification statements, the DØUBLE PRECISIØN statement must precede the first use of the variable name in an executable command.

Constants

A computer program may use quantities that do not change. Such a value is known as a *constant* and is represented by itself rather than symbolically by some data name.

Constants are used in computation or in certain control commands. They may never be read in or written out.

Real Constants. A single precision real constant is some number in the program which contains a decimal to the left, right, or between its digits. In the statement

$$XINT=PRIN*TIME/365.*.06$$

drawn from the illustrative program in Figure 2–2, both 365. and .06 are floating-point constants. So long as this statement is used, these values cannot change. This may be contrasted with a variable, where an item is represented symbolically and where the value of the item may change from time to time as new amounts are read in or computed.

Real constants follow the rules set out above for real values. They may contain up to seven significant digits in the single precision form of FORTRAN and about 16 positions in double precision mode. Unless the D or E exponent is used, they *must* contain a decimal, which may be to the left or right of the numerals, or lie between two digits. A decimal omitted from an "E" or "D"-type constant is assumed to lie to the right of the least significant digit.

The constant is left unsigned if positive; a negative value is indicated by a minus sign as the leftmost character.

Double Precision Constants. A double precision constant is some real number containing a "D" exponent. In discussing the nature of double precision data above, the value .123456789123D+14 was given as an example. This typifies a double precision constant.

The double precision constant may contain approximately 16 significant positions, the exact number of places depending on the computer used. A decimal may be omitted, on it may appear to the left, right, or between significant digits. The true location of the decimal is indicated by the exponent. A sign, if used, appears as the leftmost character. Signs are optional with positive constants but required with negative values.

Integer Constants. These must conform to the rules of the integer number system. For the IBM 360–370 and WATFIV, they may contain up to 10 digits and *must not* contain a decimal. Other size limits may apply to other computers. A minus sign is written immediately to the left of a negative number; positive numbers are left unsigned.

Integer constants may be used as data in FORTRAN, and they also serve as parts of the instructions themselves. For example, all statement numbers must be integer constants, and a review of the programming illustration in Figure 2–2 will find this rule applied.

THE LOGICAL DATA SYSTEM

Another kind of data is available for processing in FORTRAN IV. This is called "logical data." It may be read in, tested, assigned logical values, or written.

Like numeric data, logical items may be present as constants or variables.

Logical Constants

The two logical constants are:

.TRUE.
.FALSE.

These are the only logical constants in the language. When written, they must be immediately preceded and followed by periods as shown above to distinguish them from variable names.

Logical Variables

These are variables which have been assigned a logical nature by the type statement described below.

The LOGICAL Type Statement.   Before a logical variable can be cited in an executable command, its nature must first be established in a type statement. This is of the form

LØGICAL $a_1, a_2, \ldots, a_n$

where "a" represents a variable name. Any number of variables may be declared of logical nature in the same type statement, using commas to separate the items in the list. The type statement must appear in the program before the logical variable is cited in an executable command.

Variable Name.   Like any other variable name, the logical name may consist of from one to six characters, the first character being alphabetic. Because the nature of the variable is specified by the type statement, however, its first letter is not restricted and may be any alphabetic character.

Values Assigned to Logical Variables.   A logical variable may only assume the values .TRUE. or .FALSE. The value may be assigned by reading it in or by the evaluation of a logical expression.

Example of Logical Data.   As an example of the input of logical data, assume that two logical values, A and B, are to be read in. The type statement, format statement (described in Chapter 3), and read command might appear as follows:

$$\text{LØGICAL A, B}$$
$$1 \qquad \text{FØRMAT(L5,L5)}$$
$$\text{READ(5,1)A,B}$$

The LØGICAL statement indicates that variables A and B are of logical mode. The FØRMAT statement defines the fields for the logical values. The READ statement commands the computer to read a record containing two variables, A and B. Taken together, the three statements cause the definition and input of logical data.

CHAPTER SUMMARY

The nature of FORTRAN data may appear to be somewhat different from information commonly considered in business problems, although the difference really lies in the method of defining the data rather than in the data items themselves.

In FORTRAN, numerical data are considered to be of two types: integer and real. Integer data items are always whole numbers; inasmuch as many kinds of quantitative business information may not be represented by such numbers, this kind of representation is of somewhat limited use. Real values may contain decimal fractions and are frequently used for business data representation. Double precision values are a special form of real numbers and permit a larger number of significant positions to be carried than is possible in the single precision mode.

Within the divisions of integer and real data, elements may also be classed as variable or constant. Variable data items are those which can assume different values at different times, depending on the results of input or computation commands. Constant items are assigned a value in the program, which never changes.

The logical data system is a recent addition to the FORTRAN language. It includes logical constants and variables and, as will be seen in subsequent chapters, permits the creation of logical expressions. This data system allows the computer to be easily used in areas of symbolic logic.

Later chapters will indicate that both numerical and nonnumerical values are essential to proper computer utilization and that variables and constants will be employed according to the needs of the particular operation. A knowledge of basic data characteristics is essential to a mastery of the FORTRAN commands that follow.

Summary of FORTRAN Statements

This chapter introduced the following FORTRAN statements:

INTEGER $a_1, a_2, \ldots, a_n$
REAL $i_1, i_2, \ldots, i_n$
DØUBLE PRECISIØN $x_1, x_2, \ldots, x_n$
LØGICAL $x_1, x_2, \ldots, x_n$

In the statements above *"a"* represents a data name starting with some letter A–H or Ø–Z; *"i"* represents a data name starting with some letter I–N; and *"x"* a data name starting with any letter. The purpose of each specification statement is to declare the mode of the variable when not indicated by the data name itself.

QUESTIONS

1. What are the three types of data? Which type is most commonly processed by FORTRAN programs?
2. What is the integer numeric system? How many numeric positions may an integer have?
3. What is the real numeric system? How many significant digits may a real number have?
4. Is the magnitude of a real number limited by the number of significant digits it contains? Explain the meaning of "significant digits."
5. What is the "E" notation?
6. What is the relation between the double precision and real numeric systems?
7. What does the exponent of a double precision number indicate?
8. How are double precision variables distinguished from single precision variables?
9. Name and give the use of the specification statements introduced in this chapter.
10. May double precision variables start with a letter of the set I through N?
11. What is a logical constant? Give two examples.

12. What is a logical variable?
13. How are logical variables distinguished from arithmetic variables?
14. What is a variable?
15. How are integer and real variable names distinguished from each other?
16. How many characters can a data name contain?
17. What characters are acceptable in a data name?
18. May a constant be cited as a data item in an input command? An output command?

EXERCISES

1. Each of the following is legitimate in some aspect of FORTRAN. Indicate what each item may be:
   - (a) −12345
   - (b) X12345
   - (c) .TRUE.
   - (d) 123E+4
   - (e) .0002
   - (f) DALLAS
   - (g) 1975
   - (h) 1975.
   - (i) ALPHA
   - (j) NEW
   - (k) READ
   - (l) XIJKL
   - (m) .1234E−6
   - (n) ID6
   - (o) 1D6

2. Indicate the error(s), if any, in the following data names:
   - (a) A-14
   - (b) BØSTØN
   - (c) CHICAGØ
   - (d) 1X
   - (e) END
   - (f) DØL-$
   - (g) X25Y
   - (h) A2.1
   - (i) STØP
   - (j) XYZ3

3. Write each of the following values without the E notation:
   - (a) 1234E4
   - (b) 456.789E−3
   - (c) 1.E7
   - (d) .004E−3
   - (e) 1.E−3

4. Indicate which of the following are not legitimate real constants:
   - (a) 1975
   - (b) 3.1416
   - (c) +6E4
   - (d) 1.234−
   - (e) 0−1234.
   - (f) 25.4M
   - (g) 16D
   - (h) A20
   - (i) 12345678912
   - (j) 0

5. Indicate which of the following are not legitimate integer constants:
   - (a) −1234
   - (b) −123E6
   - (c) X17
   - (d) 22K
   - (e) I24
   - (f) 1234−
   - (g) +123
   - (h) 123.4
   - (i) 0−123
   - (j) 0

6. Several values written in double-precision form are given below. Write these as they would appear in regular single-precision notation (for example, item 0 would appear as 12345.).

0.	.12345D+05
a.	−.12345D−3
b.	.12345D−4
c.	−123.45D−3
d.	123.45D3
e.	12345D−5

7. Assume that a FORTRAN program is to use the data names given below in the manner cited:

Data Name	*Manner of Use*
ABEX	Logical
INCH	Real
LB	Integer
RØD	Integer
DØLR	Double Precision
TØN	Real

Give the specification statements necessary to provide proper definition.

8. Assume that a FORTRAN program is to use the data names given below in the manner cited:

Data Name	*Manner of Use*
FØØT	Real
MILE	Integer
YARD	Logical
PØUND	Double Precision

Give the specification statements necessary to provide proper definition.

3 Basic Input, Output, and Control Commands

The computer is ordinarily considered a calculating machine, and of course it was for the purpose of computation that the instrument was devised. However, data must be submitted to the computer and computational results retrieved in useful form if the machine is to serve its purpose. Further, certain control instructions are necessary to permit the programmer to guide the computer.

This chapter covers some basic means of data handling and computer control. The instructions permit simple programs to be written, and they can be executed if desired. More sophisticated input-output and control instructions are discussed in Chapters 5 and 6.

DATA ORGANIZATION

Any computer use requires certain facts as the raw material with which the machine is to operate. These facts, or data, must be organized before they can be submitted to the computer, and the results of computation must also be arranged in an orderly manner for transmission from the machine to its user. Thus, some knowledge of data organization is essential to effective input and output.

In data processing, particular facts are called *data items* or *data elements*. These are grouped in some rational manner into sets called *records*. Sets of records of similar nature are called *files*.

As an example of data organization, consider the type of information gathered in a typical firm for the computation of employees' gross pay where hourly rates are used. Assume that the following facts must be available for each employee:

1. Employee identification number,
2. Pay rate,
3. Hours worked,
4. An indication as to whether overtime is to be paid at an advanced rate or not.

These facts constitute data elements. Data on a particular employee will be grouped in a record. The set of records for all employees comprises the pay file.

Data Elements.   A data element is a basic fact not amenable to further subdivision. Just what is to be considered a data item in a given situation is largely a matter of choice. For example, an address might be used as a data item or it might be further subdivided into street, city, and state. The computer user may define as data items whatever units of information are meaningful in the particular circumstance.

FORTRAN programs are primarily designed to process numeric data, although nonnumeric information can also be handled. The numeric data items may be in either floating-point or integer mode, as defined in Chapter 2. Logical and alphanumeric data may also be processed. All types may be intermixed in any fashion.

Records.   A record may contain any series of data items. The data elements will have some logical relation to each other; therefore, this is properly called a *logical record*.

Records may contain fixed locations for their data items; in this case they are designated as having a *fixed format,* and are called *formatted records.* In other instances the data items are simply allowed to occupy whatever space they require in the record. These are considered to have *free format,* and are called *unformatted* records.

The computer is able to recognize the nature of an item only by its location in the record or position in the sequence of data elements. Computers cannot "tell" a date from an amount, or a person's name from his address, for example, except by noting where the item appears in the record or its position in the sequence of data items. Recognition of this limitation is essential when organizing and processing records.

Punched cards are frequently used to record input records. Because the punched card has only 80 recording positions or columns, this is the maximum number of characters the fields in the record may contain. Output records may frequently contain more characters; this depends on the unit used to process them.

To illustrate the nature of the record and its data elements, assume that the employee pay information introduced above has been analyzed as follows:

1. Identification number: a five-place integer value.
2. Pay rate: a five-place number, with three places to the right of the decimal.
3. Hours worked: a three-place number, with one place to the right of the decimal.
4. Overtime indicator: a one-place logical variable.

A punched card record designed as in Figure 3–1 contains the information for a single employee. The four data fields occupy adjoining columns. This is the typical design structure.

The floating-point fields for recording the pay rate and hours worked do not contain a space for punching the decimal. Decimals are not ordinarily recorded in input data; instead, their location is provided by the FØRMAT statement described below.

FIGURE 3–1
A Data Record

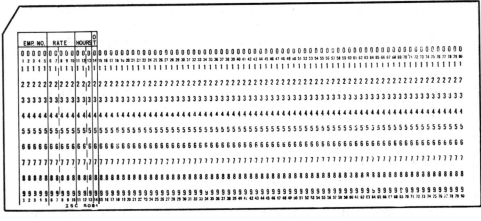

An inspection of Figure 3–1 indicates that most of the punched card containing the input record is unused. This is quite often the case, for it is normally not desirable to maintain two records on the same card.

Files.   A file is a set of records, grouped by some common characteristic. For example, student records might be grouped in the transcript file, or records pertaining to employees in the personnel file.

Business data processing is in large part a matter of handling data files. Records must be updated with the results of events, and so "file maintenance" becomes an important operation. Preparation of business information frequently requires that data from two or more files be merged to give particular meaning to events, or records in a file must be rearranged, or sorted, to highlight descriptive characteristics. An orderly data system, in which data items exist in records, which are components of files, is essential if the myriad business facts are to be reduced to useful information.

FORTRAN INPUT-OUTPUT COMMANDS

Input and output commands in FORTRAN cause the computer to read an entire input record or write an entire output record. It is not possible to read or write part of a record, nor (with the exception of data arrays) is it possible to read or write files at a single execution of an instruction.

The READ Command

The basic input instruction is of the following nature:
Command Structure.

$$k \qquad \text{READ}(i,j)list$$

In this input statement, k represents an optional statement number, i represents an unsigned integer constant referring to the input unit used in reading the record, j represents the FØRMAT number, and *list* represents the list of variable names to be read. Input unit number and FØRMAT number are enclosed in parentheses.

Input units are assigned numbers by the computer manufacturer, and the input unit number must be obtained from the manufacturer for any particular machine. In this text "5" will be used to designate the input unit in all examples. This is the IBM 360–370 and WATFIV designation of the card reader.

Specifying Data Names.   All values are read in as variables; that is, they are assigned names and are referred to by name rather than as constants. Therefore, the READ command must contain a data name for each data item to be read on the input record. Single-precision numeric names must conform to the mode of the data being read unless a type statement is used. Double precision and logical variables may begin with any letter. Within these limits, any name may be used so long as it is unique.

Data names in the READ command must appear in the same order as the input record's data items. Names refer to data items starting from the left and continuing to the end of the record on the right. Data items in the input record may be in any sequence, and so the names may also appear in any order.

Example of the READ Command. Figure 3–1 depicts an input record containing four items of data relating to employee payroll. The first data item is the employee's identification number. In designing an input statement, this is assigned an integer name, inasmuch as it is not a decimal quantity. Second in the input record is the employee's pay rate, which is assigned a floating-point name as is the third item of data, the hours worked. The last data item is a logical variable and is so designated by a type statement. Once it has been identified as a logical item, its name may begin with any letter.

Names such as NØ, RATE, HØURS, and ØTME are suggestive of the type of data contained in the input record and so are used to identify the variables.

Using these names, the statements necessary to define, describe, and read a logical record would appear as in Figure 3–2.

FIGURE 3–2
The READ Command

COMM.	STATEMENT NUMBER	CONT.	FORTRAN STATEMENT
			LOGICAL ØTME
	1		FØRMAT (I5, F5.3, F3.1, L1)
	10		READ(5, 1, END=50) NØ, RATE, HØURS, ØTME

The LØGICAL type statement declares the variable ØTME to be of logical mode, as discussed in Chapter 2. The FØRMAT statement, described later in the chapter, indicates the nature and size of data fields. Finally, the READ command instructs the computer to read a logical record and assign to the data elements contained therein the data names cited in the statement list. The statement number assigned the READ command is optional.

Punctuating the READ Command. The READ command must contain a comma between the input device number and the FØRMAT statement number and also between items in the list of data names. No other punctuation is permitted. Spaces may be left between the elements of the command (command name, input device number, FØRMAT number, and data names), but this is not required.

Effect of the READ Command. Execution of the READ command causes a record to be read and its contents transferred to the computer's memory. There, data items are stored at locations that are given the names of the variables designated in the input command. After executing the READ command in Figure 3–2, the first employee's identification number will be stored in the computer's memory at a location called NØ. Pay rate and hours worked are stored at locations RATE and HØURS respectively. A symbol indicating overtime status will be stored at ØTME. Thus, data names are really computer memory addresses.

Once the values of data items have been read into the computer's memory, they are not destroyed until some new value is stored at the location, either by reading or by computing. Only one value may be associated with a data name at a time, however, and so a subsequent read or computational command does erase the contents of the computer's memory. For example, if two commands

$$READ(5,1)NØ,RATE,HØURS,ØTME$$
$$READ(5,1)NØ,RATE,HØURS,ØTME$$

were written and executed in that order, the values read and stored by the first would be erased by the values read by the second. Thus, it is said that reading is *destructive:* the process erases any values previously stored at the named data locations.

The END Option. FORTRAN IV (and WATFIV) permits the recognition of an end-of-file condition by inclusion of the END option in the READ command. When used, it causes the READ statement to appear as follows:

$$READ(i,j,END=k)list$$

i and j are input-unit and format numbers, as described previously. k represents the statement number to which the program is to transfer when no more input records are available for reading.

The END option is illustrated in Figure 3–3. Here, the computer is instructed to read an input record and perform certain simple processing steps. However, should no record be available for reading, the program is to transfer to statement 50. There the computer is instructed to halt by the STØP command, described later in the chapter.

Using the READ Command.   As will be seen later in this chapter, computers may be made to execute the same program more than once in a processing run. If this is done, a READ command may be executed with each repetition, reading similar records.

Complex programs may contain more than one READ command, and each may refer to a different design and set of data. In a payroll processing situation, for example, the program is almost certain to refer to at least two sets of information—current pay data and historical data. When this occurs, the program will contain more than one READ command. This is quite acceptable and adds to the flexibility of the computer's use.

The WRITE Command

The output instruction transmits data from the computer's memory to the designated output unit. It is of the following nature:

Command Structure.

$$k \qquad \text{WRITE}(i, j)list$$

where i and j are unsigned integer constants. As in the READ command, the first specifies the computer unit to be used and the second the FØRMAT number. k represents an optional statement number.

The effect of the WRITE statement depends on the output device selected. Cards will be punched if the designated unit is a card punch. By the same token, the output may be written on a printer or transmitted to a tape unit or some other device. The use of output unit 6, a printer, will be assumed throughout this text, in conformance with IBM 360–370 and WATFIV standards.

Specifying Data Names.   Only data names may be included in the output list; it is not possible to write out constants by including them in the output instruction. *The variables listed in the command must have previously been "defined";* that is, they must have been assigned a value by either reading or calculating.

Data names may appear in any order in the output list.

Punctuation Requirements.   A comma must be used to separate the output unit designation and the FØRMAT statement number, and commas must separate the data names in the list of variables. As in the READ command, spaces may be left between elements of the command, although this is not required.

Example of the Output Command. Figure 3–1 contains a copy of an input record containing four data items: employee number, pay rate, hours worked, and overtime indicator. Figure 3–2 provides a command for reading these items, using data names NØ, RATE, HØURS, and ØTME, for the respective fields.

Assume that a listing of these records is desired. It is to contain only employee pay rates and employee numbers, in that sequence. A program for preparing such a list appears as Figure 3–3.

FIGURE 3–3
Using the WRITE Command

COMM.	STATEMENT NUMBER	CONT.	FORTRAN STATEMENT
			LØGICAL ØTME
	1		FØRMAT(I5, F5.3, F3.1, L1)
	2		FØRMAT(1X, F6.3, 5X, I6)
	10		READ(5, 1, END=50) NØ, RATE, HØURS, ØTME
			WRITE(6, 2) RATE, NØ
			GØ TØ 10
	50		STØP
			END

In this program, an input record is first read. Then, by citing the desired variable names in the proper order, the appropriate data items are written. The control statement, GØ TØ 10, is discussed below. Its effect is to cause the computer to return to statement 10 for its next instruction where the READ command is again encountered. Then, the next statement, WRITE . . . will be executed, the GØ TØ 10 will transfer, and so on, until all input records have been processed. Then, the END option of the READ command will transfer control to statement 50, where the program will halt.

Effect of the Output Command. It was noted earlier in the chapter that the READ instruction is destructive; that is, its execution destroys values previously stored at locations cited in the list of variable names. This is not true of output commands. The act of transmitting a value to an output unit does not disturb that item in the computer's memory at all. It is still available for use in computation, for other writing, or for any other use. The value will remain unchanged until it is redefined by reading or computing a new quantity.

DESCRIBING DATA IN FORTRAN

In very simple data handling situations, items in the input or output data list may appear in free form. Data elements are separated from one another by spaces or punctuation. In this instance, the input and output records are *unformatted*. In most business processing, however, a record may contain several data items of various types, occupying adjacent positions in the record. These records are called *formatted*. Some means must be available to describe to the computer just how these records should be treated. This is the function of the FØRMAT statement, one of the major FORTRAN instructions.

The FØRMAT Statement

Unless unformatted input-output is used, every input and every output command must refer to a FØRMAT statement. The FØRMAT statement may be written anywhere in the program, above or below its related input or output command. More than one input or output statement may refer to the same FØRMAT.

The FØRMAT statement is of the general form

$$k \qquad \text{FØRMAT}(s_1, s_2, s_3, \ldots, s_n)$$

where k represents the FØRMAT statement number and s represents a FØRMAT specification. The FØRMAT statement in Figure 3–2 would be appropriate for the record depicted in Figure 3–1, and in Figure 3–3 may be seen the FØRMAT statement used in writing the desired output.

The FØRMAT Number

Each FØRMAT statement must have a number, written in the coding space provided for statement numbers. This serves as the link relating the FØRMAT statement to its input or output statement. The number must be an unsigned integer constant and must be different from all other statement numbers. This is illustrated by the example cited earlier in the chapter, and the following FØRMAT and READ statements are given in Figure 3–2:

```
 1        FØRMAT(I5,F5.3,F3.1,L1)
10        READ(5,1,END=50)NØ,RATE,HØURS,ØTME
```

A similar relation exists between output and FØRMAT statements, as may be seen in Figure 3–3.

FØRMAT Specifications

The nature, location, and field size of data in the input or output record is indicated by the FØRMAT specification. These specifications must follow the statement name in the FØRMAT command, and all specifications are surrounded by a set of parentheses. An example of specifications may be seen in Figure 3–3.

The specifications must define the record, starting from the leftmost recording position through all used fields. It is understood that successive FØRMAT specifications define successive record fields, not allowing for any skips. Unused positions to the right of the record may be ignored.

Specifications are available for the definition or numeric, logical, and alphanumeric data fields, and also provide for the transmission of alphanumeric messages. Simple numeric and logical specifications are described in this chapter. More sophisticated specifications are covered in Chapter 6.

Defining Integer Fields: The I Specification

A data field which is to contain integer data is defined by the specification

$$I_w$$

where w represents the field width or number of positions. Thus, in Figure 3–2, the first field specification is I5, meaning that the field defined is to contain integer data and that it is five positions wide. Inasmuch as this is the first FØRMAT specification, it refers to the first five positions of the record.

In the specification, w must be an unsigned integer constant (such as 5, in the example above). The maximum field size depends on the computer used; on many computers it may be as large as the record length. Thus, if the record is in a punched card, I80 would be the largest specification allowed.

The Relation between I FØRMAT Specifications and Data

The nature and width of each data field in the input or output record is controlled by a specification in the FØRMAT statement. Input records must be prepared in conformity with the FØRMAT specification, and output records will be constructed by the computer according to FØRMAT requirements. The following rules govern the recording of data in input records and the appearance of data in output.

Input Requirements. A field may be as small as I1 or as large as I80 (for card records). In the actual input record, data may be recorded anywhere in the field. However, if the data are not right-justified in the field, zeros are filled into the unused positions to the right. Thus, in a field defined as I5, a value recorded as b12bb (where "b" stands for blank) would be treated as 1200.

An input amount may be left unsigned, in which case it is assumed to be positive. A sign, if used, must lie immediately to the left of the most significant data digit.

The maximum number of positions of data that may be read in by IBM 360–370 computers is 10, regardless of the FØRMAT specification (other computers have other limits). When a space is allowed for a sign, the maximum usable number of positions in the 360–370 input document is 11; a FØRMAT specification of more positions implies the existence of unused positions to the left of the input field.

Examples of I FØRMAT specifications and the treatment of field contents are provided in Figure 3–4.

Output Requirements. The output field specified may be wider than required by the data to be written; in this instance, the output is automatically right-justified. Making the FØRMAT field specification too large insures spacing between data elements and enhances readability.

The field specification must be large enough to contain the output data. Using a field too small causes an error. Furthermore, the leftmost position in an output field must be reserved for the sign when writing negative data. Thus, where negative data may be written, the minimum field size is $c + 1$, where c represents the number of positions of actual data.

Illustrations of the I Specification. Assume that a specification of I6 is used to read and write data. The results of processing certain data are shown in Figure 3–4. "Input Value" represents the input value as it exists in the input record. "Stored Value" shows how the amount would appear in the computer's memory when read by an I6 specification;

"Output Value" indicates how the amount would appear when written again by the I6 specification; "b" represents a blank in the field.

FIGURE 3-4
Examples of the I FØRMAT Using Specification I6

Input Value	Stored Value	Output Value
012345	012345	b12345
bbb123	000123	bbb123
123bbb	123000	123000
+12345	012345	b12345
−12345	−12345	−12345
1.2345	*	
bbbbb0	0	bbbbb0
0bbbbb	0	bbbbb0
bbbbbb	0	bbbbb0
—	−123456	†

* Error: field may not contain any character other than numerals, with optional sign in leftmost position.
† Error: output field too small for sign and significant digits.

Defining Single Precision Floating-Point Fields: The F Specification

A data field to contain single precision floating-point data is defined by the specification

$$F w.d$$

where w indicates the width of the field and d the number of places to the right of the decimal. For example, the second specification in Figure 3–2, F5.3, indicates a five-position floating-point field with three positions assumed to lie to the right of the decimal.

The letter F, indicating the nature of the specification, and the decimal must be used just as indicated. Unsigned integer constants must be used as w and d.

Numerous examples of the F specification may be found in Figure 3–5.

The Relation between F FØRMAT Specifications and Data

Input Requirements. The FØRMAT specification can call for a field of any width from a single position up to the maximum size of the record. It need not allow any places to the right of the decimal, or it may provide any number of places—even more than the width of the field itself in some FORTRAN systems. Thus, specifications such as F8.0, F4.4, and F6.8 are all valid. Many more examples may be seen in Figure 3–5.

In preparing input data, the decimal is not ordinarily written because its location will be indicated by the FØRMAT specification. Instead, all field positions are used for data. For example, using the input record described in Figure 3–1, a pay rate of $4.125 per hour would be recorded as 04125. The position of the decimal is supplied by the related FØRMAT specification of F5.3, meaning that in the five-place field, three places are to be assumed to lie to the right of the decimal. Thus, the rate punched as 04125 would be interpreted as 04.125.

Input data may have the decimal actually recorded. When this occurs, the written decimal overrides the FØRMAT specification. For example, assume that in a field defined as F5.3 were punched the amount 12.50. In this case, the punched decimal will override the FØRMAT designation and the computer will read the value as 12.50. This may also be seen in lines 8 and 9 of Figure 3–5.

An unsigned data value is assumed to be positive. A negative value is indicated by a minus sign to the left of the most significant digit in the value. Line 2, Figure 3–5, shows the proper treatment of negative values.

Arithmetic signs and written decimal points occupy data positions. Therefore, a data element so punctuated can contain fewer digits in any given field than an unsigned data item without a decimal.

The width specification in the FØRMAT statement may exceed 7; however, only seven data positions will be read from the input record. These will be the seven most significant positions recorded in the field. For example, assume that a value 1234567891234 is read from an input record under the FØRMAT specification F13.8. The value would be stored as 12345.68, using the most significant positions in the data field. The proper magnitude of the number in the data field will be determined even though the decimal lies outside the eight positions; for example, a FØRMAT specification of F13.3 would cause the above value to be read as 1234568000. This is also illustrated on line 15 of Figure 3–5.

Output Requirements. Determining the appropriate size of a single precision floating-point output field is somewhat more complicated than establishing the dimensions of an integer field. Three elements must be given consideration: the number of answer positions to the left of the decimal, the number of places to the right of the decimal, and punctuation requirements.

1. *Places to Left of Decimal.* The FØRMAT specification must be large enough to permit the output of the largest amount which might be written in the field. A size deficiency will cause an error condition to be noted, and the answer will not be written. Line 11, Figure 3–5, contains a FØRMAT specification adequate for input but inappropriate for output because too few positions are allowed to the left of the decimal.

On IBM 360 and 370 computers, and WATFIV, one very important rule sets a minimum on the number of integer recording positions. One digital position to the left of the decimal should always be provided, even when the value to be written cannot possibly use it. This is not the position provided for the sign discussed below, but an extra position allocated exclusively to digital output. For example, the computer must be able to write a decimal fraction, such as .25, in the form 0.25. Other examples of incorrect and correct field sizes are shown on lines 18 and 19 of Figure 3–5.

The computer is unable to "borrow" positions from the right of the decimal and use them on the left, even if they are available. Thus, a basic determinant of field size is the size of the integer portion of the anticipated output.

2. *Places to Right of Decimal.* This depends entirely on the wishes of the programmer. He can allow as many or as few places as he wishes. If the computer carries a value to more places than allowed for in the output FØRMAT, the extra places will be truncated by the machine without notice. Whether or not the computer will round into the least significant retained position depends on the machine and the version of FORTRAN being used. Zeros will be written in any extra places. These points are illustrated in lines 10 and 16 of Figure 3–5.

3. *Punctuation Requirements.* A field specified as F FØRMAT and used for output must provide *two* positions for punctuation: one for the decimal, and one for the sign. *This is always required.* Failure to satisfy the requirement results in output errors such as those shown on lines 5 and 6 of Figure 3–5. While decimals and signs may not be used in input, they must be allowed for in output. The sign will not be written if the value is positive. The decimal will always be written.

Thus, the proper field size may be computed as $c + d + 2$, where c represents the maximum integer size of the output, d stands for the desired places to the right of the decimal, and the addition of 2 provides for punctuation requirements. However, c must be at least 1. A w specification of $10 + d$ is large enough to write out any value, allowing for punctuation.

Illustrations of the F Specification. Several examples of the F specification and its use in input and output are provided in Figure 3–5. They are based on IBM FORTRAN and WATFIV; other systems might differ slightly. In each instance, the specification is shown in the "Specification" column, "Input Value" depicts the value as it appears in the input record, "Numerical Equivalent of Stored Value" shows approxi-

FIGURE 3–5
Illustrations of F FØRMAT Specifications

	Specification	*Input Value*	*Numerical Equivalent of Stored Value*	*Output Value*
1.	F6.3	001234	001.234	b1.234
2.	F6.3	−01234	−01.234	−1.234
3.	F6.0	bb1b34	001034.	b1034.
4.	F6.6	001234	.001234	†
5.	F6.3	−12345	−012.345	*
6.	F5.4	00002	0.0002	†
7.	F6.4	b00002	00.0002	†
8.	F6.3	01.234	001.234	b1.234
9.	F7.3	01.2345	001.2345	bb1.235
10.	F8.3	123.45bb	00123.45	b123.450
11.	F8.3	12345bbb	12345.000	*
12.	F6.0	123.45	123.45	bb123.
13.	F4.6	1234	.001234	†
14.	F11.5	00123456789	1234.568	b1234.56800
15.	F11.0	12345678912	12345680000.	*
16.	F8.4	‡	0.1234567	bb0.1235
17.	F8.4	‡	123.4567	*
18.	F6.4	‡	00.0002	†
19.	F7.4	‡	000.0002	b0.0002
20.	F6.3	‡	00.0002	b0.000
21.	F6.3	bbbbb0	000.000	b0.000
22.	F6.3	0bbbbb	000.000	b0.000
23.	F6.3	bbbbbb	−0	−0.000
24.	F10.4	‡	1234567.	*
25.	F10.4	‡	.1234567	bbbbb.1235
26.	F11.0	‡	12345670000	§
27.	F10.4	bbb1234567	123.4567	bb123.4567
28.	F12.2	‡	12345.67	bbbb12345.67
29.	F12.2	12345.67bbbb	12345.67	bbbb12345.67

* Value too large for output by this specification.
† Not a valid output specification.
‡ Example not designed to show input.
§ Cannot be written by F notation.

mately how the value read in would appear in the computer's memory, and "Output Value" represents the value written by the designated FØRMAT specification. "b" indicates a blank position.

Specifying Logical Items

Logical variables are identified in the FØRMAT statement by the specification Lw, with w indicating the field width. For example, the specification L5 would identify a logical field of five positions. A logical FØRMAT specification may be seen in Figure 3–2, where L1 is used to define the field named ØTME.

Logical Values in Input.   Only the leftmost nonblank character in a logical field is transmitted from the input record, and it must be a T or an F. Other characters in the input field are ignored. As may be expected, "T" stands for true, and "F" for false—the only logical conditions permitted.

To illustrate the process of identifying and reading logical variables, assume the following input record:

TABLETRUETFFALSEF1234

The following program is written to read this record:

LØGICAL A,B,C,I,J,K
10   FØRMAT(L5,L4,L1,L1,L5,L5)
READ(5,10)A,B,C,I,J,K

The first field has been assigned five positions in the input record and the data name A. However, when the record is read, only the first character, T, is transmitted from the input record and associated with the data name. By the same token, B is assigned a value of T (the first letter in TRUE); C is assigned the value T; and I, J, and K are each assigned the value F.

Logical Values in Output.   Regardless of the field size, only the letter T or F will be output in a logical field. It will occupy the rightmost position of the output field, preceded by $w - 1$ blanks.

Skipping Fields: The X Specification

It is sometimes desirable to skip parts of records. This is done by using the X FØRMAT specification. It is of the nature

wX

where *w* defines the width of the skipped field. Note that while the field width is specified after the key character in integer, floating-point, and logical specifications (for example, I4 and F3.0), the width is written first in the X specification.

The X Specification in Input. When the X specification is used in an input format, the positions to which the specification applies are ignored. From 1 to 80 positions (or the entire record) may be skipped.

For an example of the X notation, reference may again be made to the input of employee payroll, as it exists on the record depicted in Figure 3–1.

Here, the following fields occupy the indicated card columns:

Field	*Columns*
Employee number	1–5
Pay rate	6–10
Hours worked	11–13
Overtime key	14

Assume that it is necessary to read the employee number, hours worked, and overtime key from the record but that the pay rate is not to be read. This could be accomplished by the following related FØR-MAT and READ commands:

    1   FØRMAT(I5,5X,F3.1,L1)
         READ(5,1)NØ,HØURS,ØTME

NØ will be extracted from the first five columns of the record, and the next five positions will be ignored. HØURS will be extracted from columns 11–13, and ØTME from column 14. Thus, it may be seen that the X notation in an input FØRMAT specification causes the computer to treat the skipped field as if it did not exist, permitting the READ command to reference only those data items desired.

The X Specification in Output. Use of the X specification in an output FØRMAT causes blanks to be placed in the output record. For example, if it were desired to write out the data elements NØ, HØURS, and ØTME in a well-spaced report, the following FØRMAT and WRITE statements might be used:

    2   FØRMAT(1X,I5,8X,F5.1,8X,L1)
         WRITE(6,2)NØ,HØURS,ØTME

The X Specification in Printer Control. Whenever a record is designed for printing on the computer printer, the left-most character is not available for data. Instead, it must contain a printer carriage control symbol.

A blank in this position causes the printer to single space its output. It is essential that all output record formats contain a blank in this position, until more advanced carriage control is covered in Chapter 6. Therefore, the format of all output records should begin with wX, thus assigning one or more blank positions at the left of the record. The output record format in Figure 3–7 can be seen to satisfy this requirement.

Creating Messages in Output

It is possible to create messages to be included in computer printout in two ways. The simplest, available in WATFIV and many FORTRAN IV versions including that used on IBM 360–370 computers, is described in this chapter. The other, operable on all FORTRAN IV versions, is somewhat more complicated. It is described in Chapter 6 below.

Messages to be included in output are created in the FØRMAT statement to be used with a WRITE command. In the simplest form, the message to be written is enclosed in single quotes. All characters enclosed in quotes (but not the quote marks themselves) will be written as part of the output.

Example of Output Messages. As an example, assume that the value SALE (format xxx.xx) is to be read in an input record, and then written with the caption

THE AMOUNT OF SALE IS

in an output record. A program to accomplish this appears as follows:

```
1    FØRMAT(F5.2)
2    FØRMAT(1X,'THE AMØUNT ØF SALE IS', 5X, F7.2)
10   READ(5,1,END=25) SALE
     WRITE(6,2)SALE
     GØ TØ 10
25   STØP
     END
```

Upon execution of the WRITE command the message will be inserted, even though it is not a part of the data read in or a member of the WRITE specification list. For example, if the value 256.43 is written, execution of the WRITE statement will cause the following to be printed:

THE AMØUNT ØF SALE IS 256.43

Messages can be created for writing in the output stream even though no variable is associated. For example, an output statement such as the following, with its associated FØRMAT statement, will also generate an output message:

    1   FØRMAT(' END ØF PRØCESSING ')
         WRITE(6,1)

In this instance, when the WRITE command is executed the message

    END ØF PRØCESSING

will be written. It may be noted that the required blank space at the left of the output record is created by provision within the quote signs, rather than by the 1X specification used previously.

Punctuating FØRMAT Statements

Numeric and logical FØRMAT specifications may be separated by a comma, one or more blanks, or a comma followed by one or more blanks. However, this is not required, and the specifications may be written without any separator at all. For example, both the following FØRMAT statements are correct:

    3   FØRMAT(F6.4,F3.3,I2,I5)
    3   FØRMAT(F6.4F3.3I2I5)

Obviously, the first statement is easier to read, but the separators are not required.

An X specification immediately following a numeric specification must be preceded by a comma. Its field width precedes the specification symbol, and if the notation were not set apart by a preceding comma, it would be confused with the width of the numeric specification.

Repeating Specifications

If the same specification is to be used more than once in adjacent positions, its multiple use may be indicated by a repetition number preceding the specification. Thus, the following FØRMAT statements are the same:

    3   FØRMAT(I5,F6.3,F6.3,F6.3)
    3   FØRMAT(I5,3F6.3)

More than one specification may be repeated by enclosure in parentheses after the repetition number. For example, the following FØRMAT statements are alike in their meaning:

3   FØRMAT(I5,I2,F4.2,I2,F4.2)
3   FØRMAT(I5,2(I2,F4.2))

AN INTRODUCTION TO CONTROL STATEMENTS

Ordinarily, the computer reads a program just as we do; from left to right, down the page. It is sometimes necessary to interrupt this reading sequence and direct the computer to some other program statement, and a means of ending the program must also be available. These activities are performed by *control statements*.

Unconditional Transfer

This instruction is of the general form

$$k \qquad GØ \ TØ \ n$$

where k is an optional statement number and n the number of a statement appearing anywhere in the program. The instruction written at n must be an executable statement. It may not be a FØRMAT or specification statement, nor may it be the END statement discussed below.

An example of this statement is shown in Figure 3–7. Here, the program sequence proceeds down the page until the sixth statement,

$$GØ \ TØ \ 10$$

is encountered. At this point the sequence is interrupted, and the computer transfers to statement 10 for its next instruction.

Command Purpose. The function of the GØ TØ instruction is to cause a transfer or "jump" in the executable program sequence. It is called an "unconditional transfer" because it permits no alternative to jumping to the numbered instruction. Chapter 5 discusses certain conditional transfers where transfer may or may not occur.

Punctuation and Spacing. No punctuation is permitted in this instruction. Spacing is unimportant; GØTØ10 and GØ TØ 10 have the same meaning, although the latter form is recommended for readability.

The STØP Instruction

All programs have a logical terminal. Some programs are executed once or a determinable number of times, after which they are to stop.

Others are executed so long as input data are available; data exhaustion signals their logical termination.

At the logical end of the program should appear the STØP command. It is of the nature

$$k \qquad \text{STØP}$$

where *k* denotes an optional statement number.

It should be noted that this instruction should appear at the *logical,* not the *physical,* end of the program. It may be written anywhere in the program, so long as it will not be executed until the program is finished.

An example of this instruction is shown in Figure 3–7. Statement 50, on the seventh line, instructs the computer to STØP. When this instruction is encountered, program execution will be terminated and the computer released for some other duty.

The END Instruction

This command signals the *physical* end of the program. Generally speaking, it says to the computer: "All the program has now been read in. You may begin compilation. If any statement numbers do not match transfer commands or FØRMAT numbers do not correspond with input-output instructions, an error must exist because no more of the program is to be submitted." Thus, the computer "knows" that all the program is in, and it can begin the work of translation.

Thus, the END instruction is a signal to the computer to be used at compile time. It is not a part of the program to be used in execution. It is of the simple nature

$$\text{END}$$

and must physically be the last command in the program. It *cannot* have a statement number.

A Complete Computer Program

Complete, executable programs can be written with the commands introduced above. As an illustration, assume that records containing personnel data—employee number, pay rate, hours worked, and overtime indicator—such as shown in Figure 3–6 are to be processed. Only the employee number, hours worked, and overtime indicator are to be read from the input records, and these data are to be printed on a report.

FIGURE 3–6
Input Record

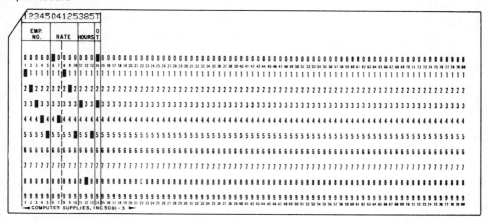

Space is to be provided between elements of the output record.

An appropriate program is shown in Figure 3–7. First, ØTME is declared a logical variable. Next, a format statement properly describes the input record. Because the pay rate is not needed in the report, the field is skipped in the input record by use of the X specification.

Statement 10, a READ command, instructs the computer to use unit 5 as its input device, and to read records according to FØRMAT 1. Input values, selected from the input record in the size, location, and mode indicated by the format statement, are to be named NØ, HØURS, and ØTME. The program is to transfer to statement 50 when the input file is exhausted.

FIGURE 3–7
FORTRAN Program

```
      LOGICAL  ØTME
    1 FORMAT(15, 5X F3.1, L1)
    2 FORMAT(1X, I6, 8X, F5.1, L5)
   10 READ(5,1,END=50)NØ, HØURS, ØTME
      WRITE(6,2)NØ, HØURS, ØTME
      GØ TØ 10
   50 STØP
      END
```

Using the sample data from figure 3–6 as an example, READ command execution will cause the contents of the record to be transferred into the computer's memory. The value 12345 will be stored at the memory location called NØ. The pay rate will be ignored because of the 5X specification in the input FØRMAT statement. HØURS will be stored as 38.5, the FØRMAT specification supplying the decimal. ØTME will receive the logical value T.

Next, the computer is instructed to WRITE, on output unit 6 by FØRMAT 2, the variables NØ, HØURS, and ØTME. This will transfer to the printer the values just read from the input record.

The output line will appear as follows, where b represents a blank space:

b12345bbbbbbbbb38.5bbbbT

Nine blank spaces separate the numeric data: eight spaces provided by the 8X notation and one by the F5.1 specification used to define the HØURS field. The logical value T is right-justified in the five-place field causing four blanks to be inserted to the left.

The next command, GØ TØ 10, is an unconditional branch. After executing the WRITE statement, the computer must come here, and at this point it must return to statement 10 for its next instruction.

The STØP command, statement 50, can be reached only by exhausting the input file and taking the END= branch of the READ command. It serves as the logical end of the program, and causes execution of this program to cease.

Finally, the END instruction signals the physical end of the program, and indicates that compilation is to begin.

CHAPTER SUMMARY

Almost every use of the computer requires data to be transmitted to the machine and information obtained from it. Therefore, input and output instructions appear in almost every program, and an understanding of them is basic to programming comprehension. The READ command controls data transmission, record by record, from an external file to the central processor. The WRITE instruction transmits data, organized as records, from the central processor to an output unit where the elements are written in acceptable form.

These instructions work with the FØRMAT statement (unless unformatted records, discussed in Chapter 6, are used), which describe the nature of the input or output records. This statement indicates the location, size, and nature of each data field.

The above statements, with a few simple control instructions, permit programs to be written and executed. The control commands required are GØ TØ, an unconditional branch; STØP, which serves as the logical end of the program; and END, the physical terminal.

Summary of FORTRAN Statements

The FORTRAN commands covered in this chapter are:
1. *k*   READ(*i,j*,END=*n*)list
   k = optional statement number
   i = code number of computer input unit (5 references the card reader in IBM FORTRAN and WATFIV)
   j = number of associated FØRMAT statement
   END=*n* = optional terminal branch designation; *n* = statement number to which program transfers when input file is exhausted
   list = set of variable names, each referencing a field in the record
2. *k*   WRITE(*i,j*)list
   k = optional statement number
   i = code number of computer output unit (6 references printer in IBM FORTRAN and WATFIV)
   j = number of associated FØRMAT statement
   list = set of variable names, each referencing a field in the record
3. *k*   FØRMAT(list)
   k = required statement number
   list = set of format specifications taken from the following:
      I*w* specifying an integer numeric field of *w* positions
      F*w.d* specifying a real numeric field of *w* positions, of which *d* are to the right of the decimal
      L*w* specifying a logical field of *w* positions
      *w*X specifying that *w* spaces are to be skipped
      Characters in quotes ' ' comprising a literal to be transmitted
4. *k*   GØ TØ *n*
   k = optional statement number
   n = a statement number to which transfer must unconditionally be made
5. *k*   STØP
   k = optional statement number
6.   END

QUESTIONS

1. What is a data item? A record? A file?

2. "A transcript is maintained for each student. The transcript contains information on courses carried, hours passed, and quality points." What file is implied in this quotation? What are its records? What data items are mentioned?

3. "Payrolls are prepared with data from two sources. One source is the employee master file, which contains information pertaining to the employee's pay rate, social security number, income tax status, and year-to-date earnings. The other source contains information about the current pay period—hours worked and employee number. From these sources is prepared the weekly earnings report showing each employee's regular and overtime pay, his withholdings, and his net pay. His master file is also updated."

   What files are mentioned above? What records? What data items may be found in each record?

4. What is a field, as the term is used in data organization? How many positions may it contain?

5. How does the computer "know" where data items are located in records?

6. Assume that a data field has been set up to contain unit prices and the sales date which is of the same size is punched here by mistake. What will happen when the record is processed?

7. In the READ command, how is the computer input unit to be used indicated?

8. Is the END clause required in the READ command? What is its effect?

9. What values may be assumed by logical variables?

10. How is the presence and size of a logical field indicated?

11. How wide may a logical field be? How many characters are transmitted when reading from a logical field?

12. How is the computer "told" that a data field should contain a decimal? The location of the decimal?

13. In the FØRMAT statement, how are integer fields distinguished from floating-point fields?

14. How does the computer "know" where to find the data items listed in a READ command?

15. What is the relation between the READ command and its associated FØRMAT statement?

16. Assume the input statement: 10   READ(5,4)A,B,C
    How is the nature of the data fields A, B, and C indicated? How is

the location of the data items in the input record indicated? The items' size? Does the input statement indicate that these fields are adjacent to one another in the input record?

17. Given the same numeric quantity to be processed, input and output FØRMAT specifications are apt to differ from one another. Why?

18. What is the general form of the output command?

19. What punctuation is required of input and output commands?

20. What punctuation is required of the FØRMAT statement?

21. Why does a program which uses a READ command also need a FØRMAT statement?

22. "Input and output statements cannot refer to the same FØRMAT." Is this true or false?

23. What happens when an attempt is made to write a data item having more places to the left of the decimal than the FØRMAT specification allows?

24. What happens when an attempt is made to write a data item having a value 123.45, using the FØRMAT F6.3?

25. What happens when an attempt is made to write a data item having a value .12345, using the FØRMAT F6.5?

26. What is the function of the X FØRMAT specification?

27. What is the reason for having a 1X specification at the beginning of an output FØRMAT?

28. What is the function of the STØP statement?

29. What is wrong with the statement   10   GØ TØ 10?

30. Where should the STØP statement appear?

31. What is the function of the END statement?

32. What is the difference between the STØP and END statements?

33. What is the difference between GØTØ25 and GØ TØ 25?

34. What is an "unconditional transfer"?

35. Where must the statement to which an unconditional transfer refers be written?

36. "A program that has a STØP instruction does not need an END command." Is this true or false? Why?

37. How can messages be inserted in output records?

EXERCISES

1. List the errors in the following program, assuming that it is to process many input records:

```
10      FØRMAT(I5,F3.2)
        READ(10,1,END=50)A,B
        WRITE(6,2)B,A
        STØP
        GØ TØ 10
        END
 2      FØRMAT(F3.2,X5,I5)
```

2. The following values are to be read in according to the given FØR-
   MAT specification. Indicate how each value will appear in the computer's memory. Mark any values "incorrect" that do not conform to
   the FØRMAT style.

	FØRMAT Specification	Value
1.	F4.3	1234
2.	F4.3	−123
3.	F6.2	1234.5
4.	F6.4	bbb123
5.	F6.2	123bbb
6.	L2	TF
7.	F4.6	1234
8.	F6.4	bbbbbb
9.	F6.0	12b345
10.	I6	123bbb
11.	L4	TRUE
12.	I2	bb
13.	8X	12345678
14.	F10.0	1234567812
15.	F6.0	0.123−
16.	6X	b$1.25
17.	L5	12345
18.	I5	1.234
19.	F5.0	−1.b3
20.	F5.0	.−123
21.	F3.3	100

3. The following values are stored in the computer's memory. Indicate
   how each will appear when written out by the designated FØRMAT
   specification. Mark "incorrect" any wrong specifications or values not
   appropriate for the FØRMAT specification.

	FØRMAT Specification	Value
1.	I5	1234
2.	F8.0	123.45
3.	F6.0	123
4.	F8.4	1.2345
5.	F6.3	123.45
6.	F3.2	.25
7.	F8.4	−123.4567

	FØRMAT Specification	Value
8.	I4	−123
9.	F5.2	.25
10.	F8.0	1234.
11.	F6.3	12.345
12.	5X	FALSE
13.	I4	TRUE
14.	L5	FALSE
15.	F4.3	.123
16.	I5	123

4. The values shown below are to be considered as being read in by their associated input FØRMAT specification. Indicate their appearance when written out by their given output FØRMAT specification. Mark "incorrect" any item incompatible with its related output FØRMAT specification.

	Input Value	FØRMAT Specification Input	FØRMAT Specification Output
1.	−1bb	I4	I5
2.	bb−1	I4	I3
3.	12345	F5.0	F7.0
4.	12345	F5.0	F6.0
5.	1bbb	F4.2	F6.2
6.	1bbbb	I5	I6
7.	123.4	F5.0	I6
8.	12345678123	F11.0	F15.0
9.	0002	F6.0	F6.4
10.	25	F2.2	F5.2
11.	123	I3	I5
12.	FALSE	L5	L5
13.	1234	4X	4X
14.	TTFF	L4	L1
15.	bbb3	F4.1	F4.0
16.	1234	F4.6	F8.4
17.	1bbb	F5.0	F5.0

5. Given below are several input values and stored values. Give the FØRMAT specification by which each value was read.

	Input Value	Stored Value
1.	1234	01234
2.	1234	01234.00
3.	1234	.001234
4.	1234	12.34
5.	1234	123
6.	1234	bbbb
7.	TRUE	T

6. Given below are sets of input records, FØRMAT statements, and READ commands. Assuming that any required type statements have been provided, give the value assigned to each input data element.

1. Input record contents: 12345678TF

        1   FØRMAT(I3,F3.2,2X,L2)
               READ(5,1)I,X,Y

2. Input record contents: 12345−12b3456

        1   FØRMAT(5X,F5.0,I3)
               READ(5,1)X,K

3. Input record contents: TTFF12345

        1   FØRMAT(2X,L1,L1,3X,F2.2)
               READ(5,1)A,B,C

4. Input record contents: 12345678F123T123

        1   FØRMAT(I3,2X,F3.1,L4,L4)
               READ(5,1)I,X,Y,Z

5. Input record contents: AA1.2345bbbbb1

        1   FØRMAT(2X,F6.2,3X,I3)
               READ(5,1)X,K

6. Input record contents: TBA12.3−12b12

        1   FØRMAT(L3,F4.0,I4,F2.2)
               READ(5,1)A,B,I,C

7. Input record contents: −123456.789

        1   FØRMAT(1X,I3,F7.0)
               READ(5,1)N,A

8. Input record contents: −123456.789

        1   FØRMAT(F5.3,I2,F4.0)
               READ(5,1)A,K,X

9. Input record contents: −123456.789

        1   FØRMAT(I7,1X,I3)
               READ(5,1)K,L

10. Input record contents: b12bb12.3bbTF

        1   FØRMAT(I5,F5.0,F1.0,L2)
               READ(5,1)N,A,B,C

7. Refer to Exercise 6 above. Given below is a FØRMAT and WRITE statement for each part of Exercise 6. For each input set, give the output line that will result from the indicated FØRMAT.

    1.   2   FØRMAT(1X,L1,' X= ',F8.2,I5)
                               WRITE(6,2)Y,X,I

    2.   2   FØRMAT(5X,I5,5X,' THE VALUE OF X IS ',F7.0)
                               WRITE(6,2)K,X

    3.   2   FØRMAT(2X,F5.2,L5)
                               WRITE(6,2)C,A

    4.   2   FØRMAT(1X,L1,'RUE',5X,I3)
                               WRITE(6,2)Z,I

    5.   2   FØRMAT(1X,F6.2)
                               WRITE(6,2)X

    6.   2   FØRMAT(1X,L1,'RUE',5X,F8.2)
                               WRITE(6,2)A,C

    7.   2   FØRMAT(1X,I3,3X,F7.0)
                               WRITE(6,2)N,A

    8.   2   FØRMAT(1X,I2,5X,F7.3)
                               WRITE(6,2)K,A

    9.   2   FØRMAT(1X,I3,I4)
                               WRITE(6,2)L,K

   10.   2   FØRMAT(I5,5X,F6.0)
                               WRITE(6,2)N,A

8. Prepare type, FØRMAT, and READ statements for the records described below. Fields occupy adjacent positions. The number of x's denotes the field size for logical and numeric variables; an assumed decimal is indicated by a caret ($_\wedge$). Numeric fields without carets are of integer mode. Use the data names given.

Data Name	*Field Size and Type**
IND	xxxx
SMAN	xxxxx
GRØSS	xxxxxx$_\wedge$x
TAX	xxx$_\wedge$xx
NET	xxxxx$_\wedge$xx
DISC	xxxxxx, logical

    * Numeric unless otherwise specified.

9. Prepare type, FØRMAT, and READ statements for the records described below. A six-place field is to be skipped between FRT and

TØTAL. The number of x's denotes field size for logical and numeric variables; and assumed decimal is indicated by a caret ($\wedge$). Omission of a caret from a numeric field indicates integer mode. Use the data names given.

Data Name	Field Size and Type*
NØ	xxxxx
STØRE	xxxxx
SALE	xxxxx̭xx
FRT	xxxx̭xx
TØTAL	xxxxxx̭xx
DISC	xxxxx, logical

* Numeric unless otherwise specified.

10. Prepare a FØRMAT and WRITE statement for Exercise 8 above. Allow five spaces between each item in the output list.

11. Prepare a FØRMAT and WRITE statement for Exercise 9 above. Allow five spaces between each item in the output list.

PROBLEMS

The following problems, while very simple, have been designed so that they may be compiled and run on a computer. Therefore, in coding them, the requirements of the computer to be used should be followed. Particular attention should be paid to the size of data names and constants and to the requirements of the input and output units.

The following rules are to be observed in coding solutions to the problems.

Rules Pertaining to Input

1. Data fields begin at the left of the record and occupy adjacent positions.

2. The number of x's in the "Field Size" column of the problem indicates the size of the data field.

3. Decimals are not recorded in real numeric values. Instead, they are to be provided by the FØRMAT statement, and their location is indicated by a caret ($\wedge$) in real fields.

4. Numeric fields without a caret are of integer mode.

Rules Pertaining to Output

1. The first output position should be left blank.

2. All data values should be separated by five blank spaces.

3. The number of *numeric* positions in a field is indicated by the number

of x's in the "Field Size" column of the problem. This does not allow for sign or decimal.

4. The proper decimal location is indicated by the printed decimal in "Field Size."
5. Use the END = option in the READ statement if appropriate.
6. Integer numeric fields are indicated by the absence of a decimal.
7. Use the data names set out in the problem.

Problems

1. The Ajax Company maintains certain sales data on computer records. Prepare a program to read the records indicated as "input record" below, and prepare the required output record. The program is to print the message 'PRØCESSING CØMPLETE' and terminate when no more input records are available.

	FORTRAN	
Item Description	*Name*	*Field Size*
Input record:		
Inventory item number	INVNØ	xxxxx
Date of sale	DATE	xxxxxx
Salesman number	SMNØ	xxxxx
Sales department	DEPT	xxx
Sales amount	SALE	xxxẋx
Sales tax	TAX	xẋxx
Total sales amount and tax	TØTAL	xxxxẋx
Output record:		
Sales amount	SALE	xxx.xx
Sales tax	TAX	xx.xx
Total sales amount and tax	TØTAL	xxxx.xx

2. An output record containing the indicated information, including the indicated message, is to be prepared for each input record of the type below. The program is to be terminated when all input records have been processed.

	FORTRAN	
Item Description	*Name*	*Field Size*
Input record:		
Payment date	DATE	xxxxxx
Check amount	CASH	xxxxẋx
Purchase discount	DISC	xẋxx
Gross amount charged	GRØSS	xxxxẋx
Account charged	ACCT	xxxxx
Output record:		
Payment date	DATE	xxxxxx
Message	'ACCØUNT NUMBER'	
Account charged	ACCT	xxxxx
Check amount	CASH	xxxx.xx

3. Personnel records contain the data described under "Input record." From this, a report containing the information listed beneath "Output record," including the indicated message, is to be prepared. The message 'PRØCESSING CØMPLETE' should be written and processing should be terminated when no more input records are available.

	FORTRAN	
Item Description	*Name*	*Field Size*
Input record:		
Employee number	NØ	xxxx
Date employed	EDATE	xxxxxx
Department employed in	DEPT	xxxx
Annual salary	SALARY	xxxxx̭xx
Output record:		
Employee number	NØ	xxxx
Message	'SALARY AMØUNT'	
Annual salary	SALARY	xxxxx.xx
Date employed	EDATE	xxxxxx

4. This problem has one input record image, and three output record images, indicated as "Output record 1," "Output record 2," and "Output record 3." An input record is to be read, and then the required data extracted from it and written out in Output record 1 (including message), Output record 2, and Output record 3. The process is then to be repeated, and continued until no more input records are available. The program should then be ended.

	FORTRAN	
Item Description	*Name*	*Field Size*
Input record:		
Item number	NØ	xxxx
Warehouse location	LØC	xxxx
Number of parts on hand	PARTS	xxxxx
Unit cost	UCØST	x̭xxx
Output record 1:		
Item number	NØ	xxxx
Message	'NUMBER ØF UNITS'	
Number of units on hand	PARTS	xxxxx
Output record 2:		
Item number	NØ	xxxx
Warehouse location	LØC	xxxx
Output record 3:		
Item number	NØ	xxxx
Unit cost	UCØST	x.xxx

5. An input file has interspersed in it two types of records. First appears a Type 1 record, then a Type 2. This sequence is repeated throughout the file.

Prepare a program that will read a Type 1 record, then a Type 2, and then prepare the required output record. Processing is to terminate when no more input records are available; this should be sensed when attempting to read a Type 1 record.

	FORTRAN	
Item Description	*Name*	*Field Size*
Input record, Type 1:		
Item number	NØ	xxxx
Number of units on hand	UNITS	xxxxx
Input record, Type 2:		
Item number	NUM	xxxx
Unit cost	UCØST	xxxx
Output record:		
Item number	NØ	xxxx
Number of units on hand	UNITS	xxxxx
Unit cost	UCØST	x.xxx

4 Assignment Statements

The computer was first planned and constructed as a calculating device, and while it has evolved into an information-processing instrument, its computational abilities are still very important. These are expressed through "assignment statements," which evaluate the relationship of constants and variables and assign the result to a variable name.

FORTRAN IV includes two assignment statements. One, created to handle numeric data, is called the arithmetic statement. Because the arithmetic statement is an essential component of almost every FORTRAN program, it is covered in this chapter. The other, the logical assignment statement, is found much less frequently.

THE ARITHMETIC ASSIGNMENT STATEMENT

There is only one arithmetic statement in the FORTRAN IV, but it is quite powerful. It can set up very complex computations, consisting of any mixture of arithmetic manipulations.

Statement Nature

The command is of the general form

$$k \qquad \text{Variable} = \text{Expression}$$

where k is an optional statement number. "Variable" must be a data name. "Expression" can be any valid arithmetic expression, as described below. The command means "evaluate the expression and store the results at the location specified by the variable"; or stated another way "set the variable equal in value to the expression."

Rules Controlling the Arithmetic Statement

The arithmetic statement must be constructed and used in accordance with certain rules. In setting out these rules below, "variable" is used to indicate the left-hand member of the command and "expression" the right-hand member. This is slightly improper because the expression may itself contain variables, as will be seen later in the chapter. However, it is convenient to use the terms in this manner for the sake of brevity.

Rule 1: Arithmetic must be performed in a unique command. In FORTRAN, it is not possible to do arithmetic as a part of any other instruction.[1] Thus, the arithmetic statement cannot be a part of a READ command, or a WRITE command, or any other instruction in the language.

Rule 2: The left-hand statement member may be only a data name. It is not possible to have any part of the computation to the left of the equal sign. Thus, the following forms of the arithmetic statement are not permitted:

$$A + B = C$$
$$A + B = X{-}5.3$$
$$-3 = Z̶$$

However, rearranged as shown below, these equations may be converted into acceptable arithmetic statements.

$$C = A{+}B$$
$$A = X{-}5.3{-}B(\text{or, } B{=}X{-}5.3{-}A)$$
$$Z̶ = -3$$

Rule 3: Evaluation defines the left-hand variable. The variable named as the left-hand member of an arithmetic statement need not have appeared before in the program, although it may have if appropriate. Execution of the command "defines" the variable; that is, it as-

---

[1] The DØ Statement, discussed in Chapter 7, is in some ways an exception to this rule.

signs a value to the item. This value may then be used in subsequent computations or written out.

If the variable had some value previously assigned to it, that value is destroyed when the arithmetic statement is executed. It is quite important, therefore, that any values to be retained be either written out or redefined before encountering the command.

Rule 4: The variable and the expression need not be of the same arithmetic mode. Any of the following forms of arithmetic statements are acceptable where I and J are integer items and X and Y floating-point elements:

$$X=Y \qquad I=J$$
$$X=I \qquad I=X$$

Thus, the expression and the variable may be of the same or different modes.

Rule 5: Evaluation occurs in the mode of the expression; the result is stored in the mode of the variable. Ordinarily, an arithmetic expression is evaluated in the mode of the constants and/or variables comprising it. Then, the results are stored in the mode of the expression. However, IBM 360–370 FORTRAN and WATFIV permit mixed-mode expressions. Where mixed mode exists in these FORTRAN versions the expression is always evaluated in real mode, and then stored in the mode of the variable.

Integer results will be floated if necessary; floating-point results will be truncated to integers if appropriate.

Rules 4 and 5 may result in the computation of incorrect answers where decimal fractions are a part of the result. In the following examples, each arithmetic statement is a valid command and yields the results shown to the right of the instruction.

Statement	*Results*
$X = 5./2.$	$X = 2.5$
$X = 5/2$	$X = 2.$
$I = 5./2.$	$I = 2$
$I = 5/2$	$I = 2$
$I = .999$	$I = 0$

In each of the above, evaluation occurs in the mode of the expression. Then, the result is stored in the mode of the variable. It may or may not be correct. Because of the nature of the integer mode, it is a sound practice to construct floating-point expressions unless the equation is such that accuracy may be assured.

The Command Illustrated

As an example of the arithmetic command, attention may be returned briefly to Chapter 3. Here, the instructions necessary to read certain employee data were given in Figure 3–2. The employee pay rate was read in as RATE, and the hours worked as HØURS.

The regular pay could easily be calculated from these variables by the command below where RPAY is the name chosen to represent the regular pay amount.

RPAY=RATE*HØURS

Thus, a program for reading pay records, computing regular pay, and writing selected payroll information might appear as in Figure 4–1.

FIGURE 4–1
Using the Arithmetic Statement

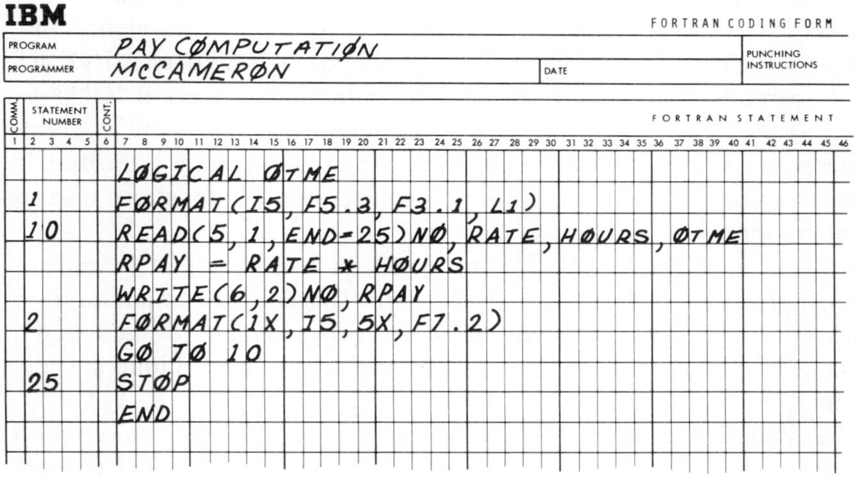
IBM FORTRAN CODING FORM

PROGRAM PAY CØMPUTATIØN
PROGRAMMER MCCAMERØN
DATE
PUNCHING INSTRUCTIONS

```
      LØGICAL ØTME
1     FØRMAT(I5,F5.3,F3.1,L1)
10    READ(5,1,END=25)NØ,RATE,HØURS,ØTME
      RPAY = RATE * HØURS
      WRITE(6,2)NØ,RPAY
2     FØRMAT(1X,I5,5X,F7.2)
      GØ TØ 10
25    STØP
      END
```

The arithmetic statement uses the values read in, RATE, and HØURS, to compute a new value, RPAY. Then, NØ (one of the input variables) and RATE are written, and the program is made to repeat.

THE ARITHMETIC EXPRESSION

In an arithmetic statement of the nature

Variable = Expression

the left-hand member can only be a data name and so does not require extended explanation. The "expression" may be quite complex, however. Its basic nature, formulation rules, and interpretation by the computer are matters which must be understood by the programmer.

The arithmetic expression is used in two places in FORTRAN: in the arithmetic statement and as the subject of evaluation in the conditional command. In arithmetic it may appear as an exponent or a function argument as well as comprising the right-hand member of the statement. The nature of the expression and its use in arithmetic are considered below; its role in conditional instructions is treated in Chapter 5.

Nature of the Expression

An arithmetic expression is any meaningful combination of *operands* and *operators*.

Operands. An *operand* is a factor to be used in computation. It may be a constant or a variable. In Figure 4–1, where the arithmetic statement RPAY = RATE*HØURS appears, both RATE and HØURS are operands. In Figure 1–4, the computational instruction XINT = PRIN*.06*TIME/365. contains a mixture of variable and constant operands. As this instruction implies, the operands may be mixed in any manner (according to rules specified below) to effect correct computation.

Use of a variable operand in an expression does not affect its value or its existence in any way. It is available for subsequent computation, or for writing, or for any other use at the programmer's discretion. Of course, this is not true of the left-hand variable in the arithmetic statement.

Arithmetic Operators. These are the *arithmetic operational symbols* that may be used meaningfully in the arithmetic statement. They represent the computer's arithmetic capabilities. The arithmetic operators are:

Symbol	*Meaning*
+	Addition
−	Subtraction
/	Division
*	Multiplication
**	Exponentiation

These symbols *must* be used when arithmetic manipulation is desired.

The computer cannot understand such words as "add" or "subtract"; it can perform these operations only when the proper operator is included in the command.

Most of the operators above are familiar and are used in ordinary arithmetic. The multiplication symbol is not common, but it must be used because ordinary multiplication signs (such as the dot, or the "X" symbol) carry other meanings in FORTRAN.

The presence of two adjacent asterisks (**) *always* symbolizes exponentiation. The power to which the value is being raised is indicated by the next operand(s).

For example, the following examples have the indicated meaning in FORTRAN:

Arithmetic Value	*FORTRAN Equivalent*
X^2	X**2
$25.^4$	25.**4
Y^I	Y**I
$Z^{.5}$	Z**.5

The exponent itself may be any arithmetic expression. Exponents may be as simple or as complex as desired. Fractional powers may be used, thus giving the root of the value when the command is executed.

Formation Requirements

The creation of an arithmetic expression requires that several rules be followed. Failure to observe any of these will prevent execution of the program; and some of the mistakes typically made in coding this command are very difficult to find and eliminate.

The rules are discussed below; then they are summarized for convenience.

Rule 1: The expression cannot contain mixed mode in many FORTRAN IV versions.[2] While some versions (including IBM 360–370 FORTRAN and WATFIV) do permit mixed mode expressions, it is best to assume that this is not allowed unless the manual of the particular computer expressly permits it. Unless mixed mode is allowed, an arithmetic expression can be written in either the fixed- or floating-point mode but it cannot mix the two. For example, each of the follow-

---

[2] That a value may be raised to a power of another mode is the one exception to this rule. See rule 5.

ing expressions is incorrect because it contains mixed mode (assume that type statements have not changed the data names' mode):

PRIN*TIME/365   The integer, 365, may not be used with floating-point variables. It must be written as follows: 365.

4*X   Again, the integer 4 may not be used with the floating-point variable X. It should be written as 4.*X.

K+A   The variables are of mixed mode, and one must be renamed.

It may be recalled that the arithmetic *statement* may be of mixed mode, even though the *expression* may not. Therefore, when two mixed-mode variables must be used in an expression, as in the third illustration above, it is possible to first redefine one and change its mode. For example, instead of writing K+A, it is appropriate to write two arithmetic statements, as follows:

$$XK = K$$
$$X = XK + A$$

The first statement changes K from fixed- to floating-point mode, without changing its value. Then, the second statement computes the sum of XK and A, both floating-point quantities.

It may be recalled that, when mixed-mode expressions are executed in IBM 360–370 FORTRAN or WATFIV, all integer members are first converted to real numeric mode and the expression evaluated in that form.

Rule 2: Variable operands must have been previously defined. Any operand used in an arithmetic expression must have been defined previously. Variables are "defined"—that is, assigned a value—by reading them in, by computing them in a prior arithmetic statement, or by definition in the DATA statement discussed below. As will be seen in Chapter 7, a variable may also be defined by a control statement.

Rule 3: No operators may be "assumed." This rule is most frequently broken in multiplication, and the infraction often involves mixed mode as well. An algebraic statement such as $X = 4Y$ is quite common. A multiplication symbol is assumed, and the statement really means "X is equal to 4 magnitudes of Y" or "X is equal to 4 times Y." This must be written out in FORTRAN, and the correct statement becomes:

$$X=4.*Y$$

Note that to write $X = 4*Y$ is still incorrect because the integer constant must be a floating-point value.

Several commonly used algebraic expression forms and their FORTRAN equivalents are shown below:

$X = 2(6Y-3Z)$	$X=2.*(6.*Y-3.*Z)$
$A = (X+Y)(X-Y)$	$A=(X+Y)*(X-Y)$
$Y = 4AC$	$Y=4.*A*C$ (assuming that A and C are two variable names)
$Y = X + AX + BX^2$	$Y=X+A*X+B*X**2$ (assuming that A, B, and X are different variable names)

Rule 4: Operators cannot occupy adjacent positions. When arithmetic operators would otherwise be next to each other, they must be divided by parentheses. For example, it is improper to write a statement such as $X = A*-4$. Instead, the operators should be divided by using parentheses and written as follows:

$$X = A*(-4.)$$

Rule 5: A value may be assigned an exponent of different mode. An exception to the rule prohibiting mixed mode in an expression is found in exponentiation. A value may be raised by an exponent of the same or different mode. The mode of the value is not affected by the mode of its exponent.

Using the symbols I and R to represent integer and real mode respectively, the following combinations of values and exponents are always permitted:

$$I^I$$
$$R^R$$
$$R^I$$

Thus, a real value may be assigned an integer exponent. In some FORTRAN versions, integer values may be raised by real exponents, but this is not always the case, and the rules of the particular computer must be observed.

Rule 6: Spacing is irrelevant. In the arithmetic expression, as in the statement itself, spacing between factors is irrelevant. It does not matter whether items are written together as, for example, $X*Y/A$, or whether spaces are interspersed. Where grouping is important, parentheses are used to provide the correct interpretation.

Summary of Rules.   A summary of the above rules follows. The rules must be observed in the creation of all arithmetic expressions; otherwise, the program will not be accepted by the computer. These rules are:

1.   The expression cannot contain mixed mode unless specifically permitted.
2.   Variable operands must be defined before they can be used in an expression.
3.   No operators can be "assumed."
4.   Operators cannot occupy adjacent positions.
5.   A value can be assigned an exponent of different mode.
6.   Spacing is irrelevant.

Evaluation of an Expression

The rules above set out requirements that must be met if the computer is to accept the FORTRAN program at all. In addition, the computer's interpretation of an expression must be understood before correct answers may be obtained.

Algorithms applied by the computer in its evaluation are discussed below in the order of their precedence. The first-described rule is applied first; then, within this, the second is followed. Finally, the third is considered. In this manner, the entire expression is interpreted.

The Effect of Parentheses.   Parentheses may be used to set off any part of an arithmetic expression. When they are used, the enclosed part of the expression is evaluated before any unenclosed portion.

Parentheses may be "nested" in an arithmetic expression; that is, pairs may be used inside one another. When this is done, evaluation occurs from the inner to the outer set. For example, in the statement

$$X = C + (((A+B)/2.)**(1./2.))$$

the sum of A and B would first be calculated, satisfying the inner set of parentheses. Then, this would be divided by 2 and raised to the 1/2 power. The fraction 1/2, being enclosed in its own set of parentheses, is all considered as the exponent. Finally, C would be added to the sum.[3]

There is no effective limit on the number of pairs of parentheses that

---

[3] The hierarchical rule, discussed below, makes the outer set of parentheses unnecessary.

may be used in an expression. However, care must be taken to see that complete pairs are used.

Hierarchy of Arithmetic Operation.   Unless parentheses intervene, arithmetic operations are given the following priority of evaluation:

1.   Exponentiation (**)
2.   Multiplication and division (*, /)
3.   Addition and subtraction (+, −)

Thus, in the evaluation of an expression or any part thereof, exponentiation is carried out first. This means that if more than one operand is to be raised to a power, the operands must be enclosed in parentheses. For example, assume that $(3X)^2$ is to be computed. If this is written as 3.*X**2, the effect is to compute $3(X^2)$. When the expression is rewritten as (3.*X)**2, the proper result is obtained because the parentheses rule forces the evaluation of 3.*X before exponentiation.

At the next hierarchical level, multiplication and division are carried out in the order of their appearance from left to right. This means that some expressions, such as $\dfrac{3X}{Y}$ will be properly evaluated when written in a straightforward manner, such as 3.*X/Y. The numerator is first calculated, as 3X, then division takes place.

However, assume the calculation to be $\dfrac{Y}{3X}$. If this is written as Y/3.*X, an improper answer will be derived because this is interpreted to mean $\left(\dfrac{Y}{3}\right)X$. Proper evaluation is obtained by enclosing the denominator in parentheses, as Y/(3.*X). According to rule one, the denominator is now computed before division is attempted.

Addition and subtraction occupy the same hierarchical level. They are evaluated last in the order of their appearance reading from left to right.

Left-to-Right Evaluation.   Expressions are evaluated from left to right after the rules pertaining to the use of parentheses and computational hierarchy have been applied. For this reason, $\dfrac{3X}{Y}$ may be written as 3.*X/Y, while $\dfrac{Y}{3X}$ must be written as Y/(3.*X). In the first instance, left-to-right evaluation gives the proper interpretation; in the second, it does not.

Examples of Expression Construction

The rules and evaluation criteria may be made clearer by reviewing the examples in Figure 4–2. In each instance, the algebraic expression is shown in the left column and its FORTRAN equivalent on the right.

FIGURE 4–2
Examples of FORTRAN Expressions

	Expression	*FORTRAN Equivalent*
1.	$A-B+4$	A−B+4.
2.	$4+2A$	4.+2.*A
3.	$4+\dfrac{2}{A}$	4.+2./A
4.	$4+\dfrac{2}{A}-B$	4.+2./A−B
5.	$\left(4+\dfrac{2}{A}\right)B$	(4.+2./A)*B
6.	$4\left(\dfrac{2}{A}\right)B$	4*2./A*B
7.	$2A+4$	2.*A+4.
8.	$4(A+B)$	4.*(A+B)
9.	$\dfrac{4A}{2B}$	4.*A/(2.*B)
10.	$\dfrac{4+A}{2B}$	(4.+A)/(2.*B)
11.	$\dfrac{A}{2+B}$	A/(2.+B)
12.	$\dfrac{4+A}{2-B}$	(4.+A)/(2.−B)
13.	$\left(\dfrac{4+A}{2-B}\right)C$	((4.+A)/(2.−B))*C
14.	$\left(\dfrac{4A}{2B}\right)C$	(4.*A/(2.*B))*C
15.	$\dfrac{1}{8}\left(\dfrac{4+A}{2-B}\right)$	(1./8.)*((4.+A)/(2.−B))
16.	$\left(\dfrac{4A}{2B}\right)^{X}$	(4.*A/(2.*B))**X
17.	$(2AB)^{X-2}$	(2.*A*B)**(X−2.)
18.	$(2AB)^{\frac{1}{2}}$	(2.*A*B)**(1./2.)
19.	$(2AB)^{-\frac{1}{2}}$	(2.*A*B)**(−1./2.)

Using Double Precision Values

A data name defined as a double precision variable can be used as the receiving area of any arithmetic statement. Double precision variables and constants may also be used in any expression not of integer mode.

Double precision values are a part of the real number set. As such, they may be used exclusively in forming an expression. They may also be used with single precision real numbers. However, to intermix double precision and integer values would create an expression of mixed mode, an error condition in most FORTRAN versions.

ASSIGNING INITIAL VALUES TO DATA ELEMENTS

Data elements are ordinarily assigned values by reading input records or by computation. It is sometimes desirable, however, to be able to assign values without resorting to either of these methods. This may be achieved through use of the DATA statement.

This instruction is of the following form:

DATA $list/i_1*d_1, \ldots, i_m*d_m/ ,list/d_1,d_2, \ldots, d_n,/ , \ldots,/$

In this statement, *list* stands for a list of variables such as might be used in a READ or WRITE statement. As many variable names may be included as are to be assigned values. They are separated by commas.

$d_1, \ldots, d_m$ and $d_1, \ldots, d_n$ are values representing integer, real, or logical data constants. They are the values that will be assigned to the variables named in *list*. They may be assigned to more than one data name by prefixing some unsigned integer constant represented as $i_1, \ldots, i_m$. Constants are separated from one another by commas, and the data list is separated from the constant set by a slash $(/)$. Data values and related names should be of the same mode. The command is ended by a slash.

As a simple example of the statement's use, assume that three variables, A, B, and C are to be assigned initial values of zero. This might be done with the following instruction:

DATA A,B,C/0.,0.,0./

The three real constants in the set of values would be assigned to the variables in the named list.

The same could be accomplished in the following manner:

DATA A,B,C/3*0./

This indicates that the value zero is to be assigned to three data items.

The DATA statement's use is somewhat restricted until data arrays are used, although the brief example above should give some indication of its value. Where a number of data items must be assigned initial values, this statement is much easier to use than the arithmetic assignment statement, which provides another means of achieving the same end. It is particularly useful when data fields must be initialized. This technique is displayed in Illustration 3 below.

MATHEMATICAL FUNCTIONS

The FORTRAN language includes several mathematical functions. These are not basic arithmetic operations such as addition and subtraction but are sets of arithmetic instructions built into the FORTRAN compiler itself. When one of the functions is called for, the arithmetic commands are inserted in the program. Thus, the programming effect is the same as if execution of the function were a basic computer ability.

The functions available vary from one version of FORTRAN to another, and also from computer to computer. Therefore, it is necessary to check before using any particular function or name. Figure 4–3 shows the basic functions available in IBM 360–370 FORTRAN and WATFIV that might be used in a business administration environment. Others are available in these FORTRAN versions, and for other computers as well.

FIGURE 4–3
Partial List of Functions in IBM 360–370 FORTRAN and WATFIV

Mathematical Function	*FORTRAN Name*
Square root	SQRT
Exponential	EXP
Sine of an angle in radians	SIN
Cosine of an angle in radians	CØS
Arctangent of an angle in radians	ATAN
Natural logarithm (base e)	ALØG
Common logarithm (base 10)	ALØG10
Absolute value, real expression	ABS
Absolute value, integer expression	IABS

Mathematical functions are used as operators in arithmetic commands. Their general nature is:

function name (expression)

where "function name" is the appropriate name from Figure 4–3 and "expression" is any arithmetic expression written in real numeric mode except where noted. The function may be used in the arithmetic statement in company with any other operands and operators.

To illustrate the function's use, assume that a standard deviation, STD, is to be computed by the formula

$$\sqrt{\frac{SUMXS - \dfrac{SUMX^2}{AN}}{AN-1}}$$

The arithmetic statement might be written as

$$STD = ((SUMXS-SUMX**2/AN)/(AN-1.))**.5$$

in which case the expression in the outer set of parentheses is taken to the 1/2 power. It could also be written as

$$STD = SQRT((SUMXS-SUMX**2/AN)/(AN-1.))$$

which uses the function SQRT.

Another example of the SQRT function might be found in the computation of one root of a quadratic equation, which may be written as:

$$R1 = (-B+SQRT(B**2-4.*A*C))/(2.*A)$$

This also illustrates that part of the arithmetic expression may be used as the argument of the function.

All mathematic functions are used in the same way as SQRT illustrated above. They are not frequently needed in data processing operations. However, they are useful in statistical analysis, and the programmer should acquire a complete list of available functions and their names before writing programs in this field.

THE LOGICAL ASSIGNMENT STATEMENT

The logical assignment statement, like its arithmetic counterpart, is of the form

$$Variable = Expression$$

"Variable" must be a logical variable, as described in Chapter 3. "Expression" is a logical constant, or some combination of arithmetic constants or variables, relational operators, and logical operators. The expression must be reducible to a true or false state.

Logical assignment statements are not frequently used. However, logical expressions are frequently employed in logical IF statements. These expressions are very comprehensive, and an understanding of them and the logical IF is essential to the effective use of FORTRAN. For this reason, their nature is covered in Chapter 5 in great detail. At that time, examples of the logical assignment statement are also provided.

EXAMPLES OF FORTRAN PROGRAMS

The commands necessary for programming logically simple situations have now been introduced. The next problem is to fit these to some purpose.

Several examples of problem situations and FORTRAN programs are provided below. Of course, these are merely suggestive of the many computer applications in the modern commercial world and of the many ways in which programs may be written to satisfy business needs.

In all the examples where input is used, it is assumed that data fields occupy adjacent record positions without any skips. Fields are numeric unless otherwise specified. The location of an assumed decimal is shown by a caret ($\wedge$) when appropriate, and the number of Xs indicates the field size.

All output records are to contain one space as the leading character, and data items are to be separated by five spaces. The number of Xs in the field size column indicates the number of *numeric positions* to be provided in the output field but does not allow for the decimal or sign.

Illustration 1. Dividend Computations

Problem.   Each input record contains a stockholder identification number and the number of shares held. Dividends are to be computed at $.25 per share, and a dividend register is to be printed showing each stockholder's number and the amount he is to receive. In addition, each printed line is to be numbered.

More than one input record is to be processed. Records appear as follows:

	FORTRAN	
Item Description	*Name*	*Field Size*
Input record:		
Stockholder number	ID	xxxxx
Number of shares held	SHARE	xxxxx$_\wedge$
Output record:		
Line number	LINE	xxxxx
Stockholder number	ID	xxxxx
Dividend amount	AMT	xxxx.xx

Analysis. This is basically a very simple problem. An input record must be read, and the amount of dividends to be paid the stockholder computed as the product of a variable (SHARE) times a constant (.25). Figure 4–4 depicts an appropriate program.

The requirement of a line number, LINE, to be printed causes a minor complication. This line number must be generated by the program, in the manner shown in Figure 4–4.

FIGURE 4–4
Dividend Computations

```
C        ILLUSTRATION 1.
  10     FORMAT(I5,F5.0)
  11     FORMAT(1X,I5,5X,I6,5X,F9.2)
         LINE = 0
  25     READ(5,10,END=30)ID,SHARE
         AMT = SHARE * .25
         LINE = LINE + 1
         WRITE(6,11)LINE,ID,AMT
         GO TO 25
  30     STOP
         END
```

LINE must be increased by one for each output record. This is done by the arithmetic statement LINE = LINE + 1. This means "take whatever value is stored at LINE, add one to it, and return the sum to LINE." Thus, with each record, LINE will be increased by one.

However, LINE must be defined before being used in the expression of the arithmetic statement of the first record. Otherwise, it will be viewed as an undefined variable. Therefore, in an early statement, LINE is defined by assigning it a value of zero. Of course, this statement must appear above the READ command; otherwise, the element would be set to zero with each record.

Illustration 2. Extension of Line Items

Problem. Input records containing a customer identification number, the number of units sold, sales price per unit, and allowable discount percentage are to be read. For each, an output record containing the identification number, number of units sold, the gross sales price, the discount amount, and the net sales price is to be prepared. Output columns are to be captioned 'NUMBER', 'UNITS SØLD', 'GRØSS PRICE', 'DISCØUNT', and 'NET PRICE', respectively.

More than one input record is to be processed. Records are to appear as follows:

	FORTRAN	
Item Description	*Name*	*Field Size*
Input record:		
Identification number	ID	xxxxx
Number of units sold	NØ	xxxx
Sales price per unit	SPR	xₓxx
Discount rate (decimal fraction) ...	RATE	ₓxx
Output record:		
Identification number	ID	xxxxx
Number of units sold	NØ	xxxx
Gross sales price	GRØSS	xxxxx.xx
Discount amount	DISC	xxxx.xx
Net sales price	NET	xxxxx.xx

Analysis. This is a typical problem involving the extension of invoice line items. It requires the computation of several amounts, but all calculations are simple.

The only complication arises from the fact that the number of units sold, NØ, is required as an integer value in output, but as a real variable in the computation of gross sales price. This poses no problem in FORTRAN versions permitting mixed mode arithmetic expressions, but the need for this item expressed as a real variable must be satisfied in other cases. The solution in Figure 4–5 suggests a means of avoiding a mixed-mode arithmetic expression.

Immediately after reading, the integer variable NØ is used to create a real counterpart, called ANØ. This is called "floating" the variable NØ, and in no way affects its existence or value. Now, computations can be written using the ANØ, the real equivalent of NØ, and the output record can use the integer form as required.

Certain values—GRØSS and DISC—are computed, used in subsequent computations, then written. This is quite acceptable. Their use in the expression does not in any way affect their value.

This problem provides some indication of the order in which programs must be executed. In this situation, data must be read before computations may be undertaken, and these must be completed before the WRITE instruction can be executed. The order of the three arithmetic instructions could be changed, but only by making subsequent computations more clumsy.

FIGURE 4-5
Extension of Line Items

IBM

FORTRAN CODING FORM

| PROGRAM | EXAMPLES | | PUNCHING INSTRUCTIONS | GRAPHIC | | PAGE | OF | |
| PROGRAMMER | MC CAMERON | DATE | | PUNCH | | CARD ELECTRO NUMBER* | | |

X28-7327-6 U/M 050
Printed in U.S.A.

C		STATEMENT NUMBER	FORTRAN STATEMENT	IDENTIFICATION SEQUENCE
C			ILLUSTRATION 2.	010
			REAL NET	020
		5	FORMAT(5X,'NUMBER',5X,'UNITS SOLD',5X,'GROSS PRICE',5X,'DISCOUNT',	030
			15X,'NET PRICE')	040
			WRITE(6,5)	050
			WRITE(6,11)	060
		25	READ(5,10,END=30)ID,NO,SPR,RATE	070
		10	FORMAT(I5,I4,F3.2,F2.2)	080
			ANO = NO	090
			GROSS = ANO * SPR	100
			DISC = GROSS * RATE	110
			NET = GROSS - DISC	120
			WRITE(6,11)ID,NO,GROSS,DISC,NET	130
		11	FORMAT(6X,I5,8X,I4,9X,F9.2,6X,F8.2,5X,F9.2)	140
			GO TO 25	150
		30	WRITE(6,12)	160
		12	FORMAT(5X,'PROCESSING COMPLETE')	170
			STOP	180
			END	190

This problem also shows how captions can be designed and printed above output columns.

First, the necessary field sizes of output data elements must be determined and appropriate columnar captions selected. Then, a line mock-up is prepared. Most printers have lines of 132 characters; this places a maximum on the length of a line to be printed. However, most output lines are substantially shorter than this.

To determine the proper placement of line captions and data elements, any vertically-ruled paper can be used. Ordinary FORTRAN coding paper is convenient, and can be spliced if an output line of more than 80 characters must be planned. By indicating where headings and data elements should be placed to provide appropriate spacing, the format of the heading and data lines can easily be determined.

Figure 4–6 contains a mock-up of the heading and data lines for this problem. First, by counting the characters in each item, it was determined that columnar heads had at least as many characters as the data over which they were to be placed. Therefore, they were written with desired spacing between each heading. Next, the location of data fields was determined, and xs placed in each data location. This made the determination of proper spacing between data elements simple.

FIGURE 4–6
Mock-up of Heading and Data Lines

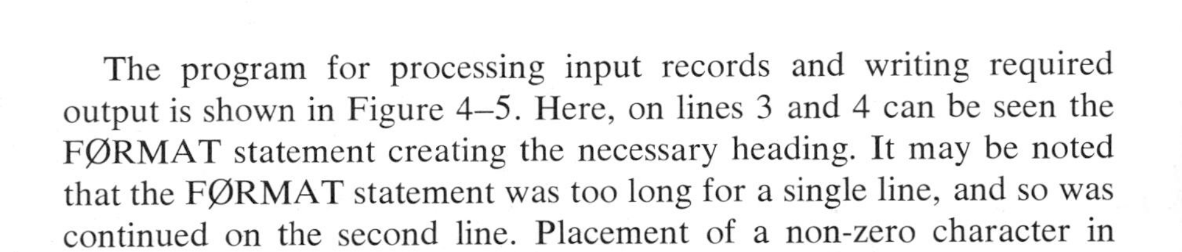

The program for processing input records and writing required output is shown in Figure 4–5. Here, on lines 3 and 4 can be seen the FØRMAT statement creating the necessary heading. It may be noted that the FØRMAT statement was too long for a single line, and so was continued on the second line. Placement of a non-zero character in column 6 of line 4 designates this a part of the FØRMAT statement.

Insertion of a blank line between the heading and contents of the report is desired. This is done by giving a WRITE command, but omitting designation of any data names. Any FØRMAT statement can be cited, so long as it does not contain an alphanumeric message.

Such a statement may be seen on line 6 of Figure 4–5.

Illustration 3. Computation of Mean

Problem.   A program is to be prepared for computing the arithmetic mean, or average, of a set of student grades. The average is calculated by dividing the number of grades read into the total of all grades. Each grade is written on a different record, and there are less than 1,000 students. Input and output records appear as follows:

	FORTRAN	
Item Description	Name	Field Size
Input:		
Student grade .... GRADE		xxx
Output:		
Number of student grade records read ... N		xxx
Arithmetic mean of grades .... AVG		xxx.xx

Analysis.   First, the records containing student grades must be read and the grades summed. As this is done, the number of records in the set must be counted.

As in Illustration 1 above, certain data fields must be initialized. The steps to accomplish this can be seen on line 3 of Figure 4–7. The reason for this initialization can be understood by imagining the processing of the first input record. If the data elements were not initialized, the computer would detect an undefined variable when attempting to execute the fifth instruction, SUMGRD = SUMGRD + GRADE.

Records are counted as they are read by the statement N = N + 1. Grade values are accumulated by the instruction SUMGRD = SUMGRD = GRADE.

The mean cannot be calculated until all grade records have been read, indicated by the exhaustion of the input file. At this time, the END = conditional of the READ statement transfers the program to statement 20. Here, the number of observations is floated to avoid mixed mode in the expression of the next statement. The average of all grades is then calculated and written with an appropriate caption, and the program halted.

Illustration 4. The Effect of Mixed-Mode Statements

It has been pointed out that arithmetic *statements* may be of mixed mode, although *expressions* (in many FORTRAN versions) may not. This means, simply, that the variable to the left of the statement may, or may not, be of the same mode as the expression. Evaluation occurs in

FIGURE 4-7

Computation of Mean

COMM.	STATEMENT NUMBER	CONT.	FORTRAN STATEMENT
C			ILLUSTRATION 3.
	1		FORMAT(F3.0)
			DATA SUMGRD, N/0., 0/
	10		READ(5,1,END=20)GRADE
			SUMGRD = SUMGRD + GRADE
			N = N + 1
			GO TO 10
	20		AN = N
			AVG = SUMGRD / AN
			WRITE(6,2)N,AVG
	2		FORMAT(1X, I3, 5X, 'VALUE OF MEAN ', F8.2)
			WRITE(6,3)
	3		FORMAT(' PROCESSING COMPLETE')
			STOP
			END

the mode of the expression; the result is stored in the mode of the left-hand variable.

However, care must be taken when writing a mixed-mode statement; otherwise the desired results may not be obtained. Several unrelated examples of mixed-mode statements are furnished below. For each, assume the following data values:

$$A = 4.75 \qquad I = 5$$
$$B = 5. \qquad J = 6$$
$$C = 2. \qquad K = 2$$

	Equation	Solution
1.	$X = I + J$	$X = 11.$
2.	$L = I + J$	$L = 11$
3.	$X = A + B$	$X = 9.75$
4.	$L = A + B$	$L = 9$
5.	$X = I / K$	$X = 2.$
6.	$X = B / C$	$X = 2.5$
7.	$L = J*K/I$	$L = 2$
8.	$X = 6.*C/B$	$X = 2.4$
9.	$L = A*2.$	$L = 9$
10.	$X = A*2.$	$X = 9.5$

These examples demonstrate the fact that in the arithmetic statement, the evaluation of the expression is carried out in its mode. If it is written in the integer mode, an integer answer is obtained. Then, the answer is stored in the mode of the left-hand variable, being fixed or floated, as necessary. If the expression is in integer mode or if the variable is integer mode, the result will be truncated to an integer.

As mentioned above, IBM 360–370 FORTRAN permits mixed-mode expressions. All integers are converted to real mode, and evaluation is executed as for a real expression.

CHAPTER SUMMARY

The arithmetic assignment statement introduced in this chapter lies at the very heart of computer utilization, for through it arithmetic computation—the evaluation of expressions—occurs. One must note the nature of the arithmetic statement carefully, for it is somewhat different from that of an algebraic equation. The arithmetic statement is as follows:

$$\text{Variable} = \text{Expression}$$

It means "evaluate, or solve, the expression, reducing it to a single number. Store the number at the location named 'variable'." Thus, a statement such as $N = N + 1$ means "take whatever value is stored at N, add 1 to it, and place the sum back at N."

The left-hand member of the statement can only be a data name, while the right portion, or expression, can consist of any meaningful combination of operands and operators.

Care must be taken in forming the arithmetic expression, and some knowledge of the computer's evaluation method is essential to proper structuring. Operands of mixed mode cause the most common error found in arithmetic expression coding. Another error frequently committed is in the use of undefined variables. Other possible errors, made less frequently, are mentioned in the chapter.

Certain computations are made so frequently that the set of instructions necessary for proper calculation have been included in FORTRAN. These are referenced by "mathematical functions." While not used nearly so frequently as the arithmetic statement itself, these functions do provide a very handy means for calling for standard calculations. Techniques for the creation of other functions are discussed in Chapter 9.

Two other assignment statements are covered in this chapter. One, the DATA statement, is used to assign initial values to data elements. It is of the following general nature:

$$\text{DATA } list/i_1*d_1, \ldots, i_m*d_m/, list/d_1, d_2, \ldots, d_n, \ldots, /$$

$list$ = list of data names
i = optional multiplier prefix
d = integer, real, or logical value
     to be assigned data-element

The last statement introduced is the logical assignment instruction, of the general nature

Variable = Expression

where "variable" is a logical variable and "expression" is some expression reducible to a true or false state. Because the statement is seldom used, and because the very important, although complex, logical expression is found most frequently in the logical IF statement, a study of its nature is found in the next chapter.

With the mastery of this chapter, one may begin writing meaningful FORTRAN programs. Therefore, the problems at the end of the chapter have been set up with all the information necessary for programming and execution. It is recommended that a group of these problems be coded and run before going to Chapter 5. Only then does the real nature of FORTRAN become apparent.

QUESTIONS

1. What is the general form of the arithmetic statement?
2. In the arithmetic statement, what is meant by "variable"?
3. What is the function of "variable"?
4. What must be on the left side of the = sign in an arithmetic statement?
5. Must the arithmetic statement have a statement number? May it have a number?
6. What is an arithmetic expression?
7. What is mixed mode?
8. Can an arithmetic statement be of mixed mode?
9. What is an arithmetic operand?
10. What is an arithmetic operator?
11. How can the word ADD be used in an arithmetic expression?
12. What is an undefined variable?

13. Assuming that no parentheses are involved, indicate which arithmetic operation will be evaluated first in the following unrelated pairs:
    (*a*) Multiplication or addition
    (*b*) Multiplication or division
    (*c*) Division or subtraction
    (*d*) Multiplication or exponentiation
    (*e*) Addition or subtraction

14. What is the evaluation order of an expression?

15. What is the symbol for multiplication? For exponentiation?

16. What effect do parentheses have on the evaluation of an expression?

17. What is the difference between X + Y/3. and (X + Y)/3.?

18. How can different answers be produced by B = X/Y and I = X/Y?

19. What is the difference between A*B/C and (A*B)/C?

20. What is the difference between A*B/C*D and (A*B)/(C*D)?

21. What is a mathematical function?

22. What is the difference between SQRT(A + B) and (A + B)**.5?

23. Give a single FORTRAN statement to achieve the same result as the two following instructions:
    X = 25.
    I = 0.

24. What values are assigned A and B after execution of the following command?
    DATA A,B/2.5,3.1416/

25. What value is assigned X after execution of the two following instructions?
    DATA X/25./
    X = X + 5.

EXERCISES

1. Indicate the errors, if any, in the following arithmetic statements:
   (*a*) I = (X*3)**K
   (*b*) A432 = I233 − X42/2K
   (*c*) X = A & B
   (*d*) I = SQR(A**2 − ((3.6*C)**.5 − D)
   (*e*) A = (B − 1.)(B + 1.)
   (*f*) I = A + B
   (*g*) A = I**J
   (*h*) ((X − Y2Z(*E**K + Y/4.)**.5
   (*i*) 4X = 2Y
   (*j*) I = I + 1

2. Indicate the errors, if any, in the following arithmetic statements:
   (a) X = ADD A AND B
   (b) K = K − 4
   (c) AI = IA
   (d) X−2. = Y + 4.
   (e) XY = (2.+(3.*A−4.)/(B+3.)
   (f) J = A**I
   (g) A = I÷J
   (h) K = 4A
   (i) I = C**2−SQR(A−B)
   (j) X = SQRT(I)

3. State the value of X or K stored as the result of each of the following arithmetic statements, and whether the result is in real or integer mode:

(a)	X = 3*(5/2)	(f)	X = 2./3.
(b)	X = 3*5/2	(g)	X = 1+2**2
(c)	X = 3.*5./2.	(h)	X = (1+2)**2
(d)	K = 3.*5./2.	(i)	K = 1.3*2
(e)	X = 2/3	(j)	X = 1.3*2

4. State the value of X or K stored as the result of each of the following arithmetic statements, and whether the result is in real or integer mode:

(a)	X = 2./5.*2.	(f)	K = 2/5*3
(b)	X = 2./(5.*2.)	(g)	X = 1/3+1/3+1/3
(c)	X = 2./5.*3.	(h)	X = 1./3.+1./3.+1./3.
(d)	K = 2./5.*3.	(i)	X = 19/4+5/4
(e)	X = 2/5*3	(j)	X = 19./4.+5./4.

5. For each of the following unrelated exercises, assume the following values: X = 4.; Y = 3.; Z = 2. Give the value of A.

(a)	A = (X*Y)**2	(f)	A = X**2+Z
(b)	A = (X−Y)**2	(g)	A = 27.**1/Y
(c)	A = X−Y**2	(h)	A = 27.**(1./Y)
(d)	A = (X+Y)**Z	(i)	A = (X+Y)**1
(e)	A = X**(2.+Z)	(j)	A = X+Y**1

6. For each of the following unrelated exercises, assume the following values: A = 4.; B = 3.; C = 2.; Give the value of X.

(a)	X = A+B*C+A	(f)	X = A*B−B*C
(b)	X = (A+B)*(C+A)	(g)	X = A/B*C
(c)	X = A*B−C	(h)	X = A/(B*C)
(d)	X = A*(B−C)	(i)	X = B−A*C
(e)	X = (A*B)−(B*C)·	(j)	X = (B−A)*C

7. Write FORTRAN expressions for the following (each variable name consists of a single letter):

   (a) $\dfrac{A+B}{A-B}$ (f) $(A+B)^{\frac{1}{2}}$

(b) $\dfrac{2A-B}{C-D}$

(c) $\dfrac{2A}{C-D}$

(d) $A+B^2$

(e) $(A+B)^2$

(g) $\dfrac{A}{B}+C$

(h) $\dfrac{A}{B}+\dfrac{C}{D}$

(i) $\dfrac{A}{B}+\dfrac{C}{DE}$

(j) $\left(\dfrac{A}{B}\right)^{\frac{1}{2}}$

8. List the errors in the following program:

```
20      FØRMAT(I5)
        READ(5,10)X = A+B
        A = (2X+Y)/5
        WRITE(6,20),X
        GØ TØ 20
        STØP
        END
10      FØRMAT,F3.2
```

9. A file contains sales records, each record consisting of the following data elements. (In "field size," the number of x's denotes number of numeric positions; a caret ($_\wedge$) the location of an implied decimal. Absence of a caret indicates that the field is of integer mode.)

	FORTRAN	
Item Description	Name	Field Size
Sales date	DATE	xxxxxx
Item number	NØ	xxxx
Sales amount ...	SALE	xxx$_\wedge$xx

Instructions: Assume that a 4% city and 2% state sales tax is assessed on the amount of the sale. Write a program that will read a sales record, and compute the appropriate taxes and write out the item number; sales amount; city sales tax (CITAX, field size xx.xx); state sales tax (STAX, field size xx.xx); total tax (the sum of CITAX and STAX, to be called TØTAX, field size xxx.xx), and sales amount plus total tax (GRØSS, field size xxxx.xx). The program should process more than one input record, and should terminate when all records have been processed.

10. Refer to Exercise 9 above. Prepare the same output records, but also accumulate the amount of total tax (as TØTAL, field size xxxx.xx) and sales amount (as TØTSL, field size xxxxx.xx). These should be written out with the captions 'TØTAL TAX' and 'TØTAL SALES' in a single record after input records have been processed.

11. Refer to Exercise 9 above. Read the input records and accumulate the total sales amount, TØTSL, and number of sales records processed,

NUM. Then, after all input records have been read, calculate the average sale size (AVGSL, field size xxx.xx). Write out 'AVERAGE SALE', AVGSL, 'NUMBER ØF SALES' and NUM (field size xxx) in a single record. The program should then terminate.

12. Refer to Exercise 9 above. The sale amount includes salesman's commission of 15% of sales before commission. Calculate the amount of sale before commission (NSALE, field size xxx.xx) and write for each input record an output record containing item number, sales amount, and NSALE. Also, accumulate the amount of commission (TØTCØM, field size xxxx.xx) from all input records and write the amount after processing all records. Write the message 'PRØCESSING CØMPLETE' before stopping the program.

13. Refer to Exercise 9 above. Assume that all sales amounts are subject to a 10% discount; then, the net amount (sales − discount) is subject to a 6% sales tax. For each input record, prepare and write an output record showing: item number; sales amount; discount amount (DISC, field size xx.xx); sales tax (TAX, field size xx.xx); and collection amount (sales amount − discount + sales tax, field size xxx.xx). Also, accumulate the sales amount, discount amount, and tax amount (as TØTSL, TØTDIS, and TØTAL, respectively, field size xxxxx.xx). After all input records have been processed, write these in different records with appropriate captions and terminate the program.

PROBLEMS

General Instructions

The following problems are designed so that they may be compiled and run on a computer, if desired. Therefore, in coding them, the requirements of the computer to be used should be followed. Particular attention should be paid to the size of data names and constants, the names of mathematical functions, and the requirements of the input and output units.

Unless other instructions are given, the following rules must be followed in preparing all problems in this and later chapters:

Rules Pertaining to Input

1. All data fields begin at the left of the record and occupy adjacent positions.
2. The number of x's in the "Field Size" column of the problem indicates the size of the data field.
3. Decimals are not recorded in real values. Instead, they are to be provided

by the FØRMAT statement, and their location is indicated by a caret ($_\wedge$) in real fields.

4. Fields without a caret are of integer mode.

Rules Pertaining to Output

1. The first output position should be left blank.
2. All data values should be separated by five blank spaces, unless to do so would exceed the allowed record length, or prevent the proper location of captions.
3. The number of *numeric* positions in a field is indicated by the number of *x*'s in the "Field Size" column of the problem. This does not allow for signs or decimals.
4. The proper decimal location is indicated by the printed decimal in "Field Size."
5. Use the END = option if appropriate.
6. Integer numeric fields are indicated by the absence of a decimal.
7. Each program should be terminated with the message 'PRØCESSING CØMPLETE'.

   You should use the data names set out in the problem. You may make up any other data names you need.

The Problems

1. The Pleasant City Water Company charges its residential customers a fixed amount of $2.70, plus $0.37 per 100 cubic feet of water consumed, as its monthly bill. Using the input and output records described below, prepare a program for the computation of bill amounts. Your program should process more than one input record, and prepare an output record for each input. It should terminate when all records have been processed, after writing 'PRØCESSING CØMPLETE'.

	FORTRAN	
Item Description	*Name*	*Field Size*
Input record:		
Customer number	NØ	xxxx
Meter reading, last month*	READ1	xxxx$_\wedge$
Meter reading, this month*	READ2	xxxx$_\wedge$
Unpaid amount from previous month	UNPD	xxx$_\wedge$xx
Output record:		
Customer number	NØ	xxxx
Charge for water used	CHG	xxx.xx

* Expressed in hundreds of cubic feet.

The charge for water used should be calculated as $2.70, plus $0.37 times the difference between the current meter reading and last month's reading, plus any unpaid amount from the previous month.

2. The Friendly Taxi Company operates a fleet of automobiles. Each month, a record is prepared that indicates the operating expenses of each auto. Because gasoline is a major operating item, it is isolated for special analysis. The automobile records, and the output record to be prepared for each input appear as follows:

		FORTRAN	
Item Description		*Name*	*Field Size*
Input record:			
Auto number	NØ		xxxx
Minor operating costs, including repairs ...	ØPEXP		xxxxx
Odometer reading, end of last month	ØDRD1		xxxxx˄
Odometer reading, end of this month	ØDRD2		xxxxx˄
Number of gallons of gas used	GAS		xx˄
Gasoline price per gallon	GASCST		˄xxx
Output record:			
Auto number	NØ		xxxx
Miles driven	MILES		xxxx
Operating cost per mile	ØPCØST		x.xxx
• Miles per gallon of gas consumed	MILGAL		xx.x

The number of miles driven can be determined by subtracting the odometer reading at the end of last month from the reading at the end of this month. Operating cost per mile is the sum of minor operating costs and gasoline cost, calculated as price per gallon times number of gallons of gas used, divided by the number of miles driven. The miles per gallon of gas consumed is determined by dividing number of miles driven by the number of gallons consumed.

In addition to preparing the above output record for each input record, the average operating cost per mile and miles per gallon for all vehicles is to be determined and written as AVGØP (field size xx.xxx) and AVGNPG (field size xxx.x), respectively, after processing all input records. This requires that the number of vehicles, operating costs, and miles driven, be accumulated as records are being processed. Then, the required averages are to be calculated and written in single output record with identifying captions and processing terminated.

3. Input records such as shown below are used by the Superior Sales Company to record its sales, and a program is to be written to prepare the depicted output record for each:

	FORTRAN	
Item Description	*Name*	*Field Size*
Input record:		
Item code number	NØ	xxxx
Number of units sold	UNITS	xxx∧
Sales price per unit	USPR	xxx∧
Freight charges on order	FGT	xxxx∧
Output record:		
Item code number	NØ	xxxx
Sales amount	SALE	xxxxx.xx
Sales tax	TAX	xxx.xx
Total invoice charge	TØT	xxxxx.xx

The sales amount is to be calculated as the product of the number of units sold times the sales price per unit, plus the freight charges on the order. Sales tax of 6% is to be assessed on this amount, and the total of sales amount and sales tax reported as TØT. Output columns are to be headed 'NUMBER', 'SALES AMT', 'TAX', and 'TØTAL CHARGE'.

In addition, the total amount of SALE, TAX, and TØT are to be accumulated from all input records as TØTSAL, TØTAX, and TØTCHG, respectively. These, with the average amount of invoice charge per record processed (AVGTØT, field size xxxxx.xx) are to be written in a single record after all data records have been processed, and the program terminated.

4. In inventory control, the economic order quantity for an item may be found by the equation $EØQ = \sqrt{\dfrac{2DC}{US}}$, where D represents the demand for the item in a given time, in units; C represents the cost of placing an order, U represents the item's per-unit cost; and S represents the cost of carrying the item in inventory, expressed as a percentage of its cost per unit.

Instructions: Using the economic order formula above, prepare a program computing the economic order quantity and purchase cost for inventory items of the Ajax Company. Input and output records appear as follows:

	FORTRAN	
Item Description	*Name*	*Field Size*
Input record		
Inventory number	NØ	xxxx
Demand	DMD	xxx∧
Cost of placing order	CØRD	xxx∧
Unit cost	UCST	xxx∧
Carrying cost	CCST	∧xxx

(Continued)

	FORTRAN	
Item Description	*Name*	*Field Size*
Output record:		
Inventory number	NØ	xxxx
Economic order quantity	EØQ	xxxxx
Purchase cost	PCST	xxxx.xx

Purchase cost is to be calculated as the unit cost times the economic order quantity.

Output columns are to be labeled 'INV.NØ.', 'ØRDER QTY', and 'CØST'.

After all records have been processed, the average economic order quantity is to be calculated as AVGEØQ (field size, xxxxx), written with an appropriate caption, and the program terminated.

5. Handisale, Inc., operates a chain of convenience stores. Sales for each store are recorded daily on the record below. A program is to be written for the preparation of an output record in the form indicated for each store, and certain control amounts, described below, are to be prepared.

Input and output records appear as follows:

	FORTRAN	
Item Description	*Name*	*Field Size*
Input record:		
Store number	STØRE	xxxx
Date	DATE	xxxxx
Cash collection amount	CASH	xxxxxx
Output record:		
Store number	STØRE	xxxx
Date	DATE	xxxxx
Sales amount	SALES	xxxx.xx
State tax collections	STAX	xxx.xx
City tax collections	CTAX	xxx.xx

The cash collection amount in each input record represents the cash collections for a certain store on a certain date and includes sales and sales taxes. State sales taxes of 4% and city taxes of 2% are computed on the amount of sales *before* tax. As each input record is read, cash is to be separated into its components—state sales tax, city sales tax, and sales. An output record is to be prepared and written for each input record.

For control purposes, the amount of cash collected is to be accumulated from the input records, and SALES, STAX, and CTAX are to be accumulated from the output records, as TØTSAL, TØTST and TØTCT, respectively (each has a field size of xxxxx.xx). These totals should be written in a single record after all data records have been processed, and the program terminated.

6. Prepare a program to process an unknown number of depreciation records of the type described below. An output record, as shown, is to be prepared for each input.

	FORTRAN	
Item Description	*Name*	*Field Size*
Input record:		
Asset number	NUM	xxxxx
Asset cost	CØST	xxxxx̭xx
Estimated scrap value	SCRAP	xxxx̭xx
Estimated units of output for		
life of asset	EST	xxxxxx̭
Units produced this period	UNITS	xxxx̭
Output record:		
Asset number	NUM	xxxxx
Units produced this period	KUNITS	xxxx
Depreciation per unit	DEP	xx.xx
Depreciation for this period	TØT	xxxxx.xx

Depreciation per unit is to be computed by subtracting scrap value from cost, then dividing by estimated units of output.

Depreciation for this period is derived by multiplying the depreciation per unit by the number of units produced.

7. Hercules Repair charges its customers the sum of labor costs, parts, and an overhead amount for repair work done. Prepare a program to process input records containing these data for each repair job, writing an output record for each one read. In addition, certain control totals described below are to be accumulated.

Input and output records appear as follows:

	FORTRAN	
Item Description	*Name*	*Field Size*
Input record:		
Work order number	NØ	xxxxx
Labor hours	HRS	xx̭x
Labor rate per hour	RTE	x̭xx
Repair parts	PARTS	xxx̭xx
Output record:		
Work order number	NØ	xxxxx
Labor cost	LCØST	xxx.xx
Parts cost	PCØST	xxx.xx
Overhead cost	ØCØST	xxx.xx
Total repair cost	TØTCST	xxxx.xx

Labor cost is to be calculated as the product of the labor hours worked times the labor rate per hour. Overhead cost is computed as 40% of the labor cost. The total repair cost is the sum of labor cost, parts cost, and overhead cost. Columns in the output report are to be labeled 'WØRK ØRDER', 'LABØR', 'PARTS', 'ØVERHEAD', and 'TØTAL'.

Labor cost, parts costs, and overhead cost are to be accumulated from all records as LABTØT, PARTØT, and ØHDTØT, respectively, field size xxxxx.xx. They are to be written with proper captions in a single record after all data records have been processed, and the program terminated.

8. Diamond Corporation prepares its employee payroll on the computer. Input records, and output records to be prepared from them, appear as follows:

	FORTRAN	
Item Description	Name	Field Size
Input record:		
Employee number	NØ	xxxx
Pay rate	RATE	xxxx
Hours worked	HØURS	xxx
Output record:		
Employee number	NØ	xxxx
Gross pay	GRØSS	xxx.xx
Social Security tax	STAX	xx.xx
Net pay	PAY	xxx.xx

Gross pay is to be calculated as the product of pay rate times hours worked. Social Security tax is computed as 5.85% of gross pay.

An output record is to be prepared for each input record. In addition, gross pay, Social Security tax, and net pay are to be accumulated from all records processed as TØTGRØ, TØTAX, and TØTPAY, respectively. After all data records have been processed, these are to be written out with proper captions by field sizes xxxxx.xx, xxxx.xx, and xxxxx.xx, and the program terminated.

9. Sales prices at the Omega Company includes a markup of 60%, based on cost. Salesmen are granted a commission of 20% of merchandise cost. Write a program that will read the indicated input records and prepare the required output records:

	FORTRAN	
Data Description	Name	Field Size
Input record:		
Salesman's number	SNUM	xxxx
Sales amount	SALE	xxxxxx
Output record:		
Salesman's number	SNUM	xxxx
Cost of item sold	CØST	xxxx.xx
Amount of markup	MARKUP	xxxx.xx
Sales amount	SALE	xxxx.xx
Salesman's commission	SCØM	xxx.xx
Company margin	MARGIN	xxxx.xx

The cost of the item sold is determined by dividing the sales amount by 1 plus the markup percent. The company's margin is calculated as the amount of markup less the salesman's commission. Columns in the output report are to be headed 'SALESMAN', 'ITEM CØST', 'MARKUP', 'SALES AMT.', 'CØMMIS.', and 'MARGIN'.

10. The Apex Manufacturing Company apportions its electricity costs to its several departments on the basis of the relative square footage occupied by the department compared to the total square footage in the building. To do this, three differently configured input records are required. There is only one record of the first and second types each, but many records of the third type.

Input and output records are as shown below:

	FORTRAN	
Item Description	*Name*	*Field Size*
Input record, type 1:		
Electric meter reading, end of last month	KWH1	xxxxxx
Electric meter reading, end of this month	KWH2	xxxxxx
Input record, type 2:		
Square footage of building	BLDFT	xxxxx‸
Input record, type 3:		
Department number	NØ	xxx
Square feet occupied by department	DPTFT	xxxxx‸
Output record:		
Department number	NØ	xxx
Departmental electricity cost	DELCST	xxxx.xx

The program should read the first input record and determine the number of kilowatt-hours of electricity used, by subtracting last month's meter reading from the reading at the end of the current month. Then, the electricity cost (ELCØST) can be calculated as electricity useage times 4.57¢ per kilowatt-hour.

Next, the single record indicating the square footage of the building should be read. Dividing the building square footage into the electricity cost determines the cost per square foot of building space.

Data records, one for each department in the building, follow. These are described above as type 3. An output record should be prepared for each, showing the departmental electricity cost (electricity cost per square foot times square feet occupied by department). Column captions 'DEPT. NØ.' and 'ELEC. CØST' should be used.

Department electricity costs should be accumulated as they are calculated, as TØTCST (field size xxxx.xx). This, and the building's electricity cost (ELCØST), should be written out in a single record after all data records have been processed with appropriate captions, and the program terminated.

11. Write a program that will read an unknown number of input records, each containing a single value of X, field size xxxx. As records are read they should be counted (as N), the sum of the X values accumulated, and the sum of the X^2 values should also be accumulated. Then, after all input records have been read, the standard deviation (field size xxxx.xx) should be computed by the following formula

$$STD = \sqrt{\frac{\Sigma X^2 - \dfrac{(\Sigma X)^2}{N}}{N - 1}}$$

and the mean computed as $AVG = \Sigma X / N$. The mean and standard deviation should be written with captions and processing should be terminated.

12. The X Company uses a method of semi-flexible budgeting, where the budgetary allowance for certain types of expenses consists of a fixed base amount, plus a fraction of sales. Using the input records below, prepare an output record for each containing the indicated data items:

		FORTRAN	
Item Description		*Name*	*Field Size*
Input record, type 1:			
Sales for period	....	SALES	xxxxxxx
Input record, type 2:			
Account number	....	NØ	xxxxxx
Basic budget allowance	....	BASE	xxxxxxx
Base sales amount	....	BSALE	xxxxxxx
Incremental allowance percent	...	PCT	xxx
Amount of actual expense	....	ACEXP	xxxxxxx
Output record:			
Account number	....	NØ	xxxxxx
Actual expense	....	ACEXP	xxxxx.xx
Total budget allowance	....	TBUD	xxxxx.xx
Budget variance	....	VAR	xxxxx.xx

A single record of the first type is to be read first. Then as type 2 records are read, the account's total budget allowance is to be calculated as the sum of the basic allowance and an adjustment amount. This adjustment is computed as the incremental allowance percent times the excess of period sales over base sales (you may assume that such an excess always exists).

Next, the amount of the budget variance is to be calculated by subtracting the amount of actual expense from the total budget allowance. In addition to the output record, the total of all budget variances is to be accumulated as TØTVAR (field size xxxxx.xx), and written with the caption 'TØTAL VARIANCE =' after all records have been processed. Then the program is to be terminated.

13. Prepare a program to process an unknown number of asset depreciation records of the type below. An output record, as shown, is to be prepared for each input.

	FORTRAN	
Item Description	*Name*	*Field Size*
Input record:		
Asset number	ID	xxxxx
Useful life—years	ULIFE	xxx_∧
Asset cost	CØST	xxxxxxx
Estimated scrap value	SCRAP	xxxxxx
Depreciation taken	ADEP	xxxxxxx
Output record:		
Asset number	ID	xxxxx
Asset cost	CØST	xxxxx.xx
Depreciation taken this period	DEPREC	xxxxx.xx
Total depreciation taken—		
including this period	ADEP	xxxxx.xx
Undepreciated value	VALUE	xxxxx.xx

The amount of depreciation, DEPREC, is to be calculated by the declining balance method. In this DEPREC is taken as R∗ Carrying Value. $R = 1 - \sqrt[n]{S \div C}$, where S is scrap value, C is original cost, and n is the number of years of useful life. The nth root of a value, X, may be expressed as X raised to the $1/n$ power. "Carrying value" is the asset's cost less depreciation taken.

The depreciation charge for this period is to be added to that taken in prior years, as read in the input record, to yield ADEP. The undepreciated value is cost less depreciation taken.

14. Prepare a program for computing depreciation for 1975 by the sum-of-years' digits method. More than one input record is to be processed, and an output record is to be prepared for each.

	FORTRAN	
Item Description	*Name*	*Field Size*
Input record:		
Asset number	IDNØ	xxx
Year of acquisition	YRACQ	xxxx_∧
Estimated useful life	ULIFE	xxx_∧
Original cost	CØST	xxxxxx_∧
Scrap value	SCRAP	xxxxx_∧
Output record:		
Asset number	IDNØ	xxxx
Current depreciation	DEPREC	xxxx.xx_∧

Current depreciation is to be calculated as the year fraction times (cost − scrap value).

The denominator of the year fraction in a sum-of-years' digits computation may be calculated as $\dfrac{n(n+1)}{2}$ where n is the useful life of the asset.

No depreciation is taken on an asset in the year of acquisition. Therefore, the years expired since an asset was acquired is the difference between its year of acquisition and the current year. For example, eight years (1975 − 1967) have elapsed since an asset was acquired in 1967. The numerator of the year fraction can then be found by subtracting this from (asset life + 1).

In addition to computing the depreciation for the year on each asset, the total of all depreciation for the year is to be accumulated as TØTDEP with the caption 'TØTAL DEPRECIATIØN', (field size xxxxx.xx) and written after all data records are processed. Then the program should be terminated.

15. The X Company uses a method of forecasting sales for the coming month that is based on sales for the prior six-month period. However, all prior months are not considered of equal importance. Instead, the following weighting scheme is followed:

   (*a*)   The oldest four months are averaged and this is assigned a weight of .5.

   (*b*)   The month before last is assigned a weight of 1.5.

   (*c*)   Last month's sales and sales forecast are averaged and this is assigned a weight of 3.

   (*d*)   The sum of (*a*), (*b*), and (*c*) above is divided by 5, and this is used as the next month's forecast.

   Using the input data below, prepare a program for computing sales forecasts for an unknown number of inventory items. The output record is to be prepared as indicated for each input record. Output columns are to be captioned 'ITEM NUMBER' and 'FØRECAST', respectively.

	FORTRAN	
Item Description	*Name*	*Field Size*
Input record:		
Item number	ID	xxxx
Last month's sales forecast	FØRLM	xxxxxx͏ˬ
Last month's actual sales	SALE1	xxxxxx͏ˬ
Sales, 2nd month prior	SALE2	xxxxxx͏ˬ
Sales, 3rd month prior	SALE3	xxxxxx͏ˬ
Sales, 4th month prior	SALE4	xxxxxx͏ˬ
Sales, 5th month prior	SALE5	xxxxxx͏ˬ
Sales, 6th month prior	SALE6	xxxxxx͏ˬ
Output record:		
Item number	ID	xxxx
Next month's forecast	FØRC	xxxxxx.

16. Prepare a program for adjusting account balances by relative index numbers. Input records are as shown below, and an output record is to be prepared for each. A number of records is to be processed.

	FORTRAN	
Item Description	*Name*	*Field Size*
Input record, type 1:		
Current index number	CINDX	xxxx
Input record, type 2:		
Account number	NØ	xxxxx
Account balance	AMT	xxxxxxxx
Index number of period in which		
balance was recorded	ØINDX	xxxx
Output record:		
Account number	NØ	xxxxx
Unadjusted account balance	AMT	xxxxx.xx
Amount of index adjusted	ADJ	xxxxx.xx
Adjusted account balance	ADAMT	xxxxx.xx

The first input record contains only the current index number and should be read by a unique FØRMAT. Then, account records are read and an output record is prepared for each. Original account balances are to be adjusted by multiplication by a fraction, the numerator of which is the index of the current year and the denominator the index of the period in which the balance was recorded. The adjusted amount is to be written out as ADAMT. ADJ is the amount of the adjustment and should be positive if the adjusted amount exceeds the original balance.

The sum of unadjusted account balances, index adjustments, and adjusted account balances should be accumulated as TØTØRG, TØTADJ, and TØTNEW, respectively, and each assigned a field size of xxxxx.xx. After processing all data records these three totals should be written in a single record and the program terminated.

5 Basic Conditional Statements

The computer commands introduced thus far control much of the computer's power. They cause the computer to accept data from an external source, perform arithmetic manipulation, and write contents of the instrument's storage, repeating the operation as many times as required.

With the single exception of the END= option of the READ command, all instructions covered so far have been imperative. They have been unequivocal orders to perform a certain function. This chapter introduces three conditional control statements. While they do not perform data manipulation themselves, these instruct the computer to make an analysis of specified conditions and then proceed along one of two or more optional routes.

The conditional statements themselves are quite simple. At the same time, their availability allows the programmer to prepare a set of computer instructions describing any quantitative situation. No matter how many alternative processes exist, or how complex each one is, the computer can be instructed to handle all circumstances.

Because computers cannot be given instructions as they execute a task, all possibilities must be anticipated and provided for. This normally involves the use of conditional statements in sophisticated combinations. When programs are to be created at this level, they must first be outlined before they can be reduced to code form, because logical analysis is by far the most difficult aspect of accurate computer use.

Logical outlines are prepared as flowcharts. This is a schematic showing of events that must occur, with each possibility that can prevail. Flowcharting techniques are introduced in this chapter, and are to be used in program preparation.

COMPUTED GØ TØ

The first conditional statement is very simple. Called the computed GØ TØ, it is of the general form

$$k \qquad GØ \ TØ(n_1, n_2, n_3, \ldots, n_m), i$$

where n represents a set of statement numbers and i is an integer variable which refers to an unsigned value. There may be any number of statement numbers in the set. The statement itself may have a number, represented above by k.

Statement Punctuation. The statement numbers are enclosed in parentheses and are separated by commas. The variable name, represented by i in the general form above, must be separated from the statement number set by a comma. As in other instructions, spacing is unimportant.

Statement Function. This command serves as a multichannel branch. The statement numbers enclosed in parentheses refer to executable statements appearing anywhere in the program. Before using the statement, the variable called i in the general form above must be defined and its value must not exceed in magnitude the number of statement numbers in the parentheses. Then, when the computed GØ TØ is encountered, "i" is queried and the program is transferred to the ith statement number in the set, reading from the left.

The magnitude of i does not represent the statement number to which transfer is made, but rather the position of that number in the set. Its value should never exceed the number of statement numbers in the set. For instance, the following would be quite improper:

$$J = 5$$
$$GØ \ TØ \ (5,2,10), J$$

Inasmuch as only three statement numbers are specified in the set, J should never have a value greater than 3. In the above instance, an error condition exists, for there is no fifth statement in the set to which the program may transfer.

The set of statement numbers may refer to commands appearing above or below the computed GØ TØ. The numbers may appear in any order. Of course, they must be logically consistent with the use of the variable by which they are referenced.

The Statement Illustrated.   Assume that a firm makes both wholesale and retail sales. A variable, K, in the sales record indicates the type of buyer where 1 stands for wholesale and 2 for retail. Wholesale and retail sales records are mixed indiscriminately in the input file.

Sale prices are to be computed. Then, wholesale customers are to be granted a 40% discount, while no discount is permitted on retail sales. Different output records are to be prepared according to sales type.

A program for processing sales records appears in Figure 5–1. Formats and record contents are assumed.

FIGURE 5–1
The Computed GØ TØ

```
C            ILLUSTRATION ØF THE COMPUTED GØ TØ INSTRUCTION.
      1      FØRMAT(I5,I1,F3.0,F3.2)
      2      FØRMAT(1X,I6,5X,F8.2,5X,F8.2,5X,F8.2)
      3      FØRMAT(1X,I6,5X,F8.2)
     10      READ(5,1,END=30)NØ,K,UNITS,UPRICE
             GRØSS = UNITS * UPRICE
             GØ TØ (15,20),K
     15      DISC = GRØSS * .4
             XNET = GRØSS - DISC
             WRITE(6,2)NØ,GRØSS,DISC,XNET
             GØ TØ 10
     20      WRITE(6,3)NØ,GRØSS
             GØ TØ 10
     30      STØP
             END
```

The amount of gross sales is required for both types of customers. Therefore, it is computed before entering the different retail and wholesale routines. Then the computed GØ TØ command is encountered.

The value of the code variable K is queried by the computed GØ TØ. If K has a value of 1, the first statement number is chosen and the program transfers to statement 15. Should K have a value of 2, the program will transfer to statement 20. These statements represent the beginning of the unique wholesale and retail processing routines, respectively. Each sales type is then processed as required.

When a program has more than one branch, great care must be taken to see that they do not improperly overlap. The wholesale routine in Figure 5–1 ends with an unconditional transfer command, GØ TØ 10. If the GØ TØ statement had been omitted, a wholesale record would have been processed through its routine; then, the program would have overrun into the retail branch and it, too, would have been executed. This sort of logical error is very serious, for it does not prevent the program's operation but gives wrong results.

The program illustrated in Figure 5–1 illustrates a situation where more than one logical path is available. The program permits the computer to follow one of two branches when it accepts an input record. In practice, as many branches can be available as are logically acceptable, and each branch may be as long or short as necessary. The branches may rejoin later in the program, or they may remain separate. This depends entirely on the logic of the situation.

While the computed GØ TØ does provide for the detection of differences and the unique treatment of each possible situation, it is rather limited in its application. It cannot compare two magnitudes and indicate which is the larger. Making this sort of comparison is the role of IF statements and is the computer's most important logical ability.

IF STATEMENTS

The two IF statements are the most powerful logical commands in FORTRAN. One, called the logical IF, tests a logical expression and provides two alternative paths for the program to follow, one if the expression is true and another if it is false. The other conditional, called the arithmetic IF, evaluates an arithmetic expression and provides for branching to three different program locations—one for a negative, one for a zero, and the third for a positive result. While each statement is technically simple, its use is limited only by the ability to quantify data and the creativity of the programmer.

THE LOGICAL IF STATEMENT

Nature

The logical IF statement is of the following general form:

k IF(logical expression) True-statement
m Continue-statement

In the above, k and m represent optional statement numbers. Other parts of the logical IF statement and its related command, "Continue-statement," are described below.

Coding Requirements

The logical expression must be enclosed in parentheses. "True-statement" is written on the same line; spacing after the right-hand parenthesis is optional. "Continue-statement" is written on the next coding line.

True-Statement. "True-statement" may be any FORTRAN instruction except a specification statement, DØ statement, or another logical IF command.

The instruction is executed if the expression in the logical IF statement is true. After execution of the command, the program normally proceeds to the statement following the IF, called "continue-statement" in the general form above. If written as "true-statement," a transfer instruction such as a GØ TØ would, of course, override this normal execution sequence and cause a jump to some other part of the program.

Continue-Statement. As mentioned, the true branch of the logical IF statement transfers to this command after executing "true-statement" unless the normal sequence is interrupted.

In addition, if the logical expression in the IF statement is false, the program sequence leads directly to this command. This statement is then the first on the false branch of the command.

Analysis of the Logical IF Statement. Thus, the logical IF statement provides for one unique statement on its "true" branch. A transfer command written in this location starts a branch of any length. However, unless a transfer is written at this point, the "true" and "false" branches of the IF rejoin at the immediately following instruction.

The nature of the logical IF statement can perhaps be best shown in a diagram, as presented in Figure 5–2. Here the position of "true-statement" on the true branch may be clearly seen. Also evident is the normal return of the true branch to the main program stream after executing the single statement.

Logical Expression

The logical expression may consist of any meaningful combination of numeric operators, variables and constants; logical variables and

FIGURE 5–2
Diagram of the Logical IF Statement

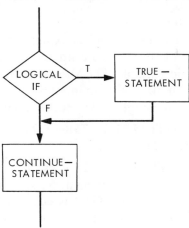

constants; relational operators; and logical operators. To be meaningful, the expression must be reducible to a logical state of either true or false.

The numeric operators, constants, and variables that may be used are the same as in the arithmetic statement. Logical constants are only two in number—.TRUE. and .FALSE., as described in Chapter 2. Logical variables are represented by data names which have been declared to be of logical mode and assigned a logical value. Relational operators and logical operators are described below.

Relational Operators.   These are symbols expressing the relation between two arithmetic constants, equations, or variables. The six relational operators and their meanings are:

Relational Operator	*Meaning*
.LT.	Less than
.LE.	Less than or equal to
.EQ.	Equal to
.NE.	Not equal to
.GT.	Greater than
.GE.	Greater than or equal to

A period must immediately precede and follow each symbol to distinguish it from a data name.

The relational operator is used to establish the relation between two arithmetic items. The general form of use is:

$$\left.\begin{array}{l}\text{Arithmetic}\\\text{expression,}\\\text{variable or}\\\text{constant}\end{array}\right\}\quad\begin{array}{c}\text{Relational}\\\text{Operator}\end{array}\quad\left\{\begin{array}{l}\text{Arithmetic}\\\text{expression,}\\\text{variable or}\\\text{constant}\end{array}\right.$$

These operators are used in a logical expression to establish the truth or falsity of a relation between two arithmetic items. For example, assume that if a numeric variable, ITEM, is less than 25, the program is to transfer to statement 50; if not, an input record containing A, B, and C is to be read. This is accomplished by the following pair of statements:

```
IF(ITEM .LT. 25)GØ TØ 50
READ(5,1)A,B,C
```

The logical expression ITEM .LT. 25 is evaluated. If the statement is true, the program branches to statement 50 for its next instruction. A false statement, indicating that ITEM is equal to or greater than 25, will cause the READ command and instructions following it to be executed.

Relational operators can only be used to test the truth or falsity of some relation between real or integer arithmetic values. Many computers do not permit relational expressions to be of mixed mode. However, some (such as IBM 360–370s) are capable of mixed-mode processing, and each computer's manual should be checked to determine its capabilities.

Logical Operators.   These are the connectives .AND. and .ØR., and the inverter .NØT. Each must be preceded and followed by a period.

.AND. and .ØR. are used to connect two logical variables or constants, or expressions containing relational operators. These may be intermixed in any manner, and the only requirement is that they must consist of, or be reducible to, a true or false state.

The connective .AND. requires that both items connected be true if the expression is to be true. .ØR. requires that either, or both, items connected be true for the expression to be true.

.NØT., written preceding a logical variable or relational, causes the expression to be true only when the variable or relational is false. .NØT. may appear immediately after either of the logical operators .AND. or .ØR.. This is the only time two logical operators can occupy adjacent positions.

Relational Operators and Logical Operators Compared

Although they may be used in the same logical expression, a careful distinction between relational operators and logical operators must be made.

Relational operators specify that a *comparison* between *arithmetic* items is to be made. The result of the relational comparison is stated as true or false.

Logical operators cause the evaluation of the truth or falsity of *logical items,* which may be logical variables, constants, or relational expressions.

A clear distinction between logical relationals and operators may be gained by comparing the ordinary meaning of certain phrases with their meaning in FORTRAN. For example, the statement "if A is greater than B and C" is ordinarily interpreted to mean "if A is greater than B, and A is also greater than C." However, in FORTRAN the statement is interpreted in an altogether different way.

In FORTRAN, the expression A .GT. B .AND. C is evaluated as follows: First, the relational operator A .GT. B is evaluated. (For convenience, call the result X.)

Then, the truth status of X and C is evaluated. If X is true and C is true, the expression is considered true. In this evaluation, C is not a factor in the relational evaluation but a logical variable. The expression in no way determines whether A is "greater" than C—only that A is greater than B, and C is true.

It must be remembered that only arithmetic expressions can be combined by the relational operators. Any attempt to use the logical operators as a part of the relational expression is improper.

The Hierarchy of Evaluation.   With the use of relational operators and logical operators, logical expressions may become very complex. In the absence of parentheses, they will be evaluated from left to right in the expression in the following order:

Operation	*Hierarchy*
Evaluation of functions (discussed in Chapter 9)	1
Arithmetic operations:	
Exponentiation	2
Multiplication and division	3
Addition and subtraction	4
Relational operators	5
Logical operators:	
.NØT.	6
.AND.	7
.ØR.	8

For example, assume the rather complex logical IF statement:

IF (.NØT. A .AND. B .EQ. C ** 2.ØR. D—4. .LT. E * 25.1) GØ TØ 25

This would be evaluated in the following order (for convenience, symbols are assigned to represent the results of each step) :

C ** 2 (Call the result T) Exponentiation
E * 25.1 (Call the result U) Multiplication
D—4. (Call the result V) Subtraction
B .EQ. T (Call the result W) Relational
V .LT. U (Call the result X) Relational
.NØT. A (Call the result Y) Highest logical
Y .AND. W (Call the result Z) Next highest logical
Z .ØR. X (Final operation)

Arithmetic operations must be carried out first, reducing computations to quantities amenable to comparison with one another. Then, the actual operation of evaluation begins.

Moving left to right in the expression, all relationals are reduced to true, or false. The logical operator .NØT. is then exercised, followed by .AND.. Thus, all the first portion of the expression is reduced to true or false. This is related to the logical result of D—4. .LT. E * 25.1. If either or both of these expressions is true, the statement is accepted as true.

Using Parentheses. Parentheses may be used in logical expressions to control the grouping of elements. When they are used, evaluation of the expression occurs from the inner to the outer set just as when used in an arithmetic expression.

Parentheses can change the meaning of expressions using logical operators. For example, consider the following pairs of expressions:

A. 1. X .AND. Y .ØR. Z
2. X. .AND. (Y .ØR. Z)
B. 1. .NØT. X .AND. Y
2. .NØT. (X .AND. Y)

In Example A–1, the operator .AND. will be evaluated first. Both X and Y must be true for this segment of the expression to be true. Then, the result of the X and Y test is compared with Z. If either or both is true, the expression is true.

In Example A–2, enclosure of Y .ØR. Z in parentheses causes this portion of the expression to be evaluated first. If either or both is true, this segment of the expression is considered true. The results of (Y .ØR. Z) are compared with X, and if both are true, the expression is true.

Example A–2 yields a result of true if X and Z̄ are true but Y is false. This yields a false result in A–1, and so the two statements are not the same.

Example B tests the effect of .NØT. as a logical operator. In B–1, the expression is true only if X is false and Y is true.

However, Example B–2 will be true only if both X and Y are false.

Thus, parentheses have a real effect on the meaning of logical statements. A detailed exploration of this subject must be left to texts on symbolic logic where the construction of truth tables may be discussed in depth. However, the examples above should serve to suggest the meaning of logical operators and the effect of parentheses on their evaluation.

Examples of the Logical IF Statement

To provide the framework for examples, assume the following variables:

> Real Variables: A, B
> Integer Variables: I, J
> Logical Variables: X, Y

Example 1. If A + 13.2 is less than or equal to B − 5. the program is to transfer to statement 50; otherwise, the program is to transfer to statement 75.

This can be coded as follows:

> IF(A + 13.2 .LE. B − 5.)GØ TØ 50
> GØ TØ 75

Example 2. If X is true and I is less than J, compute M = N + 1 and then add 1 to K. Otherwise, merely add 1 to K.

This is accomplished as follows:

> IF(X .AND. I .LT. J)M = N + 1
> K = K + 1

This example makes several important points. First, to test the truth or falsity of the logical variable X, the variable name is included in the expression. Testing of logical status occurs automatically, because the variable has been declared to be of logical mode.

Second, the use of the logical operator .AND. should be noted. The entire expression will be true only if X is true and I is less than J.

Third, the route to be taken by the two branches should be traced. If the expression is true, the command $M = N + 1$ will be executed; then, the program will proceed to the next instruction and execute $K = K + 1$. Should the expression be false, the program will still execute $K = K + 1$. Thus, the true and false branches rejoin after one unique command on the true branch.

Example 3. If X is true or Y is false go to statement 25; otherwise, go to statement 50.

This may be coded as folows:

IF(X.ØR..NØT.Y)GØ TØ 25
GØ TØ 50

This illustrates the use of the inverter .NØT. and the logical operator .ØR.. If X is true, or Y is not true (false), or if X is true and Y is not true, the program will transfer to statement 25.

Example 4. If A and/or B is greater than 50. go to statement 25; otherwise, go to statement 50.

This cannot be coded exactly as implied, because the logical operators .ØR. and .AND. cannot appear next to one another. Therefore, the conditional must be rephrased somewhat as follows:

IF(A.GT.50..ØR.B.GT.50.)GØ TØ 25
GØ TØ 50

Use of the logical operator .ØR. means "If the first member is true, or the second member is true, or both are true, the statement is true." Therefore, .AND. is not needed to state the expression properly.

An expression such as IF(A.ØR.B.GT.50) will not properly state the required condition. It says "If A (assumed by its context to be a logical variable) is true or B is greater than 50, the statement is true." Because A is not a logical variable, this is not at all what is intended. Neither relational operators nor relational objects can be implied in compound expressions such as this. Both the relational operator (.GT., in this example) and the object of the test (50.) must be explicitly included.

Example 5. If I is equal to J compute $M = K - 1$; otherwise, read an input record containing P, R, and S.

In this instance the true branch of the conditional contains a statement to be executed, but the true branch cannot be allowed to rejoin the false branch and cause the execution of its unique command. Therefore, the true branch must be diverted to some other program area, such as in the following:

IF(I.EQ.J)GØ TØ 25
READ(5,1)P,R,S
. . .
. . .
25 M = K — 1

Whether the false branch can be allowed to rejoin the true branch at statement 25 depends on the logical requirements of the program. It may be that it must jump away from statement 25 and transfer elsewhere. In any event, M = K — 1 cannot be written beside the conditional as "true-statement," for it would then lead to the false statement READ(5,1)P,R,S and constitute a logical error. In this instance the arithmetic IF statement described below is easier to use, and less likely to cause a mistake than its logical counterpart.

The Logical Assignment Statement

The logical assignment statement, introduced in Chapter 4, is of the general nature

$$\text{Variable} = \text{Expression}$$

where "Variable" is a logical variable and "Expression" a logical expression. The expression is evaluated and reduced to a true or false state. The variable is therefore set to either true or false, according to the results of evaluation.

An understanding of this command can be gained by considering again the five examples of the logical IF statement above. In each instance below a logical variable, W, will receive the results of the logical expression's evaluation.

Example 1.   This can be stated as follows:

$$W = A + 13.2 \text{ .LE. } B — 5.$$

If A + 13.2 is less than or equal to B — 5., W will be assigned a true value.

Example 2.   The logical statement

$$W = X \text{ .AND. } I \text{ .LT. } J$$

will be true if X is true, and if I is less than J; otherwise the logical variable will be assigned a value of false.

Example 3.   In the statement

$$W = X .ØR..NØT. Y$$

W will be true if X is true, or if Y is false, or if both X is true and Y is false.

Example 4. The logical assignment statement will be written as

$$W = A .GT. 50..ØR. B .GT. 50.$$

It means "Is A greater than 50? Is B greater than 50? If either, or both, of these is true, assign a true value to W."

Example 5. Again, the statement W = I .EQ. J means "Assign a value of true to W if I is equal to J."

Statement Analysis. Like the logical IF statement, the logical assignment statement analyses a logical expression. Where the IF statement causes a branch based on the evaluation, however, the assignment statement sets a logical variable to either true or false.

The logical assignment statement is essential to logical analysis. However, it is not widely used in business data processing, because most manipulative assignment is of quantitative, not logical, data.

THE ARITHMETIC IF STATEMENT

Nature

The arithmetic IF statement is of the following nature:

$$k \qquad IF(\text{expression})n_1, n_2, n_3$$

k represents an optional statement number. The word IF is required as shown. "Expression" is any arithmetic expression, as simple or as complex as necessary to express the situation to be evaluated. "n_1, n_2, n_3" are the numbers of executable statements appearing elsewhere in the program; they must not refer to statements of the following type:

> FØRMAT
> EQUIVALENCE
> CØMMØN
> DIMENSIØN
> LØGICAL
> REAL
> INTEGER
> DØUBLE PRECISIØN

The arithmetic expression is evaluated. If its results are negative, the program transfers to the statement number designated as n_1. If the expression is zero, the program transfers to statement n_2; a positive result causes transfer to n_3. Thus, the arithmetic IF statement provides a three-way branch. The branch taken by the program at execute time depends on the results of the expression's evaluation.

Coding Requirements

In writing the IF statement, punctuation must be provided just as shown above. Commas must be used as separators between the statement numbers. No other symbols are permitted.

The expression must be surrounded by parentheses. It may consist of any symbol combination meeting the requirements of an arithmetic expression. It may be as short as a single data name or as long as the most complex expression.

Three statement numbers must always be assigned as the transfer objects, even though the logic of the expression is such that one of them cannot be used. However, any two of the numbers may be the same; therefore, when only two of the three branches are required, the unused alternative may be assigned the same number as one of the active alternatives.

Examples of the Arithmetic IF Statement

Note that the IF statement tests an arithmetic *expression,* not a statement. This sometimes leads to awkwardness in writing the command. For example, assume a situation where if $A = B$ the program is to go to statement 50, if not, to 75.

To code this as IF $(A = B)75,50,75$ is improper because the arithmetic statement may not be used. The condition must be restated as follows:

$$IF(A-B)75,50,75$$

Thus, if $A - B = 0$, the program will branch to statement 50. The statement $A = B$ has been converted into the expression $A - B$.

Other statement characteristics may be seen in the following examples. For each, assume the following values:

$$A = 0.$$
$$B = -5.$$
$$C = 10.$$

(*a*) IF(C—3.)10,20,30

The program will transfer to statement 30, the expression C—3. being positive.

(*b*) IF(A)10,20,30

The program will transfer to statement 20 because the expression is zero. Note that the expression may have only one term.

(*c*) IF(B + 2.)10,10,20

The program will transfer to statement 10, the expression being negative. Note that negative and zero results were assigned the same statement number; indicating that these results are to be treated alike.

(*d*) IF(A * (B + 5.))5,4,5

This expression is slightly more complex than those illustrated above but is quite acceptable. Because the expression has a value of 0, the program will transfer to statement 4.

(*e*) IF(C/B)8,22,22

The expression is evaluated algebraically. Therefore, the program will transfer to statement 8.

(*f*) IF(B—8.)10,10,5

Again, the expression is evaluated algebraically and the program will transfer to statement 10.

(*g*) IF(C + 2)8,8,2

Mixed mode in the expression may cause an error condition to be recognized. The expression must follow the rules set out in Chapter 2.

PREPARING LOGICAL FLOWCHARTS

The basic FORTRAN commands have now been introduced. With the instructions explained thus far, any computer-amenable situation can be programmed.

The meaningful use of these instructions requires that they be combined in the proper way. Most of the problems and illustrations contained in this text are quite simple. However, even they raise such programming questions as the following:

1. When must data be read, and what initialization steps must be taken before reading?
2. When conditionals are used, what steps must lie on the program branches?
3. What steps are common to all branches and should be written in the program's mainstream?

4. When must computation take place?
5. When must values be tested?
6. When must writing occur?

Of course, these questions no more than exemplify the many that arise when longer programs are written.

Flowcharting

Questions such as the above may be resolved and sound logic assured by preparing logical diagrams of a program before undertaking its coding. These diagrams are simulations of the paths to be followed by the computer in executing the program. They are drawn in flowchart fashion and use a few widely recognized symbols. Each symbol indicates the operation to take place at that point and contains the details of the operation. The relation between operations is depicted by the lines joining the symbols.

Flowchart Symbols. A selected set of basic flowcharting symbols is shown in Figure 5–3 below. While others are also used, these are sufficient for outlining most simple computer programs.

ILLUSTRATIONS OF FORTRAN PROGRAMS

Like all FORTRAN instructions, both versions of the IF statement are quite simple in construction. Appropriate use is most complex, however, because these commands permit the programming of any situation where the logic may be described and the variables quantified. Therefore, several examples are discussed below. These, ranging from simple to complex, are but indications of the operations that may be reduced to computer-sensible terms when the IF statement is used. In several cases, the solution is presented with both the logical and arithmetic IF forms used, thus presenting the relative advantages of each.

Illustration 1. Recognizing a Terminal Condition

Even if the FORTRAN version being used does not accept the END= option as part of the READ command, terminal conditions can still be recognized and handled. Exhaustion of an input file may be signaled by placing a pseudo-transaction record at the end of the data set. This, while complying with the format requirements of the file, contains as one of its data elements some value known to be false. It is known as a *transfer record*.

FIGURE 5–3
Basic Flowchart Symbols

Function	Flowchart Symbol
1 Input–output. Used with READ and WRITE commands.	
2 Processing. Used with arithmetic, specification, and other commands for which no special symbol is available.	
3 Conditional. This is mainly used with the IF statement.	
4 Terminal. The STØP and PAUSE commands are symbolized in this manner.	
5 Connector. Used, with appropriate linkage, when processing lines would be too long.	
6 Off–page connector. Used when flowcharts are drawn on more than one page.	

As input records are read, the transfer record is sought by using a conditional to check the field containing the false value. The record is processed if the false value is not found. When it is found, the processing loop is broken.

This may be illustrated in the following situation.

Problem. Sales records are to be processed, and the gross sales price calculated as the number of units sold times the sales price per unit. An unknown number of records is to be processed. Input and output records appear as follows:

	FORTRAN	
Item Description	*Name*	*Field Size*
Input record:		
Inventory number	NØ	xxxxx
Number of units sold	UNITS	xxx︵
Sales price per unit	PRICE	x̬xx
Output record:		
Inventory number	NØ	xxxxx
Number of units sold	KUN	xxx
Sales price per unit	PRICE	x.xx
Gross sales price	GRØSS	xxxx.xx

The last record does not contain a transaction. It has 99999, known not to be a valid inventory number, in the NØ field. When this is recognized, all data records have been processed and the program is to stop.

Analysis. The programs depicted in Figure 5–4 show how the processing of an indeterminant number of input records may be halted. As may be seen, the NØ field in the input record is queried just after reading. If the field does not contain the known transfer amount—99999—the program processes the data record. However, when the transfer amount is recognized, the IF statement in each version branches to the STØP command.

Using the Arithmetic IF. Version A, Figure 5–4 shows how the problem may be programmed using the arithmetic IF. It may be noted that the test cannot produce a negative result because 99999 is the largest integer that may be written in a five-place field. The expression must

FIGURE 5–4
Illustration of Program Termination

```
C          ILLUSTRATION 1 - PROGRAM TERMINATION.
C          VERSION A. USING THE ARITHMETIC IF.
    1      FORMAT(I5,F3.0,F3.2)
    2      FORMAT(1X,I6,5X,I4,5X,F5.2,5X,F8.2)
   10      READ(5,1)NO,UNITS,PRICE
           IF(99999-NO)20,3,20
    3      STOP
   20      KUN = UNITS
           GROSS = UNITS * PRICE
           WRITE(6,2)NO,KUN,PRICE,GROSS
           GO TO 10
           END

C          VERSION B. USING THE LOGICAL IF.
    1      FORMAT(I5,F3.0,F3.2)
    2      FORMAT(1X,I6,5X,I4,5X,F5.2,5X,F8.2)
   10      READ(5,1)NO,UNITS,PRICE
           IF(NO .EQ. 99999) STOP
   20      KUN = UNITS
           GROSS = UNITS * PRICE
           WRITE(6,2)NO,KUN,PRICE,GROSS
           GO TO 10
           END
```

be either positive or zero, and so only the last two statement numbers in the IF specification are useful. However, all three statement numbers must be provided. The logically impossible branch is, therefore, assigned the number of one of the other branches. This is an easy, acceptable means of compromising the technical requirements of the command with the logical requirements of the problem.

Using the Logical IF. When a test has only two possible results, as in this instance, the logical IF statement frequently offers a more useful programming tool than does its arithmetic counterpart. As may be seen in Version B, Figure 5–4, the STØP command is assigned to the true branch of the conditional. Therefore, when the test (NØ .EQ. 99999) is true, the program will be halted. On the other hand, the "continue-branch" will be followed in other cases.

In both versions, the STØP command appears physically in the center of the program. This is quite satisfactory, for all processing will be terminated when this command is executed. This illustrates clearly the difference between the STØP and END commands, for the latter must physically be the last in the program.

Illustration 2. Multiple Conditionals

While each IF statement permits only a single test, the conditionals may be related to form a very sophisticated logical pattern.

Problem. For example, assume that a firm grants sales discounts according to the following schedule:

Sales Amount		Discount Rate
0	−$ 250.00	0%
$ 250.01–	500.00	1
500.01–	1,000.00	2
1,000.01	....	3

Input records contain the data listed below. Output records containing gross, discount, and net prices are to be written. In addition, these three values, as well as the number of units sold, are to be accumulated and written as control totals when all input records have been processed.

Analysis. Because this problem is somewhat more complicated than that of Illustration 1, a logical flowchart is prepared before attempting to code a FORTRAN program. This indicates the general logical flow,

	FORTRAN	
Item Description	*Name*	*Field Size*
Input record:		
Inventory number	NØ	xxxxx
Number of units sold	UNITS	xxx͈
Sales price per unit	PRICE	x̂xx
Output record:		
Inventory number	NØ	xxxxx
Gross sales price	GRØSS	xxxx.xx
Discount amount	DISC	xxx.xx
Net sales price	NET	xxxx.xx
Control totals:		
Gross sales prices	TGRØSS	xxxxx.xx
Discount amounts	TDISC	xxxx.xx
Net sales prices	TNET	xxxxx.xx
Total number of units	TUNIT	xxxxxx.

steps to be taken on the major path, and steps to be performed on unique branches.

The problem flowchart is shown in Figure 5–5. Here, the program may be seen to begin with a READ command, followed by the computation of GRØSS. This must be done before testing for appropriate discount rates can occur.

Testing begins immediately following the computation of gross amount. Note that, on the unique branch initiated by the three IF statements, only the appropriate discount amount is computed. Computation of the net amount is delayed until the branches rejoin; this is a step common to all routes.

Programming is routine once the discount amount is calculated. NET is computed, and control totals accumulated. Then, the output record is written and processing returns to the READ command.

When the END condition is sensed by the READ statement, processing branches out of the regular routine to the terminal path. Here, control totals are written out and the program terminated.

The logical flowchart does not attempt to include every FORTRAN statement that will ultimately be required. FØRMAT statements are routinely omitted. Initialization statements, such as required to assign starting values to the control total data elements, may be included or omitted. Other statements may be indicated generally, rather than by giving their true form. However, the logical flow of the problem is made clear by the flowchart, and coding becomes a simple task. Flowcharting

FIGURE 5–5
Illustration 2 Flowchart

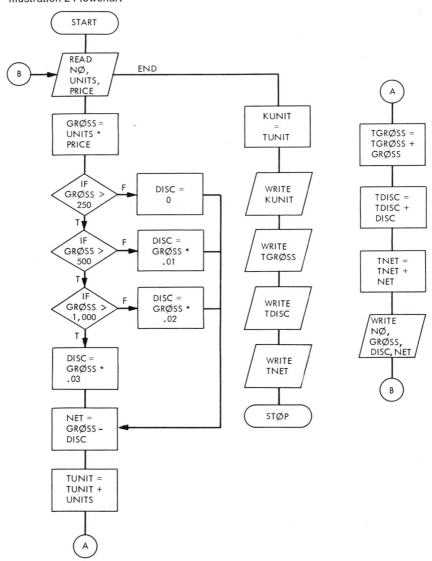

is essential in programming complex situations, where a logical error may cause the production of erroneous information.

Because coding technique is still important, the program shown in Figure 5–6 should be carefully studied. To make tracing easier, all

FIGURE 5–6
Compound Conditionals

COMM	STATEMENT NUMBER	CONT	FORTRAN STATEMENT
C			ILLUSTRATION OF MULTIPLE CONDITIONALS.
	1		FORMAT(I5,F3.0 F3.2)
	2		FORMAT(1X, I6,5X,F8.2,5X,F7.2,5X,F8.2)
	3		FORMAT(1X,'TOTAL UNITS ',I10)
	4		FORMAT(1X,'TOTAL CHARGES,GROSS ',F10.2)
	5		FORMAT(1X,'TOTAL DISCOUNTS ALLOWED ',F10.2)
	6		FORMAT(1X,'TOTAL CHARGES,NET ',F10.2)
	7		REAL NET
	101		DATA TUNIT,TGROSS,TDISC,TNET/4*0./
	10		READ(5,1,END=50)NO,UNITS,PRICE
	102		GROSS = UNITS * PRICE
	103		IF(GROSS .GT. 250.)GO TO 11
	104		DISC = O
	105		GO TO 20
	11		IF(GROSS .GT. 500.)GO TO 12
	106		DISC = GROSS * .01
	107		GO TO 20
	12		IF(GROSS .GT. 1000.)GO TO 13
	108		DISC = GROSS * .02
	109		GO TO 20
	13		DISC = GROSS * .03
	20		NET = GROSS - DISC
	110		TUNIT = TUNIT + UNITS
	111		TGROSS = TGROSS + GROSS
	112		TDISC = TDISC + DISC
	113		TNET = TNET + NET
	114		WRITE(6,2)NO,GROSS,DISC,NET
	115		GO TO 10
	50		KUNIT = TUNIT
	116		WRITE(6,3)KUNIT
	117		WRITE(6,4)TGROSS
	118		WRITE(6,5)TDISC
	119		WRITE(6,6)TNET
	120		STOP
			END

statements except END have been assigned statement numbers. Those used for discussion only begin with 101; the statement numbers essential to the program are those of 50 or less.

The logical IF statement is used throughout the program. Because all tests permit binary results, the arithmetic IF is less satisfactory than its logical counterpart.

The complex of IF statements and related commands necessary to evaluate GRØSS for proper discount computation may be seen between numbers 103 and 12. The conditional expressions may be written in several ways. Here, they are so coded that GRØSS is measured against the upper limit of a discount category; if GRØSS is equal to or less than the upper limit, the discount is computed; otherwise the program continues for further testing. Finally, with the conditional written as statement 12, all possibilities are exhausted. Gross amounts equal to or less than the limit are granted a discount of 2% ; others receive a 3% discount. No further conditional tests are required.

Steps to prevent the computer's erroneous execution of a branch may also be seen. Statements 105, 107, and 109 all command: GØ TØ 20. If these were omitted, the computer would branch to the proper computational command and calculate DISC. Then, it would overrun the other branches and DISC would be erroneously recomputed. Finally, regardless of the discount properly granted, DISC would be computed at the 3% rate for all sales because this is the variable's last computation. In any program containing a conditional, care must be exercised in bringing the branches back together only at the proper time.

Note that DISC is assigned some value, regardless of the quantity of GRØSS. If no discount is allowed, the variable is set to zero. It must be remembered that values in a computer's memory are erased only by redefinition. If no discount were justified and the variable, DISC, simply ignored, it would still contain the value assigned from the previous data record. To erase this, the field must be set to zero.

The development of control totals, shown previously in Chapter 4, is another illustration segment that deserves comment. In business data processing, the computation of control totals is a major aspect of internal check. Totals are taken before sending data to the electronic data processing center. Then, the data will be summed again as a part of the processing routine. Agreement between the totals indicates proper processing, while any discrepancy means that an error has been committed. Thus, errors may be detected before the identity of the data is lost.

Sometimes reference or classification data, such as account numbers, will be added. The result, called a "hash total," is verified by comparison with totals maintained outside the data processing center. The total of all units sold, called TUNIT, is an example of such a sum.

In this illustration, the amounts of gross price, discount, and net price are also accumulated from all processed input records. The four control fields are first defined by assigning them zero values. Then, as records are processed, the amounts are accumulated. The totals are printed after all transaction records have been processed.

Note that separate FØRMAT statements are used for each total and that each is given a caption. This is ordinarily done, for these amounts must be transmitted to parties outside the data processing center and their nature would not be known otherwise.

The alignment of the fields in FØRMAT statements 3, 4, 5, and 6 should be noted. The longest caption was set up first, then the other three were designed to conform to it. In this fashion, when the totals are printed, they will be neatly arranged, as follows (amounts are assumed):

TØTAL UNITS	75000
TØTAL CHARGES, GRØSS	10000.00
TØTAL DISCØUNTS ALLØWED	200.00
TØTAL CHARGES, NET	9800.00

Illustration 3. Checking a Counter

Many computer programs are designed to loop, that is, to repeat themselves a fixed or determinable number of times. Looping may be controlled by the IF statement, or the DØ statement discussed in Chapter 7 may be used.

Problem. To illustrate this kind of problem and its FORTRAN program, assume that depreciation schedules are to be prepared by the sum-of-years' digits method for assets of any cost, scrap value, and useful life. Input and output records are to appear as shown at the top of page 132.

The first output record is to contain only the asset's identification number and its cost, the latter to be written in the BAL field. Subsequent output records are not to show the identification number but should contain the year, beginning with 1975, the amount of depreciation for the year, the accumulated depreciation to date, and the undepreciated balance.

Analysis. The sum-of-years' digits depreciation method requires that a year's depreciation be computed by multiplying the asset's cost less its scrap value by a fraction. The numerator of the fraction is the year number, written in reverse order. The denominator is the sum of all years of the asset's life and may be calculated as $n(n+1)/2$. This frac-

| | *FORTRAN* | |
Item Description	Name	Field Size
Input record:		
Asset identification number	NØ	xxxxx
Asset cost	CØST	xxxxxͺxx
Asset scrap value	SCRAP	xxxxxͺxx
Estimated useful life–years	USE	xxxͺ
Output record:		
Asset identification number	NØ	xxxxx
Year	YR	xxxx
Current depreciation amount	DEPR	xxxxx.xx
Accumulated depreciation	ADEP	xxxxx.xx
Undepreciated balance	BAL	xxxxx.xx

tion must be modified with each program iteration. The program, illustrated by flowchart in Figure 5–7 and programmed in Figure 5–8, computes depreciation according to these requirements. Statement numbers have been put beside certain steps in the flowchart for easy reference.

By inspection of the flowchart in Figure 5–7, steps to be written before entering the loop, and those to be inside the loop can be seen. This program begins by reading an input record. The example assumes that the END= option is not available; therefore, a record containing 99999 in the NØ field is to be used to terminate the program. The input record is checked in the manner discussed in other illustrations.

If the record contains asset data, certain initial program steps must be taken. The asset's cost must be moved to the BAL field, ADEP must be defined as zero, and the year must be established as 1975. Then, the iterative portion of the program begins.

In statement 20, the numerator of the fraction is partially set up by subtracting 1975 from the "year" field. Then, the year fraction is calculated. The numerator reflects the year's rank in reverse order, and the denominator the sum of its years of useful life.[1]

Statement 102 computes the actual depreciation. Statements 101 and 102 could easily be written together; they are divided here only for discussion purposes.

---

[1] To verify the accuracy of this step, shown in Figure 5–8 as statement 101, assume that an asset with a use-life of 10 years is being processed and depreciation for its first year is to be computed. Statement 20, AKYR = YR − 1975, would set AKYR to 0. Then, in statement 101, deducting this from USE would result in a numerator of 10. The denominator, computed as $(10*(10+1))/2$, would be 55. The year fraction would therefore be 10/55. Next year, AKYR would be increased by 1 through the action of statement 12, and the numerator would be reduced to 9. This would continue through the asset's useful life.

FIGURE 5–7
Illustration 3 Flowchart

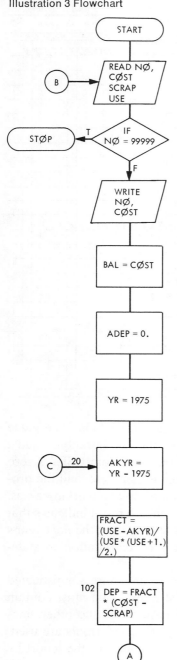

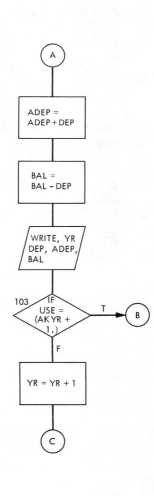

FIGURE 5–8
Using a Counter

```
C         ILLUSTRATION 3.  DEPRECIATION COMPUTATION.
          INTEGER YR
    1     FORMAT(I5,2F7.2,F3.0)
    2     FORMAT(1X,I6,45X,F10.2)
    3     FORMAT(12X,I5,3(5X,F10.2))
   10     READ(5,1)NO,COST,SCRAP,USE
          IF(NO.EQ.99999) STOP
          WRITE(6,2)NO,COST
          BAL = COST
          ADEP = 0
          YR = 1975
   20     AKYR = YR - 1975
  101     FRACT = (USE - AKYR)/(USE*(USE+1.)/2.)
  102     DEP = FRACT*(COST - SCRAP)
          ADEP = DEP + ADEP
          BAL = BAL - DEP
          WRITE(6,3)YR,DEP,ADEP,BAL
  103     IF(USE.EQ. AKYR+1.)GO TO 10
          YR = YR + 1
          GO TO 20
          END
```

Statement 103 is used to determine the end of the loop. The value
called AKYR is always 1 less than the number of iterations made.
Therefore, 1 is added to it and the result subtracted from USE. A zero
result indicates that the depreciation schedule is complete, and the program returns to read another data record, reinitialize its working areas,
and prepare a schedule for another asset. A nonzero result indicates that
this schedule is incomplete, YR is increased by 1 to start the next year's
computations, and the program returns to the computation in statement 20.

The program illustrated in Figure 5–8 contains more sophisticated
output than do previous examples. The first output line must contain
only the asset's identification number and cost, while the other lines
must contain other data. To effect this, two different formats are used.
The first line is written by one format, and the balance of the report by
the other. This is the technique used when report headings are prepared.

Illustration 4. Using a Three-Way Branch

Sometimes an IF statement may refer to three alternatives.

Problem.   As an example of this, assume that a program for preparing depreciation records is to be written and that assets may be depreciated in one of three ways—by the straight-line, sum-of-years' digits, or declining-balance methods. A variable, I, in each asset record indicates the depreciation method to be used, where 15 represents straight-line; 20, sum-of-years' digits; and 25, declining balance.

Analysis.   If the code designations were 1, 2, and 3 the computed GØ TØ could be used to direct the program, somewhat as follows:

	GØ TØ (40,50,60),I
40	(straight-line routine)
50	(sum-of-years' digits routine)
60	(declining-balance routine)

(In each instance, the depreciation program is not written out because it is not essential to the example.)

However, the code designation in this illustration does not lend itself to use in the computed GØ TØ. An arithmetic IF statement may be set up as follows to accomplish the same end:

	IF(I—20)40,50,60
40	(straight-line routine)
50	(sum-of-years' digits routine)
60	(declining-balance routine)

Should the expression be negative, some code less than 20 is indicated, and the program transfers to the straight-line routine. A zero expression indicates the need for a sum-of-years' digits computation, and a positive result transfers to the declining-balance program segment. Thus, all three branches of the IF statement are used.

The logical IF statement does not work as well in this situation as its arithmetic counterpart, for a single test can only provide binary results. No matter what relational operators are used, two IF statements will be required. They might be constructed as follows:

	IF(I .EQ. 15)GØ TØ 40
	IF(I .EQ. 20)GØ TØ 50
60	(declining-balance routine)
40	(straight-line routine)
50	(sum-of-years' digits routine)

The first test determines if the straight-line process is to be used. The second establishes whether the sum-of-years' routine is proper or, by elimination, if the computer is to execute the declining-balance routine. Thus, for *n* alternatives, n — 1 IF statements must be used.

Illustration 5. Checking Sequence

In many business data processing situations, records must be kept in a carefully controlled sequence. They are frequently maintained in order according to some key data element in the record. The most commonly used sequence is called "ascending order" meaning that the magnitude of the key value increases from records in the front of the file to those at the end.

Problem. Programs processing such sequentially-arranged files routinely check to see that records are in the proper order, and draw attention to any apparent errors. To demonstrate such sequence check-

FIGURE 5–9
Sequence Checking Flowcharted

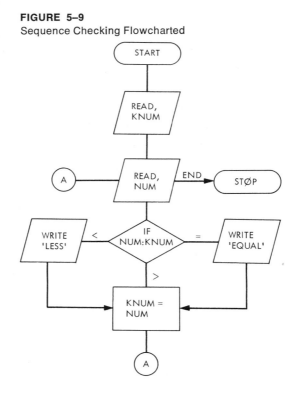

ing, assume that records in a file contain a variable called NUM (FØRMAT xxxx). Records are maintained by ascending sequence in this data field. A program is to be written to check the sequence of these records, and write out the value of NUM for any duplicate number or value less than that from the preceding record (this is called a "step-down").

Analysis.   A flowchart for sequence checking is shown in Figure 5–9, and the related FORTRAN program in Figure 5–10.

Although sequence-checking routines are quite simple, they do require some thought. First, a value must be read in to initialize the routine. Then, another input record is read and a comparison made. Should

FIGURE 5–10
Coded Program for Sequence Checking

IBM   FORTRAN CODING FORM

| PROGRAM | SEQUENCE | PUNCHING INSTRUCTIONS |
| PROGRAMMER | MCCAMERØN | DATE |

```
C     ILLUSTRATIØN 4. CHECKING SEQUENCE.
1     FØRMAT(I4)
2     FØRMAT(1X,'EQUAL',5X,I4)
3     FØRMAT(1X,'LESS ',5X,I4)
      READ(5,1)KNUM
10    READ(5,1,END=50)NUM
      IF(NUM-KNUM)4,5,6
4     WRITE(6,3)NUM
      GØ TØ 6
5     WRITE(6,2)NUM
6     KNUM = NUM
      GØ TØ 10
50    STØP
      END
```

the key number of the second be greater than that of the first, all is assumed to be in order (although, as shown below, this may not be the case). Should the condition not exist, an error is detected and signalled. In either instance, the second key value must be moved into the location of the first, to be used as the basis for the next comparison.

To understand how the routine works, assume the following key values in the first several input records:

Value

1111
1112
1112
1000
1113
1119
1114

Upon reading the first record, the value 1111 is stored as KNUM. Then, the second input record is read and NUM assigned the value 1112. In the IF statement, NUM is found to be greater than KNUM, an acceptable condition. NUM is moved to KNUM, and the program returns to the second READ statement.

This time, a comparison determines NUM and KNUM to be equal, each having a value of 1112. Therefore, an error message is written. The next record contains 1000 as NUM. When tested, this is determined to be less than KNUM, and a step-down is therefore signaled.

The test does not always indicate which record is out of sequence. For instance, it appears that record 1119 is out of place. However, when tested, this will be determined to be greater than 1113 and accepted. Upon testing the next record, 1114 will be found a step-down from 1119 and will trigger an error signal. Determining which record is out of sequence requires visual inspection, or a checking routine much more sophisticated than the one shown.

Illustration 6. Merging Sequential Files

Many business data processing situations require that data from records in two or more files be combined, as when data on current happenings must be combined with historical accumulations, or unchanging data from one file merged with variable data from another. The current or variable data records are frequently called "detail records," and their file the "detail file." Historical or unchanging records, frequently called masters, are maintained in the "master file."

The merger process is normally complicated by the fact that not all records in the master file will be active at any processing run; that is, some master records will not have corresponding records in the detail file.

Problem.   As an example of this type of processing, assume that the employee master file contains a record for each employee. An employee record contains employee number and hourly pay rate. Time cards, showing the time worked, are prepared daily for each employee and kept in the time card detail file. The master file is kept in employee number sequence, and time cards are sorted into this sequence before processing. Not all employees work in every pay period, and employees who do work may have one or more time cards in the detail file. The time cards for each employee are grouped together.

A program to compute gross pay for each employee by accumulating hours worked and multiplying by his pay rate is to be prepared. Input and output records are as follows:

| | FORTRAN | |
Item Description	*Name*	*Field Size*
Employee Master Records:		
Employee Number	MSTRNØ	xxxxx
Hourly pay rate	RATE	xxxx
Time Card Records:		
Employee Number	DETNØ	xxxxx
Hours worked	HØURS	xxx
Pay Records:		
Employee Number	MSTRNØ	xxxxx
Gross pay	GRØSS	xxx.xx

Analysis.   While this is a very simple merge problem, its logic is rather sophisticated. Preparation of a flowchart, such as shown in Figure 5–11, is essential to proper coding.

The most critical problem in merging is finding the proper reading sequence. One file usually contains a less complete set of records than the other, based on presence by key data element (employee number, in this example). In this instance, the master file has a record for every employee but the detail file does not; hence the detail file is less complete.

A record from the less complete file should be read first. Then, reading from the more complete file should start, and should continue until matching control numbers are found. An error condition exists if a search of the entire file fails to detect a record matching the detail. In this illustration, an error message, UNMATCHED DETAIL, is written, and processing ended. More sophisticated error routines are frequently used in practice.

In Figure 5–11 flowchart, these instructions are written in Block 1,

FIGURE 5–11

Illustration 6 Flowchart

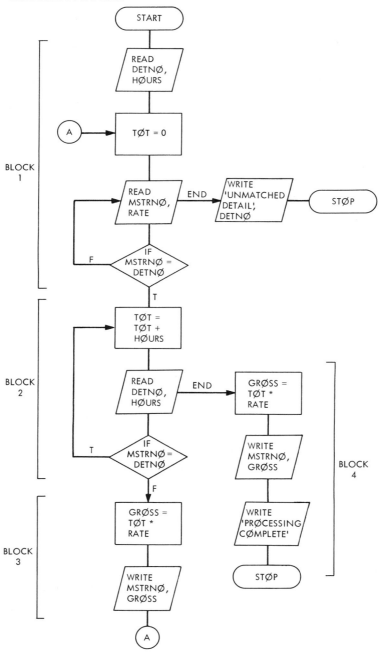

where a field for accumulating hours worked is prepared by the command TØT = 0, also.

After finding the proper master record, records from the detail file must be read and their contents (HØURS) accumulated. This must continue until a detail record with a different control number is read, a condition known as a "control break." When this happens the gross pay can be calculated, and an output record written. Steps in the accumulating process are shown in Block 2 of the flowchart; computation and output steps are contained in Block 3. The program then returns to Block 1, TØT resets to zero, and the search for a new matching master record repeated.

Care must be taken to write the last total after exhausting the detail file. This is done in Block 4, just before the program is terminated.

The logical process can best be followed by using test data. Assume that input records containing depicted data appear in the following sequence:

	Master File			Detail File	
Read Step	MSTRNØ	RATE	Read Step	DETNØ	HOURS
2	111	2.00	1	112	8
3	112	3.00	4	112	6
7	113	5.00	5	112	7
8	114	4.00	6	114	8
	115	4.50	9	114	8

The sequence in which records will be read is shown in the two "Read Step" columns.

First, a detail record is read, followed by a master record. MSTRNØ and DETNØ are then compared; since they are unequal, the program returns and reads another master record as Read Step 3. Employee numbers are again compared, and this time they agree. The program therefore passes to block 2, and hours are accumulated. Another detail record is read, as Read Step 4. As its employee number agrees with MSTRNØ, hours worked are again accumulated, bringing the total to 14, and another detail record read (Read Step 5). Control numbers again agree, hours are accumulated to a sum of 21, and in Read Step 6, another detail record is read.

This time, the employee number in the detail record, 114, does not agree with MSTRNØ, 112. Therefore, all hours records for employee number 112 have been read; his gross pay is calculated as 21×3.00, and an output record is written. These steps occur in flowchart Block 3.

Now, the master record corresponding to the most recently read detail record (DETNØ=114) must be found. To do this, the program returns to block 1 and the master search is repeated. Using the test data, this would cause Reads 7 and 8. A match is found after reading the step 8 record, and the program passes into the accumulation of hours once again. This time, processing is terminated after read step 9 when the detail file is exhausted. The gross pay of employee number 114 is calculated and written, and the program terminated.

Once the flowchart is completed and tested, coding the FORTRAN program is a routine matter. The program for this problem is shown in Figure 5–12.

Illustration 7. Using Compound Conditionals

The final illustration demonstrates the use of compound conditionals, intermixing relational and logical operators. It also illustrates the use of logical data.

Problem. A program is to be written which will scan personnel records, selecting and writing the employee number of any employee who has at least a college degree and earns more than $15,000 annually, or who is over 35 years of age and married with three or more children. Only records meeting the test are to be written; others will be ignored.

Assume that records in the input and output files contain the following:

		FORTRAN	
		Field	
Item Description	*Name*	*Size*	*Type*
Input record:			
Employee number ... NØ		xxxx	Integer
Age, in years .... AGE		xx	Integer
Educational level .... EDUC		x	Integer (college degree=4)
Marital status .... MARR		x	Logical (Married=T)
Number of children .. CHILD		xx	Integer
Annual salary .... PAY		xxxxx̂xx	Real
Output record:			
Employee number ... NØ		xxxx	Integer

Analysis. The FORTRAN program for this problem is shown in Figure 5–13. At its heart is a complex logical IF statement testing a

FIGURE 5–12

Illustration 6 Program

IBM

FORTRAN CODING FORM

PROGRAM	*MERGING*		PUNCHING INSTRUCTIONS
PROGRAMMER	*MC CAMERON*	DATE	

```
C      ILLUSTRATION 6. MERGING RECORDS
       INTEGER DETNØ
1      FØRMAT(I5,F4.2)
2      FØRMAT(I5,F3.1)
3      FØRMAT(1X,I5,5X,F7.2)
4      FØRMAT(' UNMATCHED DETAIL ',I5)
5      FØRMAT(' PROCESSING COMPLETE')
       READ(5,2)DETNØ,HOURS
10     TØT = 0
15     READ(7,1,END=30)MSTRNØ,RATE
       IF(MSTRNØ.NE.DETNØ)GØ TØ 15
20     TØT = TØT + HOURS
       READ(5,2,END=50)DETNØ,HOURS
       IF(MSTRNØ.EQ.DETNØ)GØ TØ 20
       GRØSS = TØT * RATE
       WRITE(6,3)MSTRNØ,GRØSS
       GØ TØ 10
30     WRITE(6,4)DETNØ
       STØP
50     GRØSS = TØT * RATE
       WRITE(6,3)MSTRNØ,GRØSS
       WRITE(6,5)
       STØP
       END
```

compound expression combining logical and relational operators. Careful study of this will provide insight into the workings of this very useful command.

The logical expression is as follows:

EDUC .GE. 4 .AND. PAY .GT. 15000 .ØR. AGE .GE. 35 .AND. MARR .AND. CHILD .GE. 3

This would be evaluated in three phases, as follows (for convenience, symbols are assigned to represent the results of each evaluation):

Phase 1: 1. EDUC .GE. 4 (Call the result A) Relational operator.

FIGURE 5–13
Illustration 7 Program

IBM   FORTRAN CODING FORM

| PROGRAM | *PERSONNEL SELECTION* | | PUNCHING INSTRUCTIONS | GRAPHIC | | | |
| PROGRAMMER | *MC CAMERON* | DATE | | PUNCH | | | |

```
C        ILLUSTRATION OF COMPOUND CONDITIONALS
         INTEGER AGE, EDUC, CHILD
         LOGICAL MARR
   10    FORMAT(I4, I2, I1, L1, I2, F7.2)
   11    FORMAT(' EMPLOYEE NO ' I5, ' MEETS REQUIREMENTS ')
   50    READ(5, 10, END=75) NO, AGE, EDUC, MARR, CHILD, PAY
         IF(EDUC .GE. 4 .AND. PAY .GT. 15000. .OR. AGE .GT. 35
        1 .AND. MARR .AND. CHILD .GE. 3) WRITE(6, 11) NO
         GO TO 50
   75    STOP
         END
```

2. PAY .GT. 15000 (Call the result B) Relational operator.

3. AGE .GT. 35 (Call the result C) Relational operator.

4. CHILD .GE. 3 (Call the result D) Relational operator.

Phase 2: 5. A .AND. B (Call the result E) Logical operator.

6. C .AND. MARR (Call the result F) Logical operator.

7. F .AND. D (Call the result G) Logical operator.

Phase 3: 8. E .ØR. G (Final result) Logical operator.

All relationals will be resolved to a true or false state in phase 1, evaluation moving from left to right through the expression. Then, in phase 2, all statements connected by the logical operator .AND. are resolved to true or false. Finally, the .ØR. operators are evaluated in phase 3, thus reducing the entire expression to a true or false condition.

CHAPTER SUMMARY

This chapter introduces the control statements necessary to create programs with more than one branch. At this point, coding techniques become of less consequence than design logic in the preparation of valid computer programs. One may, with practice, learn to avoid the standard coding errors which so hamper proper execution in the beginning. However, the challenge of logic design is an integral part of every program.

Real computer ability is tapped when the IF statement is used. It is the logical center of FORTRAN and the key to the success of the modern electronic computer. It provides a means by which data may be tested and the program channeled in more than one way according to the results obtained.

Both the arithmetic and logical IF statements serve very important roles in FORTRAN. The arithmetic version tests arithmetic expressions and provides a three-way branch, reflecting whether the results of the evaluation are negative, zero, or positive. The logical IF provides a two-way branch, testing a logical expression. The form of the statement to be used depends on the user's preference and the needs of the program; however, most programmers seem to exhibit a preference for the logical IF version as being quite versatile and easily fitted to the nature of most logical patterns.

Summary of Instructions

FORTRAN instructions introduced in this chapter are of the technical character indicated below.

1. Computed GØ TØ

> k GØ TØ $(n_1, n_2, n_3, \ldots, n_m), i$
> k = optional statement number
> n = statement number
> i = integer variable

2. Logical IF

> k IF (logical expression) True-statement
> m Continue-statement
> k and m = optional statement numbers

3. Arithmetic IF

> k IF (arithmetic expression)n_1, n_2, n_3
> k = optional statement number
> n = statement number

QUESTIONS

1. What is the difference between the GØ TØ and the computed GØ TØ commands?

2. What is the difference between the computed GØ TØ and IF statements?

3. Assume the following statements:

$$IF(A.EQ.B)X=Y$$
$$C=D$$

When will $X=Y$ be executed?
When will $C=D$ be executed?

4. How does the logical IF statement differ from its arithmetic counterpart?

5. What are the punctuation requirements of the computed GØ TØ instruction?

6. What are the punctuation requirements of the logical IF statement?

7. Are the commas in the arithmetic IF statement optional?

8. What is evaluated in an arithmetic IF statement? A logical IF statement?

9. Is a value destroyed when it is used in an IF expression?

10. Must the IF statement have a statement number?

11. Assume the following FORTRAN statement: $IF(A=B)1,2,3$
    What is wrong with the command? How might this be written using logical IF statements?

12. How many addresses must the arithmetic IF statement specify?

13. How is the "true-statement" of a logical IF designated?

14. How is the expression set off from the remainder of an IF statement?

15. May nonquantitative data be evaluated in the arithmetic IF statement? The logical IF statement?

16. Assume the following statement: $IF(X-Y)10,20,30$
    To which statement will a negative evaluation transfer? A positive evaluation?

17. Identify the following flowchart symbols:

EXERCISES

1. Indicate the errors, if any, in each of the following commands:
    (*a*) 25 $IF(X=5.)10,20,30$
    (*b*) 20 $IF (X*2.-10.*Y), 10,20,30$
    (*c*) 20   IF X .GT. 25, GØ TØ 50
    (*d*) 25 $IF(X-2Y)10,15,20$

(e)   25   IF(X + Y) GØ TØ 20
(f)   25   IF(X) GØ TØ 20
(g)   20   IF(A − N),1,1,10
(h)   20   IF(A = B) GØ TØ 10
(i)   20   IF(SQRT((AK − (U − 1.)/(V*(V* + 1.))/(A − 2.))4,5,5
(j)   20   IF(X LE Y) GØ TØ 20
(k)   20   IF(X .MT. Y) X = Y

2. Point out any errors in the following statements or statement sets:
   (a)   GØ TØ (110,16,43)K
   (b)   GØ TØ (110,16,43),A
   (c)   GØ TØ (110,16,43),2
   (d)   K = 5
         GØ TØ (110,16,43),K
   (e)   GØ TØ (110 16 43)2K

3. Describe the errors in the following program:
   10   FØRMAT (2F5.1)
   11   FØRMAT (1X,2F7.1)
   1   READ10, CØST, UNIT
   2   UCST = CØST/UNIT
   3   IF(UCST − 1.)10,3,12
   12   WRITE(6,11),CØST,UCST
         GØ TØ 11
         END

4. The directive "if both X and Y are greater than Z, go to 200" has been coded as follows:

   IF(X .AND. Y .GT. Z)GØ TØ 200

   Criticize this statement as adequate for the execution of the directive given.

5. List all errors in the following program. Punctuation mistakes in a single command count as one error. The program is to process the following input and output records:

Item Description	FORTRAN Name	Field Size
Input record:		
Account number	NACT	xxxx
Number of units sold	NØ	xxx
Sales price per unit	PR	xxx
Output record:		
Account number	NACT	xxxx
Sales amount	SALE	xxxx.xx
Discount amount	DISC	xxx.xx
Net price	ANET	xxxx.xx

SALE is to be calculated for each input record by multiplying sales price times the number of units sold. Then, if the account number is equal to or greater than 4000, a 2% discount is to be allowed. No discount is allowed on other accounts, and the discount field should be set to zero. Net price is the difference between the sales amount and discount.

A count of input records is to be kept in CTR. A transfer record with 9999 in the NACT field is at the rear of the transaction records; when this is encountered, CTR should be printed and the program should stop. The program is prepared as follows:

```
90      FØRMAT(I4,I3,F3.2)
91      FØRMAT(1X,I4,5X,F6.2,5X,F5.2,5X,F6.2)
1       CTR = 0
        READ NACT PR NØ
        IF(NACT-9999.),GØ TØ 50
3       SALE = PR * NUM
        CTR = CTR + 1
        IF(NACT-4000)4,3,10
4       DISC=SALES * 2
        ANET = SALE - DISC
10      DISC=0
        SALE=ANET
        WRITE(6,91),INV,SALE,DISC,ANET
        GØ TØ 1
70      WRITE91,CTR
        HALT
        END
```

6. Write a program to read a value, K (FØRMAT xxx) from a single input record. Then, write the commands necessary to determine whether K is odd or even. If even write "HEADS," if odd, "TAILS." The program should then be terminated.

7. Each element, X (FØRMAT xxxx$_\wedge$) of a data set is punched in a different input record. Write a program to find the largest and smallest X values, to be called BIG and SMALL, respectively. Write these values when all records have been read.

8. Assume that input records contain two values. ACT (FØRMAT xx$_\wedge$xx) represents the actual material cost and STD (FØRMAT xx$_\wedge$xx) the standard material cost of producing an article. If ACT does not differ by more than 10% of STD from STD, the program is to write 'NØRMAL'; if the difference is greater, it should write 'EXCESSIVE'.
    Instructions:
    (*a*) Write the commands necessary for this program without using the absolute value function.

(*b*) Write the command necessary for the program, using the absolute value function and a single logical IF statement.

9. The equation $Y = 10X - X^2$ produces a curve that slopes upward, then downward as X increases from 1 to infinity. Write a program to find and write the maximum value of Y, using an initial value of 2 for X and increasing X by 1 with each iteration. (Hint: Y_n is the largest Y value when $Y_n > Y_{n+1}$).

10. Write a program to read an unknown number of records, each of which contains an X and a Y value (FØRMAT 2F4.0). Accumulate the excess of X over Y and count the number of input records processed. When all records have been read, as signaled by the END= conditional, compute the average excess (EXC) and print it as FØRMAT 6.2.

11. Assume the following input sales records:

	FORTRAN	
Item Description	*Name*	*Field Size*
Date of sale (integer field)	DATE	xxxx
Sales territory (integer field)	TER	x
Customer type	KUST	x
Invoice number	INV	xxxx
Salesman's number (integer field)	SMNØ	xxxx
Number of units sold	UNITS	xxxx$_\wedge$
Unit cost price	CØST	xx$_\wedge$x
Unit sales price	SALE	xx$_\wedge$x

On sales in sales territory 1, the company allows a 35% discount to manufacturers, indicated as KUST $= 1$, and a 20% discount to wholesale firms, indicated as KUST $= 2$. Other buyers in this and other sales territories pay the regular sales price.

Instructions: Prepare an output record for each input. The END= option is to be used to terminate processing.

Output records are to appear as follows:

	FORTRAN	
Item Description	*Name*	*Field Size*
Salesman's number	SMNØ	xxxx
Number of units sold (integer field)	UNIT	xxxx
Discount rate	RATE	xx.
Gross sales price	GRØSS	xxxxx.xx
Discount amount	DAMT	xxxx.xx
Net sales price	PRNET	xxxxx.xx

GRØSS is to be computed as the product of unit sales price and number of units. Then, the discount amount, if any, is to be calculated, and this determines the net price. DAMT should be set to zero if no discount is allowed.

12.   Refer to the input records in Exercise 11 above. Assume that the firm makes sales in four territories, identified as 1,2,3, or 4 in the data field TER. Accumulate gross sales amounts by territories, calling the four amounts SAMT1, SAMT2, SAMT3, and SAMT4. When all records have been processed, write the four amounts by FØRMAT F10.2. The END= conditional is to be used to terminate processing.

13.   Refer to the input records in Exercise 11 above. Read the input records and find the largest and smallest net sales to a manufacturer, where all manufacturers are indicated as KUST = 2. Store the largest sale at BIG and the smallest at SMALL. Write these amounts by FØRMAT F9.2 when all records have been processed.

14.   Refer to the input records in Exercise 11 above. On sales to Customer type 1, a discount of 1% is to be allowed on the first $1,000 of gross sales (computed as UNITS times SALE) and a discount of 2% thereafter. Thus, a sale of $4,000 would receive a discount of .01 × 1,000 plus .02 × 3,000, or $70.00.

   Write a program to process input records, and prepare output records containing INV; the amount of gross sale, GRØSS (FØRMAT xxxx.xx); the discount amount, DISC (FØRMAT xxxx.xx); and the amount of net sale, NET, (FØRMAT xxxx.xx). Use the END= conditional to end processing.

15.   Refer to the input records in Exercise 11 above. Assuming that records should be in ascending sequence by invoice number, write a program to check sequence and write an error message containing the invoice number and the message ØUT ØF SEQUENCE for any record causing a step-down to be detected.

16.   Refer to the input records in Exercise 11 above. Assume that records are kept in two files; one for Sales territory 1 and the other for Sales territory 2. Both files are maintained in ascending sequence by date of sale.

   Using input unit 5 for Sales territory 1 and input unit 7 for Sales territory 2, write a program to merge the files by date and write a single output file on output unit 6. Territory 2 records should be merged behind territory 1 records for each date.

17.   Refer to the input records in Exercise 11 above. Assume that a "finder" record containing a salesman's number is placed in front of the sales records. This finder record contains a salesman's number, FØRMAT I4, which is to be read as KSMAN. Then, all sales records are to be processed, and the amount of gross sales made by salesman KSMAN is to be accumulated as TSALE. After all records have been processed, print out the total by FØRMAT F10.2.

18. Refer to the input records in Exercise 11 above. Write a program to process the sales records, and write out a gross profit record on all sales where the gross profit exceeds 100% of cost. Gross profit is the difference between the gross sales price and cost.

Output records should consist of the following:

	FORTRAN	
Item Description	*Name*	*Field Size*
Invoice number	INV	xxxx
Gross sales price	GSALE	xxxxx.xx
Gross cost	GCØST	xxxxx.xx
Gross profit	GPFT	xxxxx.xx
Gross profit, percent of cost	PCT	xxx.x

19. Given below are several data names and their related data type:

Data Name	*Data Type*	*Field Size*
I	Real	‸xxxx
J	Integer	xxx
K	Logical	xxxxx
W	Integer	x
X	Real	xx‸xx
Y	Logical	x

Prepare the type statements necessary to properly identify the above.

20. See Exercise 19 above. Prepare FØRMAT and input and output statements, assuming that I/Ø unit 5 is used for reading and 6 for writing. Five blank spaces are to be left between output fields.

21. "If stocks on hand are less than the recorder point and no order has been placed, an output record consisting of the inventory number and reorder quantity is to be written. In any event, processing is to continue."

Instructions: Write a program to scan the records described below, searching for and writing output records for those items requiring reorder. Use the END= option for termination.

	FORTRAN		
Item Description	*Name*	*Type*	*Field Size*
Inventory number	INV	Integer	xxxx
Number of units on hand	UNITS	Integer	xxx
Reorder quantity.	RQ	Integer	xxx
Reorder point	RØP	Integer	xxx
Order status*	ØRDER	Logical	xxxxx

* Recorded as "true" if an order is outstanding, "false" if not.

PROBLEMS

Prepare a flowchart and a FORTRAN program for the following problems. Observe the instructions preceding the Chapter 4 problems in coding the FORTRAN solution. Use the END= option to detect end-of-file conditions where appropriate if the computer being used permits; otherwise, a transfer record should be provided where needed.

1. The Pleasant Valley Electric Company bases its charges on the amount of electricity consumed, as follows:

> First 40 Kilowatt-Hours (KWH) .... 5.55¢ per KWH
> Next 60 KWH .... 4.57¢ per KWH
> Next 300 KWH .... 2.60¢ per KWH
> All other .... 2.38¢ per KWH

Prepare a program to read input records and prepare an output record for each. Input and output records appear as follows:

Item Description	FORTRAN Name	Field Size
Input record:		
Customer number	CUSTNØ	xxxx
Meter reading–last month	ØLDRD	xxxxx
Meter reading–this month	NEWRD	xxxxx
Unpaid balance	ØLDBAL	xxxxx
Output record:		
Customer number	CUSTNØ	xxxx
Electricity	USE	xxxx
Charge for current service	CUR	xxxx.xx
Balance due	BALDUE	xxxx.xx

The amount of electricity consumed is to be calculated by subtracting the last month meter reading from that of the current month. Charges for current services are to be calculated by application of the charge schedule above. This, combined with any unpaid balance, gives the balance due.

In addition to preparing customer statements as above, the amount charged all customers by applying each of the four rates used is to be accumulated as TØTR1, TØTR2, TØTR3, and TØTR4, respectively. These totals, and the total of all charges, are to be written out by FØRMAT xxxxx.xx after all customer records have been processed.

2. The Ajax Company grants discounts on large sales. The discount schedule is as follows:

Sales Amount	Discount Percent
$ 0.00–$ 500.00	0%
$ 500.01–$1,000.00	2
$1,000.01–$2,500.00	5
Over $2,500.00	10

Data input consists of the following:

	FORTRAN	
Item Description	Name	Field Size
Item Number	INØ	xxxx
Number of units	NØ	xxx
Unit sales price	SPR	xxx

Instructions: Write a FORTRAN program for computing the amount of gross sales, the discount amount allowed, if any, and net sales, preparing an output record for each input record. Output should consist of the following:

	FORTRAN	
Item Description	Name	Field Size
Item number	INØ	xxxx
Discount rate allowed	DRATE	xx
Gross sales price	GRØSS	xxxx.xx
Discount amount	DAMT	xxxx.xx
Net sales amount	SAMT	xxxx.xx

"Item number" is to be the item's descriptive number, as read in. "Discount rate allowed" should reflect the allowed rate of discount, according to the schedule above. "Gross sales price" should reflect the sales price for all units on this sale, "Discount amount" the amount of discount allowed, and "Net sales amount" should be the difference between the two.

The amount of GRØSS, DAMT, and SAMT should be accumulated as records and processed as TØTGR, TØTD, and TØTS. After all records have been processed, these should be written by FØRMAT F10.2. Then, PCT should be computed as the percent that the total discount granted is of the total gross sales amount and written by FØRMAT xx.xx. (Hint: Compute PCT by dividing TØTGR into TØTD, then multiplying by 100.)

3. The Freystone Company pays its salesmen on a commission basis. The commission rate depends on the amount of sale, as follows:

Sales Amount	Commission Rate
Above $10,000	25%
$ 7,500–$10,000	20%
5,000– 7,499	15%
below 5,000	10%

Commissions are calculated by multiplication of the appropriate rate times the sales amount.

Input and output records appear as follows:

<table>
<tr><td></td><td colspan="2">FORTRAN</td></tr>
<tr><td>Item Description</td><td>Name</td><td>Field Size</td></tr>
</table>

Item Description	Name	Field Size
Input record:		
Salesman number	SLMNØ	xxxxx
Sales amount	SALES	xxxxx.
Output record:		
Salesman number	SLMNØ	xxxxx
Commission amount	CØMM	xxxxx.xx

An output record is to be written for each input record. Output is to have the headings SALESMAN and CØMMISSIØN above the respective columns, followed by a blank line.

4.   Employees of the Crowell Company are paid a base salary, and they can earn a bonus for exceptionally high production. The schedule for determining bonus payment is as follows:

Production	Bonus
Up to 1,000 units	No bonus allowance
1,000–1,200 units	$ .50 per unit
1,201–1,500 units	$ .75 per unit
1,501–2,000 units	$1.00 per unit
Above 2,000	$1.50 per unit

The bonus is calculated in steps. For example, a worker producing 1,700 units would receive no bonus for the first 1,000 units, then $ .50 for the next 200 ($100), then $.75 for the next 300 ($225), and, finally, $1.00 for the last 200 ($200). Thus, his bonus would be $525.

Input and output records appear as follows:

Item description	Name	Field Size
Input record:		
Employee number	EMPENØ	xxxxx
Base salary	SALARY	xxxxx
Number of units produced	UNITS	xxxx
Output record:		
Employee number	EMPENØ	xxxxx
Base salary	SALARY	xxx.xx
Bonus earned	BØNUS	xxxx.xx
Total pay	TØTPAY	xxxx.xx

Columns in the printed output are to be headed EMPLØYEE, SALARY, BØNUS, and TØTAL, respectively. The heading is to be followed by a single blank line.

An output record is to be prepared for each input record. After all have been processed, the total amounts of salary, bonus, and total pay for the entire run are to be written beneath the output columns with the caption PAYRØLL TØTALS beside them. Use format xxxxx.xx for writing the total amounts.

5. The X Company uses a modified standard cost plan for its inventory. Each item of inventory has been assigned a standard unit cost, and actual unit costs are compared with this standard. If actual costs differ from standard by no more than 10% of standard, the actual cost is used as the inventory value. However, if the difference is greater than 10% of standard, standard costs are used and the difference, called a variance, is reported separately.

Data input for the program appears as follows:

		FORTRAN	
Item Description		*Name*	*Field Size*
Inventory number		INV	xxxx
Actual cost		ACØST	xxxxxxx
Standard cost per unit		STD	xxxx
Number of units		UNITS	xxxx

Processing is to take place as follows:

The actual unit cost should be computed by dividing the number of units into ACØST. This unit cost should then be compared with 90% and 110% of standard cost per unit. If the unit cost lies outside either limit, standard cost should be used as the item's value and the variance should be computed by subtracting the standard from actual. This amount, multiplied by the number of units, should be reported as VAR and accumulated as TVAR. If the unit cost lies within acceptable limits, the item's value should be its actual cost and VAR should be set to zero. An unfavorable variance (cost exceeds standard) should be reported as a positive amount.

The following output is to be prepared for each input record:

		FORTRAN	
Item Description		*Name*	*Field Size*
Inventory number		INV	xxxx
Inventory value		VALUE	xxxxx.xx
Variance		VAR	xxxxx.xx

Records are maintained in the input file in ascending sequence by inventory number. This sequence should be checked while processing the records, and the inventory number of any record causing a step-down to be detected should be written out with the message ØUT ØF SEQUENCE.

TVAR should be written out by FØRMAT xxxxx.xx after all records have been processed, and the program is then terminated.

6. Students at the Apex University fill out the Student Fee Bill below

for automatic calculation of their university tuition and fees each semester:

APEX UNIVERSITY
Student Fee Bill

1. Student Social Security number: _____

2. Credit hours enrolled for: _____

3. Residence status (check 1): _____ Resident _____ Nonresident

4. Housing:

    a. Plan: _____   3   On campus: Room $150
        1   Off campus   per semester
        2   On campus: Room $125   4   On campus: Room $200
            per semester   per semester

    b. Telephone: _____ (Indicate "yes" if telephone desired; cost
                            $20 per semester)

5. Board: _____ (Indicate "yes" if to eat in cafeteria; cost $250
                     per semester)

6. Hospitalization _____ (Indicate "yes" if hospitalization insur-
                              ance desired; cost $5.00 per semester)

7. Special Fees: Place a check beside any special fee for which you
    are charged this semester:

    a. Chemistry ($15) _____

    b. Computer Science ($10) _____

    c. Zoology ($20) _____

8. Scholarship: _____ (Indicate the amount of any scholar-
    ship already awarded that is to be deducted from the above fees)

Tuition is charged on the following schedule:

	Credit Hours			
	12 or more	*8–11*	*4–7*	*1–3*
University tuition	$300	$250	$200	$100
Nonresident fee	300	200	150	100

Out-of-state students are required to pay both the university tuition and nonresident fee. In-state students pay only the university fee.

Instructions: Write a program to calculate, from his fee bill, the amount of fees owed by each student. Output, with the column headings shown, should appear as follows:

STUDENT NUMBER	UNIVERSITY TUITIØN	NØNRESIDENT FEE	HØUSING	BØARD	HØSPITALIZATIØN	TØTAL
		LESS: SCHOLARSHIP*				
		NET AMOUNT OWED*				

* To be shown only if a scholarship is available.

The student Social Security number is a 7-digit number. A student cannot carry more than 21 hours. Scholarships are never for more than the greater of $500 or the amount of the fees owed. Other field sizes are indicated by data on the fee bill.

It is recommended that "yes" and "no" responses on the form be coded as "1" and "2" on the computer input record. A student may be subject to one or more special fee; therefore, a separate field should be set out for each. Other input design is left to the programmer.

7. The Miller Drug Company makes credit sales to customers. These sales are recorded in computer-sensible form as they occur, and the records held until the end of the month. Then, they are sorted into customer-number sequence, and monthly bills are prepared.

Input and output records appear as follows:

	FORTRAN	
Item Description	Name	Field Size
Input record:		
Customer number	CUSTNØ	xxxxx
Sales amount	AMT	xxxxx
Output record, type 1:		
Customer number	CUSTNØ	xxxxx
Sales amount	AMT	xxx.xx
Output record, type 2:		
Message	TØTAL DUE	
Total amount owed by customer	TØTAMT	xxxx.xx

Records for a customer are to be listed, and the amount accumulated. Then, when all records for the customer have been processed, a single line is to be skipped and the message TØTAL DUE written beside the account total.

8. A set of records containing asset data is to be processed. Each asset is represented by a balance record. If any changes in the asset's balance have occurred, these are contained in records immediately following the balance record. Thus, each asset is represented by a subset of records consisting of a balance document and transaction documents

if appropriate. The records appear as follows. Note that a decimal *is recorded* in the AMT field.

Item Description	FORTRAN Name	Field Size
Input record:		
Blank field		x
Account number	NACCT	xxxxx
Record type*	KTYPE	xx
Amount	AMT	xxxxxx.xx

* Recorded as 1 for a balance record, 2 for a debit, and 3 for a credit.

Instructions: Write a program for updating the asset balance records and preparing new ones in the same format as the old. An output balance record will become the input balance record of the next processing run; therefore, input and output formats are the same, and the input format must have one blank space as its first character. There are no skips between data fields.

Processing should take place as follows:

(a) The first record read will contain an asset balance. The account number and balance amount should be moved to another location.

(b) Then, another record should be read. This must be tested, for it may be:

    (1) A transaction record. If so, a debit amount should be added or a credit subtracted from the balance. The program should then return to read another record.

    (2) A new balance record. This signals the completion of the old record's posting. Therefore, the updated old record should be written out and the new one moved into its place. The new balance record should be written out by the format used in reading.

(c) Sensing an END condition by the READ statement indicates that processing is complete. The last updated balance record should be written, and the program ended.

9. Assume that input records of the following description are to be processed and output records prepared as described:

Item Description	FORTRAN Name	Field Size
Input record:		
Customer number	NØ	xxxx
Account status	RETAIL	x (logical)
Date of sale	SDATE	xxx
Amount of sale	AMT	xxxxxx

	FORTRAN	
Item Description	*Name*	*Field Size*
Output record:		
Customer number	NØ	xxxx
Account balance, if over		
90 days old	AMT1	xxxx.xx
Account balance, if 61–90		
days old	AMT2	xxxx.xx
Account balance, if 31–60		
days old	AMT3	xxxx.xx
Account balance, if under		
31 days old	AMT4	xxxx.xx

This problem requires that retail accounts be aged. These are indicated by a "true" status in the logical field RETAIL. Other types of accounts are to be ignored.

Aging requires that the date of sale (SDATE) be compared with the current date; for this, the current date must be entered into the computer in front of the data records. It is to be read in ahead of the data records as CDATE, an integer value of FØRMAT xxx.

All dates are entered as the number of the day in the year (for example, December 26 would be entered as 360). It is assumed that the current year is not leap year.

No account is more than six months old. However, an account may have originated in the previous year. When the account's age is determined, its amount is to be prepared for writing in the proper category of the output record. (For example, a very new account would be written out in the field called AMT4, etc.) The amount fields available for other ages must be set to zero. Processing is to cease when END is detected or a record containing zero in the SDATE field is read.

10. Assume that a vote has been taken on a particular issue. Each ballot has been recorded in the first position of a separate record where "T" stands for "yes" and "F" for "no."

Prepare a program to count the "yes" and "no" votes. When all have been tabulated, determine which response is the more numerous and the percent of winning votes to the total cast. Write the result in the message THE a VØTES WIN, WITH b PERCENT where "a" stands for the winning response and "b" the percent of winning to total votes.

11. When bonds are sold, two factors cause the cash proceeds on the sale to differ from the bonds' face amount. One of these is the premium or discount that may exist. Bonds are quoted at a percentage of their face; hence a $1,000 bond quoted at 101½ would sell for $1,015.00, while a bond quoted at 97¼ would bring $972.50. The difference between sales price and face is the premium or discount.

The other factor influencing the amount of sales proceeds is interest. The bond seller collects from the buyer any interest accrued since the last interest payment date. Bonds ordinarily pay interest twice annually; thus, accrued interest will be measured from the most recent payment date.

Assume that the X Company sells a number of its own bonds. In the face amount of $1,000, these pay interest at 6% per year, with interest payment dates of June 30 and December 31.

Prepare a flowchart and program for computing the amount of premium or discount and any interest accrued on the bonds as they are sold. The program is to continue processing records until all records have been processed.

Input and output records are as follows:

Item Description	FORTRAN Name	Field Size
Input record:		
Account number	NAC	xxxx
Number of bonds sold	NØ	xx
Sale date	DATE	xxx
Price quotation	PR	xxx̬xx
Output record:		
Account number	NAC	xxxx
Face amount of bonds	FACE	xxxxx.xx
Premium	PM	xxxx.xx
Discount	DIS	xxxx.xx
Accrued interest	INT	xxxx.xx
Sales proceeds	PRØC	xxxxx.xx

The sale date in the input record is recorded as the number of the day in year, beginning with January 1 as 001. Thus, for example, December 21 would be recorded as 355. June 30 may be taken as the 181st day in the year.

The price quotation is recorded in input as it is ordinarily given. Therefore, a recorded quotation of 10575 indicates that the sale was made at 105.75% of the bonds' face value.

The following comments pertain to the output record:

(a)   FACE is to be computed as the number of bonds sold times their face value.

(b)   The amount of premium or discount on the sale is to be calculated as defined above. Of course, a given sale cannot have both a premium and a discount. The unused field is to be set to zero.

(c)   Interest is to be computed as outlined above.

(d)   The sales proceeds is the face value of the bonds, adjusted by premium or discount, and interest accrued.

12.   A set of input records is to be processed. Each record contains one

observation of X (FØRMAT xxxx). Write a program that will read these records, make proper accumulations, and compute the mean and standard deviation by the following formulas:

$$\text{Mean} = \Sigma X/N$$

$$\text{Standard deviation} = \sqrt{\frac{(\Sigma X^2) - \frac{(\Sigma X)^2}{N}}{N - 1}}$$

The following accumulations should be made as input records are processed:

N, the number of observations.
The sum of the X values.
The sum of the squares of the X values.

The mean and standard deviation should then be calculated and written out by the following formats: xxxx.xx, and xxx.xxxx.

13. This program is to be used at the end of the year, December 31, to calculate the amount of discounts lost on Accounts Payable. Input and output records are as follows:

Item Description	FORTRAN Name	Field Size
Input record:		
Creditor identification number	CRDTR	xxxxx
Transaction date	TDATE	xxx
Discount granted	DISC	x(logical)
Discount period	DPER	xx
Discount rate	DRATE	xx
Net transaction amount	NAMT	xxxxxx
Output record:		
Caption*	*	*
Amount of discounts lost	DISMT	xxxxx.xx

* A message, as follows:
THE AMØUNT ØF DISCØUNT LØST IS

When credit purchases are made, the Account Payable is recorded net of any discount. At the end of the financial year, therefore, all balances in the Payables account must be checked to see if the discount period on any account has lapsed. The amount of all discounts lost in this manner must be accumulated, and written out after all Account Payables records have been processed. Specific points on processing are as follows:

(a) An input record should be read. Not all vendors grant a discount; therefore, the logical field DISC should be checked. A "T" in this field indicates that a discount is granted; "F" indicates that there is no discount, and the program should return and read another input record.

(b) When a discount is granted, the transaction date and discount period must be investigated to see if the discount period has lapsed. The transaction date is recorded as the number of the day in the year; thus, March 13 would be recorded as 072. Leap years are to be ignored.

(c) If the discount is still in force, the record may be ignored. However, if the discount has lapsed, its amount must be computed and added to DISMT. Computation is based on the discount rate and net transaction amount; it must be remembered, however, that the discount amount taken was based on the gross transaction amount.

14. This problem involves the input and output records outlined below. Input records are to be processed and an output record prepared when necessary, until END is encountered. This indicates that the program is to stop.

	FORTRAN	
Item Description	*Name*	*Field Size*
Input record:		
Inventory identification number	IDENT	xxxxx
Kind of unit	KIND	x
Number of units sold—current month ..	CURSAL	xxxxx
Number of units sold—last month	XSAL	xxxxx
Number of units sold—previous month .	YSAL	xxxxx
Number of units on hand	UNITS	xxxx
Reorder point	RØP	xxxx
Order status	STATUS	x(logical)
Storage capacity	CAP	xxxx
Output record:		
Inventory identification number	IDENT	xxxxx
Kind of unit*		
Number of units to be ordered	NØRD	xxxxx
* See instruction (c) below.		

Instructions: Prepare a FORTRAN program for listing items requiring reorder as follows:

(a) Check the number of units on hand against the reorder point. If the inventory exceeds reorder, the item does not require ordering, and a new record can be read. If the units on hand is below the reorder point, check to see if an order is already outstanding, as indicated by a T in the STATUS field. If so, an additional order is not to be placed.

(b) If an order is necessary, the amount to be ordered is three quarters of a month's average sales volume (found by averaging the three months' sales reported) less the inventory on hand.

However, storage capacity may not permit this much to be stored. If the computed amount to be ordered exceeds storage capacity less the current balance, only the difference between the current balance and storage capacity is to be ordered.

(c)   If an order is placed, the kind of unit must be indicated by a written-out message. The input field, KIND, contains a code indicating the kind of unit, where 1 represents pounds, 2 represents gallons, and 3 represents feet. Three output formats are to be set up, one containing the description PØUNDS, another GALLØNS, and the third FEET. Then, when an order is to be placed, KIND should be queried and the proper output format used.

15.   The Principal Provision Company makes credit sales to customers. Three input files are involved in processing credit sales and preparing a listing of unpaid balances.

The first is the Accounts Receivable master file. This contains a record for each customer having approved credit with the Company. The second, called the Sales file, is a detail file. It contains records with information on sales made since the last processing run. The third file, called the Cash Receipts file, is also a detail file; it contains information on cash collections made since the last processing run. Accounts Receivables are processed weekly. Before this is done, all three files are sorted into Account Number sequence, in ascending order. Records and their contents appear as follows:

	FORTRAN	
Item Description	*Name*	*Field Size*
Records in Accounts Receivable master file:		
Customer account number	MASTER	xxxxx
Unpaid balance	BAL	xxxxxx
Credit limit	LIMIT	xxxxxx
Records in Sales file:		
Customer account number	SALENØ	xxxxx
Sales amount	SALAMT	xxxxxx
Records in Cash Receipts file:		
Customer account number	CASHNØ	xxxxx
Amount of cash receipts	CASH	xxxxxx
Output record:		
Customer account number	MASTER	xxxxx
Beginning balance	BAL	xxxx.xx
Sales made to account	TØTSAL	xxxx.xx
Collections on account	TØTCAS	xxxx.xx
Ending balance	ENDBAL	xxxx.xx
Remarks*		

* If an Accounts Receivable master record contains an unpaid balance and no cash is collected, the message INACTIVE should be written here. If the ending balance exceeds the Credit limit, the message ØVER LIMIT should be written.

Instructions: Prepare output records as described above. An account may be inactive, or there may be multiple sales and/or cash receipts records for it. For an account, sales records should be processed before cash receipts records where both are active. It is suggested that processing proceed somewhat as follows:

(*a*)   Read one record from both the Sales file and the Cash Receipts file.

(*b*)   Read one record from the Accounts Receivable master file.

(*c*)   Check to see whether the Sales or Cash Receipts record applies to this account.

(*d*)   If neither record applies, determine whether the Account Receivable has an unpaid balance. If not, the record should be ignored and another Accounts Receivable record read. If it has an unpaid balance, the amount should be written out as BAL and ENDBAL, with the required message.

(*e*)   If the Sales record applies to the Master, the amount of sale should be accumulated and another sales record read. This process should continue until all applicable Sales records have been read.

(*f*)   If the Cash Receipts record applies to the Master, a procedure similar to (*e*) above should be followed.

(*g*)   If both Sales and Cash Receipts records apply, Sales should be processed first.

(*h*)   When all detail records applicable to the master have been processed, the total Sales (TØTSAL) for the account should be added to BAL, while the total Cash Receipts (TØTCAS) for the account should be subtracted. ENDBAL should be compared with the credit limit, and a message written if necessary.

16.   Write a program to prepare depreciation schedules by either the straight-line or declining-balance methods. Input and output records appear as follows:

Item Description	FORTRAN Name	Field Size
Input record:		
Asset number	NØ	xxxx
Estimated use-life, years	USELFE	xxx_∧
Cost	CØST	xxxxxₓxx
Estimated scrap value	SCRAP	xxxxxₓxx
Depreciation method indicator*	I	x
Output record:		
Asset number†	NØ	xxxx
Depreciation method†		
Year	YEAR	xxxx
Depreciation for year	DEPREC	xxxxx.xx

FORTRAN

Item Description	Name	Field Size
Accumulated depreciation	ACDEP	xxxxx.xx
Undepreciated balance	BAL	xxxxx.xx

* 1 = straight line
  2 = declining balance
† These items are to appear only on the first line of the output schedule with the asset's cost in the BAL field location. "Depreciation method" should be a message containing either the phrase STRAIGHT LINE or DECLIN-ING BALANCE, as appropriate.

Instructions:

(*a*) The "year" field should begin with 1975 and increase by one with each line in the schedule. No depreciation should be taken for 1975.

(*b*) The depreciation for the year should be calculated by one of the following ways:

(1) Declining-balance method: R* Carrying value, where R is the depreciation rate and "carrying value" the difference between the asset's cost and depreciation already taken. $R = 1 - \sqrt[n]{S \div C}$, where $n =$ the asset's estimated use-life, in years; $S =$ estimated scrap value; and $C =$ cost.

(2) Straight-line method: 1/use-life times (cost − scrap).

(*c*) Accumulated depreciation should be the total depreciation taken to date.

(*d*) BAL should represent the undepreciated balance.

(*e*) The program should continue until END is encountered.

17. The coefficient of correlation, *r*, may be computed by the following formula:

$$r = \frac{N\Sigma XY - (\Sigma X)(\Sigma Y)}{\sqrt{(N\Sigma X^2 - (\Sigma X)^2)(N\Sigma Y^2 - (\Sigma Y)^2)}}$$

A set of input records containing X and Y (FØRMAT 2F5.0) is to be read. While doing so, the following values should be accumulated:

N (the number of input records)
ΣXY
ΣX
ΣY
ΣX^2
ΣY^2

When all data records have been read, the coefficient is to be written as x.xxxx and processing is to be ended.

18. The Ajax Company wishes to use the computer in preparing its payroll register.

Input data are available as follows:

Item Description	FORTRAN Name	Field Size
Employee number	NØ	xxxxx
Hours worked this week	HRS	xxx
Shift worked	K	x
Hourly pay rate	RATE	xxxx
Number of dependents	NDP	xx
Year-to-date-earnings	YTD	xxxxxxx

The program should produce a pay record containing the following for each employee:

Item Description	FORTRAN Name	Field Size
Employee number	NØ	xxxxx
Straight pay	STGT	xxx.xx
Overtime pay	ØTIME	xxx.xx
Total pay	TØT	xxxx.xx
Income tax withheld	TINC	xxx.xx
Social Security tax withheld	SST	xxx.xx
Net pay	NET	xxxx.xx

An END condition should be used to terminate the program.

Details of computation: In output, the employee number should, of course, be the same as read in. Pay is to be computed as follows:

(a)   K, a data field in the input record, indicates the shift worked, where

$$1 = \text{regular shift}$$
$$2 = \text{shift 2}$$
$$3 = \text{shift 3}$$

(b)   The hourly pay rate is the rate paid for the regular shift. Hourly shift premiums are allowed as follows:

$$\text{Shift 2: } \$.50$$
$$\text{Shift 3: } \$1.00$$

Before attempting to compute any pay amounts, the pay rate should be adjusted if necessary to compensate for the shift worked. This gives the straight pay rate.

(c)   Straight pay is defined as the straight pay rate for all hours worked.

(d)   Overtime pay is defined as one half the straight pay rate for all hours worked in excess of 40. If no overtime is earned, this should be set to zero.

(e)   Total pay is the sum of straight pay and overtime pay.

(*f*)   Any income tax to be withheld is to be computed as follows:

(1)   Multiply the number of dependents by $14.40 and subtract the product from total pay.

(2)   If the result is positive, compute the amount to be withheld from the following table:

If the Net, Computed in (1) Above Is:		Income Tax to Be Withheld:	
Not over $11.00		0	
Over	But Not Over		of Excess Over
$ 11	$ 39	14%	$ 11
$ 39	$167	$3.92 plus 16%	$ 39
$167	$207	$24.40 plus 20%	$167
$207	$324	$32.40 plus 24%	$207
$324	$409	$60.48 plus 28%	$324
$409	$486	$84.28 plus 32%	$409
$486		$108.92 plus 36%	$486

For example, assume that an employee claiming two dependents earns $150. His income tax withholding would be computed as follows:

(1) $150.00 $-$ (2 $\times$ $14.40) $=$ $121.20

(2)   Withholding on $121.20: $3.92 plus .16 $\times$ (121.20 $-$ 39.00) $=$ $17.07

(*g*)   Social Security withholdings should be at the rate of 5.85% on the first $12,000 earned in the calendar year. In computing this amount, three cases must be allowed for:

(1)   Year-to-date earnings exceed $12,000 before this pay period, and no Social Security tax is to be withheld. In this case, SST should be set to zero.

(2)   The sum of year-to-date earnings and current pay does not exceed $12,000, so the entire amount of current earnings is subject to tax.

(3)   Only part of the current earnings is subject to tax.

(*h*)   Net pay is the amount of total pay less income tax and Social Security withholdings.

19.   Many businesses value ending inventory at its cost or its market value, whichever amount is less. This is an act of conservative accounting designed to absorb in the current period any losses that may be associated with unsold inventory. The inventory value carried forward as an asset is no more than the item can be expected to bring at a sale.

As defined by the American Institute of Certified Public Accountants, "market value" is considered as follows:

"As used in the phrase 'lower of the cost or market' the term 'market' means current replacement cost except that: (1) Market should not exceed the net realizable value (i.e., estimated selling price in the ordinary course of business less reasonably predictable costs of completion and disposal); and (2) Market should not be less than net realizable value reduced by an allowance for an approximately normal profit margin."

Thus, in applying the "lower cost or market" rule in a particular instance of inventory valuation, the following steps must be taken:

(*a*)   Select a market value. This value should be one of the following:

   (1)   The value chosen should not be more than the item's sales price less costs necessary to complete and sell the article. This is called the "net realizable value."

   (2)   The value chosen should not be less than the item's net realizable value minus the normal profit margin.

   (3)   If the replacement value of the article lies between the limits set by (1) and (2) above, replacement cost should be used to represent market value. If the replacement value lies outside the limits, the nearer limit should be used to represent market value.

(*b*)   The market value chosen in (*a*) above should then be compared with cost, and the lower amount should be used as the inventory item's asset value. If the two amounts are the same; cost should be selected as the value of the article.

Instructions: Input records contain the data shown below. You are to write a program for processing this data. For each input record, an output record is to be prepared.

	FORTRAN	
Item Description	*Name*	*Field Size*
Input record:		
Inventory number	INØ	xxxx
Number of units	UNIT	xxx $_\wedge$
Cost*	CØST	xxx $_\wedge$
Replacement market price*	REPL	xxx $_\wedge$
Cost to complete and sell*	SELL	xxx $_\wedge$
Normal profit*	PRØ	xxx $_\wedge$
Sales price*	SPR	xxx $_\wedge$
Output record:		
Inventory number	INØ	xxxx
Inventory value	VAL	xxxx.xx
Write-down	WDN	xxxx.xx

   * Per-unit amounts.

"Inventory value" is to be the value for all units of this particular item using the "lower of cost or market" rule as specified above. If an item's value is reduced from cost to market, the reduction amount is to be shown as WDN; otherwise, this field is to contain zeros.

In addition, the total of all write-downs is to be accumulated as TWDN. When processing has been completed, this should be written out with a format of xxxxx.xx and the program terminated.

20. An employer who pays all his employees in cash must know how many bills of each denomination—ones, fives, tens, and twenties—he needs to make up his payroll. You are to write a program that will read each employee's pay record and determine the bills necessary to prepare his pay envelope (ignore coins). Accumulate the requirements of all employees, and when END is encountered write the requirements out by the formats specified below.

Input and output records appear as follows:

	FORTRAN	
Item Description	*Name*	*Field Size*
Input record:		
Employee number	NØ	xxxxx
Employee pay	PAY	xxxxx
Output record:		
Caption*		
Number of bills	†	xxx

    * This should indicate the kind of bill, as ONES, FIVES, TENS, or TWENTIES.
    † This will be a different field name for each kind of bill. Data names such as K1, K5, K10, and K20 may be used.

21. The X Company maintains its perpetual inventory records by the weighted-average method.

A balance record is kept for every inventory item. This appears as follows:

	FORTRAN	
Item Description	*Name*	*Field Size**
Blank space	—	x
Inventory number	NØ	xxxxx
Record type†	K	xx
Number of units on hand	UNITS	xxxx
Cost of balance on hand	TCØST	xxxxx.xx
Cost per unit	UCØST	xx.xx
Reorder point	RØP	xxxx
Reorder quantity	RQTY	xxxx

    * Output records serve as the input records for the next period. Therefore, input and output FØRMATS should be the same and decimals are punched. The field sizes above *do* allow for signs and need not be increased in output.
    † Balance records are represented by a 1.

Receipts are recorded on records similar to those used to retain balance data. The receipts are filed behind their related balance record prior to updating. There may be more than one receipt record for an item. The receipts records appear as follows:

Item Description	FORTRAN Name*	Field Size
Blank space	—	x
Inventory number	NØ	xxxxx
Record type‡	K	xx
Number of units received	UNITS	xxxx
Cost of receipts†	TCØST	xxxxxₓxx

 * Note that the same names are assigned as in the balance record.
 † Note that field sizes are the same as in the balance record, although decimals are not punched.
 ‡ Receipt records are represented by a 2.

Inventory issues are also recorded on records similar to the balance record. However, when inventory is issued to the factory, the cost is not recorded. The inventory number and number of units issued is written down, and the issues records are filed behind the balance *and* receipts records of the particular inventory item. An item may have more than one issue record. The issues records appear as follows:

Item Description	FORTRAN Name	Field Size
Blank space	—	x
Inventory number	NØ	xxxxx
Record type*	K	xx
Number of units issued	UNITS	xxxx
Job number†	RØP	xxxx

 * Issue records are represented by a 3.
 † Note that this information is recorded in the reorder field.

Thus, each inventory item is represented by a set of records, grouped together as follows:
(*a*) First, a balance record.
(*b*) Second, receipts records, if any.
(*c*) Third, issues records, if any.
 Processing is to proceed as follows:
(*a*) A balance record is to be read, and its contents moved from the fields used in reading.
(*b*) Another record is to be read. This may be a receipts record, an issues record, or another balance record.
  (1) Receipts record. The inventory number is to be verified with that of the last-read balance record. If the numbers agree, the number of units received and cost are to be added to the appropriate balance fields, and the program is to return and read a new record. If the inventory numbers do not

agree, an appropriate message is to be written, and the program is to return and read another record.

(2)   Issues record. With the reading of the first issues record after receipts records, the processing of the latter is known to be completed. Therefore, a new per-unit cost is to be computed. A "costed inventory issues" record is to be written for each issues record, as follows:

| | *FORTRAN* | |
Item Description	*Name*	*Field Size*
Job number	JØB	xxxx
Inventory number	NØ	xxxxx
Number of units issued	UNITS	xxxx
Cost per unit	UCØST	xx.xx
Cost of units issued	CØSTIS	xxxxx.xx

After writing the costed inventory issues, the program is to return and read another record.

(3)   Balance record. The reading of a balance record signifies that all processing related to the previous inventory item has been completed. Therefore, a balance record should be written with the updated amounts pertaining to the just-finished item. This should appear in the same format used in reading balance records.

The reorder-point of the completed item should also be checked. If the balance on hand has fallen below this point, a reorder should be written. This should appear as follows:

| | *FORTRAN* | |
Item Description	*Name*	*Field Size*
Inventory number	NØ	xxxxx
Reorder quantity	RQTY	xxxx

Then, the new balance data should be moved to the balance fields.

Processing Note: The read command must be given as for a balance record because at the time of reading, there is no way of knowing what kind of record will be read. Therefore, any read instructions should use the data names and format specification of the balance record. Once a record has been read, its type can be determined by checking K. This will indicate the nature of the processing steps to follow.

22.   The Smith Company uses the standard cost method of cost accounting. The following procedure reflects data processing involved in the accounting for raw materials put into process.

Standard cost records are maintained for every item of raw material used on a different manufactured article. They are kept in the Standard Cost Master file. When processed, they are read in on input unit 7.

As raw materials are issued to production, the issuance is recorded and the record placed in the Raw Material Issues Detail file. Just before processing, these records are sorted into the same order as the standard cost records—by Raw Material number, with each raw material subdivided by the Finished Unit number on which the part is used. Thus, records are maintained in the order suggested by the following:

Raw Material Number	Finished Unit Number
1111	566
1111	567
1111	569
1112	566
1112	569
1112	575
1113	567

The Raw Materials Issues Detail file is read on input unit 5 when processed.

Input records appear as follows:

Item Description	FORTRAN Name	Field Size
Standard Cost Master:		
Raw material inventory number	RMATM	xxxxx
Inventory number of finished unit on which used	NØFGM	xxxxx
Number of pieces of raw material required per finished unit	NØPC	xxx
Standard cost per piece of raw material	STDRAW	xxxx
Raw Material Issues Detail:		
Raw material inventory number	RMATD	xxxxx
Inventory number of finished unit on which used	NØFGD	xxxxx
Number of units of raw material used	USAGE	xxxx
Number of units of finished goods produced	FINGD	xxxxxx

Processing should take place as follows:

(a) Detail records should be sequence-checked by Finished Unit and Raw Material number as they are read. A step-down should be signalled by writing the message RECØRD ØUT ØF ØRDER and the raw material and finished unit number. Processing should then continue.

(b) Records from the master and detail files should be merged. Not all master records will be active in any processing run.

(*c*) An output record should be prepared for each issues record. It should appear as follows:

FORTRAN

Item Description	Name	Field Size
Inventory number of finished unit	NØFGM	xxxxx
Quantity of finished units mfg.	FINGD	xxxxxx
Standard material cost per finished unit	STDFG	xx.xx
Standard cost for finished units produced	STDJØB	xxxxx.xx
Excess of actual cost over standard cost	VARØV	xxxxx.xx
Excess of standard cost over actual cost	VARUR	xxxxx.xx
Actual cost for all finished units produced	ACTCST	xxxxx.xx

NØFGM and FINGD should be as read in. STDFG should be the standard cost per unit of raw material times the number of pieces of raw material required to make one finished unit. STDJØB should be the standard cost of all finished units reported on the issues record.

If the actual cost for the issues reported exceeds the standard allowance determined as STDJØB, the excess should be reported as VARØV. Should actual cost be less than STDJØB, the difference should be reported as VARUR. In either event, the unused field should be set to zero. If standard and actual costs are equal, both fields should be zero.

ACTCST should be computed as the standard cost per piece of raw material times the number of units of raw material used. STDJØB + VARØV or − VARUR should equal ACTCST.

Columnar headings above the output should be provided as follows:

FIN. UNIT NUMBER	QUANTITY PRØDUCED	STD. UNIT MAT. CØST	STD. JØB CØST	VARIANCE ØVER	VARIANCE UNDER	ACTUAL JØB CØST

Total for STDJØB, VARØV, VARUR, and ACTCST should be accumulated during processing. They should be written out beneath their respective columns after all records have been processed.

23. You are to prepare a program for writing an invoice register, sometimes called a sales journal. Assignment of data names and program organization is left entirely to the programmer. The register is to contain data from invoices such as the following, where each invoice line is punched into a separate input card. Each input card contains the following invoice information in the order mentioned:

Invoice number, sales branch and salesman, city, state, customer number, inventory number (shown in the "description" part of the invoice), quantity, unit price, and cost.

The fields may be assumed to never exceed the largest data size shown on the sample invoice.

Decimals are not punched in input.

The invoice register is to contain the following: invoice number, inventory number, quantity, sales amount (calculated as unit price times quantity), cost, and gross profit (calculated as sales amount less cost).

REPRESENTATIVE COMPANY

CUSTOMER'S
ORDER NO. AND DATE

SIGNED BY

REQUISITION NO.

REFER TO INVOICE NO.   42401

INVOICE DATE   1/8/--

SALES	CITY	ST.	CUST. NO.
BR. SMN			
23	98	126	44	87631

SOLD TO   New York Stores, Inc.
1026 Madison Avenue
New York, N.Y.

SHIPPED TO AND DESTINATION

DATE SHIPPED

F. O. B. ENDICOTT, N.Y.   TERMS 30 DAYS NET

QUANTITY	DESCRIPTION		UNIT PRICE	AMOUNT	COST
70	SWEET POTATOES	23912	2.10	147.00	95.56
27	FLY PAPER	65393	2.20	59.40	38.60
80	MACARONI	12513	1.25	100.00	85.00
28	AMERICAN CHEESE	14008	.51	14.28	9.46
90	PRUNES	23735	2.80	252.00	216.10
200	COFFEE	45263	2.88	576.00	349.75
29	CHOW CHOW	23207	.34	9.86	8.44
1	ZINC BUCKET	65996	9.60	9.60	8.38
16	BROOMS	65135	3.10	49.60	44.90
40	CIDER	19216	1.40	56.00	36.35
21	KETCHUP	34464	1.88	39.48	37.07
12	NOODLES	12552	1.25	15.00	13.50
14	DOG BISCUITS	73335	4.50	63.00	56.95
50	LYE	63504	.64	32.00	28.80
150	CONDENSED MILK	76272	2.60	390.00	380.75
176	COCOA	46257	.80	140.80	133.00
130	PAPRIKA	43632	.60	78.00	74.68
20	CRACKERS	48312	3.10	62.00	55.70
30	TAPIOCA	50927	3.65	109.50	102.60
15	BEANS	58080	1.65	24.75	21.25
80	PEPPER	43672	.55	44.00	39.65
97	NUTMEG	43560	.92	89.24	81.19
140	SALT BUTTER	14785	7.50	1,050.00	68.35
50	SWISS CHEESE	14920	.33	16.50	10.72
70	PEAS	58664	2.15	150.50	128.00
1636		41314	58.30	3,578.51	2,124.75

Totals for sales amount, cost, and gross profit are to be written each time an invoice listing has been completed. In addition, the following totals are to be accumulated, and listed when all invoice records have been processed:

Quantity
Sales amount
Cost
Gross profit

The percent of gross profit to cost is also to be listed at this time.

6 Other Input-Output Topics

Chapter 3 introduced basic input, output, and FØRMAT character-istics. These were sufficient to support the computational instructions of Chapter 4, and the conditionals covered in Chapter 5. They are, in fact, adequate to permit basic data input and output in FORTRAN.

Certain other input-output capabilities enrich the FORTRAN lang-uage. Some expand processing to include non-numeric input as well as output. Others simplify the creation of FØRMAT specifications, or per-mit the elimination of them altogether. Still other input and output in-structions permit data stored in direct-access files to be manipulated without the constraints of sequential processing.

ADVANCED FØRMAT SPECIFICATIONS

The A Specification

This FØRMAT specification permits the programmer to define fields, which may contain any symbol in the computer's character set. While this set may vary from one computer to another, it usually includes all letters and numbers, and such special characters as the following:
$$+ - . , \# * ( ) \$.$$
The A specification is written as follows:

$$A_w$$

where w defines the field width. The width definition is less flexible than with other specifications, as may be seen below.

Naming A Specification Fields.   There is no first-character restriction on the name of a field defined by the A specification. The name may begin with any character of the alphabet. Alphanumeric fields do not require declaration in a type statement.

The A Specification in Input.   The exact computer treatment accorded A-defined fields varies from one machine to another. The detailed operations discussed below apply to the IBM 360–370 series and WATFIV; other computers' reference manuals should be checked to determine the exact storage and retrieval systems in use.

When fields defined by the A specification are read, their contents are stored in sets of four characters. If the field width is greater than 4, only the rightmost characters will be stored and the rest ignored. If the field width is less than 4, the characters read in will be stored in the left-hand portion of the memory word location, and blanks will be used to fill the storage space.

The A Specification in Output.   Output works in essentially the same way as input. A four-place specification permits the computer to write the entire contents of the word location. A smaller specification results in writing the leftmost characters stored, while a larger specification causes the stored data to be written in the right-hand part of the field, blanks filling the unused left-hand positions.

Examples of A Specification.   Application of the above rules may be seen in the following examples.

1. Basic Input-Output Characteristics.   Assume that an input record contains the following 24-character alphanumeric field:

BRICK BUILDING NØ. A–162

This is too wide to be read by a single A specification, but it may be treated as six adjacent alphanumeric fields and defined and read in the following way:

5   FØRMAT(6A4)
READ(5,5)A,B,C,I,J,K

The same message could be written out as follows:

6   FØRMAT(1X,6A4)
WRITE(6,6)A,B,C,I,J,K

This would cause the following message to be written (preceded by a blank):

$$\text{BRICK BUILDING NØ. A–162}$$

Should the field not be a multiple of four characters, similar results are obtained. For example, assume the following data in a 19-place field:

$$\text{123 NORTH JEFFERSON}$$

This can be specified and read as follows:

$$5 \quad \text{FØRMAT (4A4,A3)}$$
$$\text{READ(5,5)I,J,K,L,M}$$

The command WRITE(6,6)I,J,K,L,M writes the same message, assuming appropriate format.

2. *Examples:* The following should make clear the nature of the A specification. "Input Specification" and "Output Specification" refer to the FØRMAT designations used in reading and writing, respectively. "Data Field" indicates the contents of the input field, while "Storage" reflects the item's appearance in the computer's memory. "Output Field" shows the data as it would be written under the stipulated format.

Input Specification	Data Field	Storage	Output Specification	Output Field
A4	123X	123X	A4	123X
A5	1234X	234X	A5	b234X
A3	123	123b	A3	123
A3	123	123b	A4	123b
A4	123X	123X	A2	12
A3	ABC	ABCb	A6	bbABCb

3. *Illustration of Use.* Assume that customers' names and addresses are maintained on punched cards, as follows:

	FORTRAN	
Item Description	Name	Field Size
Account number	NØ	xxxxx
Customer name	X1, X2, X3, X4, X5	20 positions
Street address	Y1, Y2, Y3, Y4, Y5	20 positions
City and state	Z1, Z2, Z3, Z4, Z5	18 positions
Zip code	KZIP	xxxxxx

These records are to be read and name-address labels printed in the usual style.

Figure 6–1 contains a program designed to prepare the address labels.

FIGURE 6–1
Illustration of the A Specification

IBM FORTRAN CODING FORM X28-7327-6 U/M 050 Printed in U.S.A.

PROGRAM: ADDRESS LABELS
PROGRAMMER: MC CAMERØN

```
C     ILLUSTRATIØN ØF THE A SPECIFICATIØN
 1    FØRMAT(5X,14A4,A2,I6)
 2    FØRMAT(20X,5A4)
 3    FØRMAT(20X,4A4,A2,2X,I7)
 10   READ(5,1,END=20)X1,X2,X3,X4,X5,Y1,Y2,Y3,Y4,Y5,Z1,Z2,Z3,Z4,Z5,KZIP
      WRITE(6,2)X1,X2,X3,X4,X5
      WRITE(6,2)Y1,Y2,Y3,Y4,Y5
      WRITE(6,3)Z1,Z2,Z3,Z4,Z5,KZIP
      GØ TØ 10
 20   STØP
      END
```

An address record is read, and the fields are given names showing their grouping. Three output records are written for each input, showing name, street, and city. Thus, an input record containing the following data would be printed in the indicated manner:

Input:

62331ALBERT P. JOHNSON 1223 CENTRAL AVENUE BATON ROUGE LA 70808

Output:

ALBERT P. JOHNSON 1223 CENTRAL AVENUE BATON ROUGE LA 70808

Defining Alphanumeric Fields: The H Notation

This is also called the Hollerith notation, after the inventor of punched-card data processing equipment. Used in output format statements, it serves the same purpose as the single quote symbols introduced earlier.

The notation is of the general nature

$$w\text{Hmessage}$$

where w is an unsigned integer constant defining the field width and H is the symbol representing the nature of the FØRMAT specification.

"Message" represents the message which is actually included in the FØRMAT statement and is transmitted as a part of the output list when the write command is given. The message must contain the same number of characters (including blanks) as the number specified as w.

To illustrate, assume the following FØRMAT statement:

1   FØRMAT(14H THE VALUE IS ,F6.2)

Assume, further, that some value, X, has been calculated to be -28.48. Execution of the write command

WRITE(6,1)X

would cause the following to be written:

THE VALUE IS -28.48

Thus, the message inserted in the FØRMAT statement is transmitted as a part of the output list, even though the WRITE command does not mention it. Allusion to the proper FØRMAT statement is all that is required. Of course, the value of X was written out under the FØRMAT specification F6.2 in the manner previously described.

Note that the number of positions in the message, 14, just exactly equals the value of w in the H specification. The position count in the message was as follows:

bTHEbVALUEbISb

where "b" represents a blank space.

Note that the message count begins immediately after the H with the intervening space included as a part of the message itself.

Failure to provide a space at the end of the message would have caused X to be written without intervening space and made reading difficult, somewhat as follows: THE VALUE IS-28.48 Thus, spacing before and after the message must always be considered in setting the field width.

In compilers, such as IBM 360–370 FORTRAN and WATFIV, which support the single quote form of output message inclusion, the Hollerith specification is seldom employed. However, it is implemented in all FORTRAN versions, and is therefore available when the quote specification is not.

The E Specification

Chapter 2 describes how very large or small numbers, having their decimal outside their set of significant digits, may be written through the use of an exponent. As discussed in that chapter, such a number as 1234567.E+03 is to be read as 1234567000, a larger number than may be represented without exponent in single-precision form.

The E FØRMAT specification provides for the reading and writing of such numbers. The FØRMAT specification is of the following general form:

$$Ew.d$$

where w specifies the field width and d the number of places assumed to lie to the right of the decimal.

Relation between the E Specification and Data

Input Requirements.   The data to be read under an E FØRMAT specification should be of the same general nature as that read under the F specification. It can consist of from 1 to 7 significant digits, an optional decimal, and an optional sign. The decimal, if included, can occur anywhere to the right, left, or between significant digits. The sign, if included, must be the leftmost character.

The E-notation number is unique in that it is followed immediately by an exponent of the following general form:

$$E \pm e_1 e_2$$

This can be modified in several ways for simplicity. The letter "E" may be omitted if the exponent sign is used. Such writing may be seen in Example 4, Figure 6–2. Or, as shown in Example 3, the sign may be omitted if "E" is written and the exponent is positive. Finally, e_1 may be omitted if its value is zero; this is shown in Example 4.

Input values are shown in their standard form in Figure 6–2, Examples 1 and 2. The sign is used in both of these because the values are negative; an omitted sign may be seen in the input value of Example 3.

A decimal may be written in the input value. If so, it overrides the decimal location indicated by the FØRMAT specification. A written decimal and the related computer-sensible value may be seen in Example 2, Figure 6–2.

If desired, the decimal may be omitted from the input value. In this case, the decimal location is provided by the FØRMAT specification. It will be located "d" places from the position immediately to the left of "E" in the exponent (or the exponent sign, if "E" is omitted), plus or minus the value of the exponent.

FIGURE 6–2
Illustrations of E-type Specifications

Example	FØRMAT Specifi- cation	Input Value*	Numerical Equivalent of Stored Value	Output Value*
1.	E14.7	b−.1234567E+00	−.1234567	−0.1234567E+00
2.	E14.7	b−12.34567E+02	−1234.567	−0.1234567E+04
3.	E13.6	bbbb1234567E2	123.4567	b0.123456E+03
4.	E13.6	bbbb1234567−2	.01234567	b0.123456E−01
5.	E11.6	b1234567E−2	.01234567	(1)
6.	E16.7	bbbbb1234.567E−4	.1234567	bbb0.1234567E+00
7.	E10.0	1234567E−5	12.34567	bbbb0.E+02
8.	E8.1	bbb1.E09	1000000000.	b0.1E+10

* b = blank
(1) Format does not allow seven output spaces for sign position, zero, decimal, and exponent.

The proper decimal placement may be seen in Example 3 of Figure 6–2. Here, the value 1234567E2 is read by the FØRMAT specification E13.6. Counting from the position preceding "E" six places to the left, then adding two positions for the exponent, the actual value is read as 123.4567.

Output Requirements. Values written out under the E specification all have the same general form. Such an output contains a signed exponent, a leading zero followed by a decimal, and the number with its most significant digit just to the right of the decimal. A sign must be written as the leftmost character if the value is negative.

Example 2, Figure 6–2, depicts a typical output value. Written by the FØRMAT specification E14.7, it shows the value as −0.1234567E+04. This should be read as −1234.567.

The output field must always be seven positions or more wider than the number of significant digits to be written $(w \geqslant d+7)$. Three places to the left are required, one each for sign (even when positive), leading zero, and decimal. Four positions are required for the exponent, which is always written in its entirety.

Example 5 of Figure 6–2 indicates the results of failure to allow a field of the appropriate size. The FØRMAT specification calls for seven places to the right of the decimal; however, this leaves only five positions in the 12-place field for leading positions and exponent.

Output will be right-justified if the field width is greater than $d + 7$. Such a situation is depicted in Figure 6–2, Example 6.

The exponent of an output value is always adjusted so that the decimal precedes the most significant digit. Thus, the significant digits will always appear as a decimal fraction, and d in the FØRMAT specification must be greater than zero if any value is to be written. In Figure 6–2, Example 1, d is large enough for the writing of seven significant decimal positions. In Example 3, d is set at six, and so one answer position is lost. Example 7, with a FØRMAT specification of E10.0, does not allow any decimal positions to be written.

The D Specification

A data field to contain a double-precision value is defined by the specification

$$Dw.d$$

As in the E specification, w represents the field width and d the number of places to be allowed to the right of the decimal.

Thus, the FØRMAT specification D15.8 would define a field 15 positions wide, having 8 places to the right of the decimal.

Double-Precision Values in Input.   The function of double-precision arithmetic is to allow the carrying of more significant digits than is possible in single-precision mode. Therefore, it is not unusual to find rather large input and output fields.

As described in Chapter 2, all double-precision values must contain an exponent of the general form $D\pm ee$, with such permitted modifications as are illustrated in Figure 6–3. The field width must be great enough to permit reading of the value and its exponent. Thus, if the exponent is written in detail, the input field must be at least four places wider than the number of significant positions desired.

A decimal may be written in the double-precision value, or it may be omitted. If omitted, it is supplied by the FØRMAT specification. Written decimals override the one specified by the FØRMAT statement.

Double-Precision Values in Output.   Most FORTRAN systems cause double-precision values to be written as

$$s0.xxxD\pm ee$$

FIGURE 6–3
Illustration of Double-Precision Values and Specifications

Example No.	FØRMAT Spec.	Input Value	Numerical Equivalent of Stored Value	Output	To Be Read as
1	D19.12	bb.123456789123D+03	123.456789123	b0.123456789123D+03	123.456789123
2	D19.12	bbbbb123456789123D3	123.456789123	b0.123456789123D+03	123.456789123
3	D19.12	bbb−1234.56789123D3	−1234567.89123	−0.123456789123D+07	−1234567.89123
4	D19.12	bb−1234.56789123D−6	−.00123456789123	−0.123456789123D−02	−0.00123456789123

A space, represented by *s,* is reserved for the sign, which is written only if negative. One zero position to the left of the decimal must be allowed, and space for the decimal must always be provided. Any number of significant digits, to the maximum provided by the computer, may be written. The exponent always requires four output positions.

The output field must always be seven positions wider than the number of significant digits to be written. These are required to the left of the significant digits to allow for the sign, zero, and decimal. Four, for the exponent, must be allowed to the right.

Examples.   Examples in Figure 6–3 depict more clearly the use of double-precision values in input and output, and the use of controlling FØRMAT specifications.

Example 1 shows an input value containing a full D-type exponent. This is carried in the computer's memory in approximately the manner shown and is written out as indicated. The final column in Figure 6–3 shows how the amount should be read.

Example 2 in Figure 6–3 depicts an input value using a shortened exponent and not explicitly stating the decimal location. The exponent in acceptable form, and the decimal location is drawn from the FØR-MAT statement. Therefore, the value is stored in memory and written out as shown.

In Example 3, a negative value is read in. The sign is carried in the computer's memory, and the output will also be negative.

This example also indicates how a written decimal overrides the FØRMAT specification in input. The value is carried in the computer and written out with the decimal to the left of the number, but the exponent shows the decimal's proper location.

Example 4 is much like Example 3, except that a negative exponent is used. Again, the input value is converted to a decimal fraction, the exponent representing the true location of the decimal.

Multiline Specifications

A FØRMAT statement may cause the input or output statement to be associated with more than one record. This is done by the inclusion of a slash (/) in the list of FØRMAT specifications. Encountering the slash indicates that following items are to be read from (or transmitted to) a subsequent record.

For example, consider the following FØRMAT statement and READ command:

        10   FØRMAT(I4/I2,F2.0)
                READ(5,10)I,J,X

Upon execution of the READ command, I would be read from one input record, and J and X from the next record. Output works in the
same way; the command WRITE(6,10) I, J, X would cause I to be
transmitted to one output record, and J and X would go to the next
record.

As many slashes may be used as appropriate. Thus, a single input or
output command may be associated with any number of records.

If no specification is given preceding a slash, an input record is ignored or a blank output record is transmitted. Furthermore, in IBM
360/370 FORTRAN and WATFIV, a slash at the end of the format
specification list has a similar effect.

Assume the following FØRMAT and output statements:

        10   FØRMAT(I4,//F6.0)
                WRITE(6,10)K,A

This would be transmitted as follows: First, K would be written in a
record by itself. This would be followed by a blank record (the second
slash is not preceded by a specification). Then, A would be transmitted
to a new record, which would be followed by a blank record.

Multiline format specifications are sometimes used to group input
from more than one record in a single READ command. This avoids
the coding of multiple READ instructions, and in some instances permits the physical function of reading to agree with the logic of input.

In output, the slash may be of even greater value. It is frequently used
when multiline headings are created, and when blank lines are desired
for readability. In these instances, the slash affords an easy means of
improving the appearance of the output record.

Assume, for example, that the following heading is to be used in a
report:

                CURRENT   *UNDEPRECIATED*
        YEAR   *DEPRECIATION*   *BALANCE*

The heading is to be separated from the statement body by one blank
line.

Assuming that the heading is to begin at the report's left margin after
one space, the following FØRMAT statement would satisfy all
requirements:

1   FØRMAT(10X, ' CURRENT   UNDEPRECIATED '/
1 ' YEAR   DEPRECIATIØN ' ,5X 'BALANCE'/)

The first line will be printed by the first part of the FØRMAT specification; then, continuation to a new line is caused by the slash. After printing the second line of the heading, the final slash will cause a blank line to be left before data are written.

Carriage Control

To this point it has been assumed that all output is to be written single space; therefore, a blank has been inserted in the first, or carriage control, position of the output FØRMAT statement. This is not the only forms control possible, however; spacing can be controlled by insertion of one of the following:

CARRIAGE CONTROL

Character	Meaning
blank	Advance one line before printing
0	Advance two lines before printing
1	Advance to first line of new page
+	No advance

Consider the following FØRMAT and related WRITE commands:

```
1      FØRMAT('0',F5.0)
2      FØRMAT(' ',I3)
3      FØRMAT('+',I3)
       WRITE(6,1)A
       WRITE(6,2)K
       WRITE(6,3)K
```

The first WRITE command would cause double spacing, because the carriage control character of its associated FØRMAT statement is 0. The second WRITE command will cause single spacing; the carriage will advance one line before printing. The third WRITE statement will print without any spacing at all. This is sometimes used to print a line, such as one containing totals, extra dark for emphasis. For example, writing the two last output commands above will cause K to be written once after single spacing; then, the last WRITE statement will write K again without spacing. This will cause the printer to strike the value of K twice.

FØRMAT-FREE INPUT AND OUTPUT

WATFIV and levels G1 and H of IBM FORTRAN IV permit the use of input and output commands not associated with FØRMAT statements.

These are called "list-directed" instructions, because record layout is controlled by the input or output list, rather than by a FØRMAT statement. While these are not as versatile as their formatted counterpart, they are useful when simple input and output is being prepared and location of data in the record is not critical.

Input Statements

The following list-directed input instructions are available:

IBM G1 and H FØRTRAN	*WATFIV*
READ(a,*,END=i)*list*	READ(a,*,END=i)*list*
READ *, *list*	READ, *list*

In the above, "a" represents the number of the input unit. The END clause is optional; if used, "i" represents the statement number to which control is transferred when no more input records are available. "*List*" represents the list of variable names to be associated with values in the input record. The asterisk (*) is used as shown; it takes the place of the FØRMAT number. The READ, *list* command in the WATFIV language is automatically associated with the systems input unit; this is ordinarily a card reader.

Data in the Input Record.   Data values must be separated from one another by a comma or at least one space. They must agree in mode with the variable names in the input list except that decimals may be omitted from real values. In this case, the decimal is assumed to lie to the right of the rightmost significant digit.

WATFIV permits data values recorded in more than one input record to be accessed by a single READ command. This is true in IBM FORTRAN only in special cases and is to be avoided. The WATFIV list may specify fewer values than contained in the input record; this is not true of IBM FORTRAN. In WATFIV, unnamed data values are ignored.

Output Statements

The following output statements are available in list-directed processing:

IBM G1 and H FORTRAN IV	WATFIV
WRITE (a,*)list	WRITE(a,*)list
PUNCH *, list	PUNCH, list
PRINT *, list	PRINT, list

WATFIV and FORTRAN IV output commands are very similar. In each, *"a"* represents the number of the output unit. Where no output unit is designated, the PUNCH command transmits data to the card punch, while the PRINT instruction is associated with the printer.

Data in the Output Record.   Integer values will be written right-justified in a 12-position field; thus, some spacing is automatically allowed. Real values are written differently in WATFIV and in FORTRAN IV. In the former, a real value is written in E notation as though under the control of an E16.7 FØRMAT specification. The value will be written as bbbb.xxxxxxxE±ee, where "b" represents a blank, "x" a numeric position, and "e" a position in the exponent. IBM FORTRAN writes out real values as though controlled by the FØRMAT specification F13.7.

Example of List-Directed Processing

Assume that the following input records are to be processed in WATFIV by the program shown in Figure 6–4:

                12345 4321 12.49
                .00676 7890 123.45
                .987 222 .0054
                12.45 999 236.3

Output would appear as follows:

7890	.6760000E—02	.4321000E+04
12345	7890	987
.1245000E+02	.9990000E+04	.236300E+03
.1245000E+02	.9990000E+04	.236300E+03

The first READ instruction will extract values of I, A, and B from the first input record; then values for C and J from the second. The last

FIGURE 6–4
List-Directed Input and Output

```
        READ,I,A,B,C,J
        PRINT,J,C,A
        READ(5,*)K,L,D
        WRITE(6,*)I,J,K
        READ(5,1)X,Y,Z
1       FORMAT(F6.0,F3.3,F6.0)
        WRITE(6,*)X,Y,Z
        PRINT,X,Y,Z
        STOP
        END
```

value in the second record is lost. The output of J, C, and A is consistent with the description above. Integer data are written in I12 fields; real values are written as though by an E16.7 format. Because the input value of C, 12345, did not have a written decimal it was assumed to be a whole real number.

The next READ statement shows that it and other READ forms, both formatted and unformatted, can be mixed in the same program. Values for K, L, and D are extracted from the third input record.

A regular formatted READ statement is used to read the fourth record. Its contents are then written out in unformatted form. Finally, the PRINT command can be seen to have the same effect as its WRITE(6,*) counterpart.

List-directed input and output is very simple. It may be found advantageous in simple input-output situations, particularly when using a remote terminal, where form is not important. However, most data processing applications require that some attention be given to layout, and so formatted records are most frequently used.

NAMELIST: Another Type of Nonformatted Input-Output

This input-output form provides a very simple means of transmitting data to or from the computer.

First, the names of the variables to be transmitted are identified in a special statement, called the NAMELIST command. It is of the following general form:

$$\text{NAMELIST } /i_1/list_1/i_2/list_2/,\ldots,/i_n/list_n$$

"List" represents a list of data-names to be read or written. *"i"* is the NAMELIST name which is to be used to symbolize the associated variables. A single NAMELIST name and its related variables can be given in a statement, or multiple sets may be specified as indicated above.

For example, consider the following:

$$\text{NAMELIST/DSET1/A,B,I,J/DSET2/I,K,X,Y,}\not{Z}$$

This indicates that one NAMELIST list, assigned the name DSET1, consists of the variables A, B, I, and J. Another NAMELIST list, called DSET2, contains the variables I,K,X,Y, and $\not{Z}$. Note that I is a member of each set. This is acceptable, although of course not required.

The above would be used with input and output statements such as the following:

$$\text{READ(5,DSET1)}$$
$$\text{WRITE(6,DSET2)}$$

Neither the READ nor the WRITE instruction specifies a format number or a list of variables to be transmitted. Format specification is not required, and the list of variables to be transmitted is supplied by the NAMELIST statement itself. Thus, in reading, it is expected that the variables A, B, I, and J will be transmitted as members of DSET1.

Appearance of Data in Input. NAMELIST data records are substantially different from all others. They are of the following general form:

$$\text{b\&}ibn_1,n_2,\ldots,n_m,\text{\&END}$$

"b" represents a required blank in column 1 and after the NAMELIST name
The & is required in column 2
"i" = the NAMELIST name of the data set
"n" is a statement of the nature "data-name = constant"
&END is required to signal the end of the record

The nature of a NAMELIST input record and its relation to the input statement can be seen in the following:

$$\text{NAMELIST /DSET1/A,B,I,J}$$
$$\text{READ(5,DSET1)}$$

This can be used to read the following input record:

Column

2

↓

&DSET1 I=5,A=29.75,B=123.,J=1975,&END

The first position of the input record must be blank. It must be followed immediately by the symbol "&" and the NAMELIST name, then another blank must be left. Next, the series of data-names to be read and the values to be assigned them can appear in any order. The input record is terminated by &END.

Appearance of Data in Output.   When NAMELIST is used to write data, the form is much like that of the input record. Format control is not used; instead, each data value is given sufficient room, and multiple output records (lines, on the printer) are used if necessary.

Considering the example above, assume that the instruction

WRITE(6,DSET1)

is given. This will result in the following output:

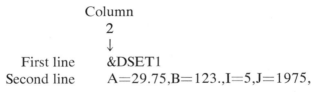

                   Column

                       2

                       ↓

First line   &DSET1

Second line   A=29.75,B=123.,I=5,J=1975,

Variables appear in output in the order of their inclusion in the NAMELIST list.

DIRECT-ACCESS DATA PROCESSING

The text has assumed records in input and output files to be sequentially accessible only; that is, that records must be processed in the order of their inclusion in the file. Most files are structured in this manner, and those maintained on punched cards or magnetic tape must be so constructed because of the nature of their storage medium. With the advent of large-scale secondary storage devices, however, a new file structure and processing method has been created. This is called *direct-access* processing. In this, any record in the file may be accessed directly, without passing through those appearing in front of it.

This change in accessing method merely relates to the method of reading from or writing into a file. All other FORTRAN and WATFIV processing instructions are used in their regular way.

Direct-Access Instructions

Four special commands are used in direct-access reading and writing.

DEFINE FILE. This instruction is used to designate a file as direct-access. Files so named cannot be processed with regular READ and WRITE statements. The statement is of the following general form:

DEFINE FILE $a_1(m_1,r_1,f_1,v_1),a_2(m_2,r_2,f_2,v_2), \ldots ,a_n(m_n,r_n,f_n,v_n)$

"*a*" represents an unsigned nonzero integer constant identifying the file. It is the *file number.*

"*m*" represents an unsigned integer constant that specifies the maximum number of records in the file.

"*r*" represents an unsigned integer constant that specifies the maximum number of characters in each record.

"*f*" is a letter indicating whether or not records are to be read and written under format control, as follows:

"L" indicates that records in the file are to be read or written either with or without format control.

"E" indicates that records in the file are to be read or written with format control.

"U" indicates that unformatted records are to be read or written exclusively. In this case, "*r*" does not represent the number of characters in the record, but the number of "words" instead. The number of words in a record can be calculated by dividing the number of characters by four and rounding to the next highest integer if a remainder is obtained.

"*v*" represents an integer data name called the "associated variable." This is a variable associated with the file and assigned a value by READ, WRITE, and FIND statements. It can also be given a value by an arithmetic assignment statement.

Example of DEFINE FILE Command. Assume that two direct-access files are to be defined. The first, to be called file number 10, is to contain a maximum of 1,000 records, and each record is 80 characters long. Records are formatted, and the associated variable is to be called KEY1.

The second file, to be assigned file number 11, is to contain 300 records of 30 characters each. Records are formatted, and the associated variable is to be named KEY2.

These files are defined as follows:

DEFINE FILE 10(1000,80,E,KEY1),11(300,30,E,KEY2)

Of course, a single file may be described in a DEFINE FILE command if desired.

READ.   This command causes a single record to be read from a file previously defined as direct-access by a DEFINE FILE instruction. It is of the general nature

READ(*a ' r,b*)*list*

The "*a*" is an unsigned integer constant or variable representing the file number from which the record is to be read. It must be followed by a single apostrophe(').

The "*r*" is an integer expression that indicates the location of the record, relative to the front of the file. It may be a constant, a variable, or any combination of the two.

The "*b*" is optional. If used, it represents the FØRMAT statement number. Files defined as containing formatted records must be read under proper FØRMAT control.

"*List*" is a typical list of input data-names.

With each execution of the READ command, the file's associated variable is augmented by one from an initial value assigned in the READ statement itself or in some other previous instruction.

Examples of the READ Command.   Assume that the third record from file 10 is to be read. This can be done by the following statements (assume proper FØRMAT and data names).

```
1     FØRMAT(8F10.2)
      READ(10 ' 3,1)A,B,C,D,E,F,G,H
```

The third record will be read from file 10 and its contents transmitted from secondary to primary storage according to the format and data names specified.

Assume the following program:

```
      K = 5
      READ(10 ' K,1)A,B,C,D,E,F,G,H
```

This time the record designated by K will be read. Because K was set to 5, the fifth record will be transmitted.

Although the file 10 associated variable, KEY1, is not cited in the READ statements above, it is affected by their execution. It will automatically be assigned a value of 4 after the first READ command, and a value of 6 after the second. The variable always points to the next record after execution of a READ command.

The associated variable can be used to select the record to be read. Assume the following program segment:

KEY1 = 25

. . .

. . .

. . .

READ(10 ' KEY1,1)A,B,C,D,E,F,G,H

1   FØRMAT(8F10.2)

A single record will be read from file 10, as designated by KEY1. In this instance, KEY1 was assigned the value 25, so the 25th record is read. After executing the READ statement, the associated variable has a value of 26.

FIND. The selection of a record directly from a secondary storage file is a fairly slow process. Once the READ command is given, program processing is halted until the record is found and transmitted to the computer's primary storage unit.

The FIND command is designed to minimize this delay. If the reading of a record can be anticipated, this instruction can be used to find the record in the direct-access file. Then, when it is required by the program, all the READ command must do is control actual transmission to primary storage.

The command is of the following general nature:

FIND(*a* ' *r*)

The "*a*" is an unsigned integer representing the file number. It must be followed by a single apostrophe (').

The "*r*" is an integer expression indicating the location of the record in the file.

After executing the FIND instruction, the associated variable is assigned as a value the number of the record found.

Example of the FIND Command. Assume that a key number is to be read in from an external record; then, after intervening processing steps it is to be used to read a direct-access record.

Such a program would appear as follows (data names and FØRMAT numbers are assumed):

READ(5,1)IDNØ
FIND(8 ' IDNØ)

. . .

. . .

. . .

READ(8 ' IDNØ,2)A,B,C

This permits the computer to find record number IDNØ in file 8 while other processing steps are being executed. Then, when the READ command is to be executed, all or part of the selection process has been completed.

WRITE.   This instruction is used to write records in direct-access files. It is of the following general nature:

WRITE (*a* ' *r,b*)*list*

The "*a*" is an unsigned integer constant or variable representing the file number. It must be followed by a single apostrophe.

The "*r*" is an integer expression representing the location of a record within the direct-access file.

The "*b*" is a format number.

"*List*" is the set of variable names representing data to be written.

This instruction transmits data as indicated by "list" from primary storage to the secondary storage location specified by the file number and record location.

The associated variable related to the direct-access file being written in is increased by 1 after the WRITE command, and points to the next record. For example, upon completion of the command WRITE (8 ' 10,2)I,J,K, the associated variable related to direct-access file 8 would have a value of 11.

Example of the WRITE Command.   Assume that records are to be read from an external source and written in a direct-access file. Assuming formats and record contents, this can be done in the following program:

```
       DEFINE  FILE  9(1000,80,E,ID)
       ID = 1
15     READ(5,1,END=10)A,B,C
       WRITE(9 ' ID,2)A,B,C
       GØ TØ  15
```

The associated variable, ID, is initialized at 1. Then, a record is read from the card reader, and written in direct-access file 9 at the location designated by the associated variable. The associated variable, ID, is incremented by 1 upon completion of the WRITE command, thus causing the next record to be written in the next position. This is a standard way to construct a direct-access file.

Extended Illustration

Assume that the Supreme Retail Company maintains its customer records in the Customer Balance File, a direct-access file in secondary storage. Sales are recorded on sales tickets, from which essential data is punched into cards. These cards are processed in random sequence against the Customer Balance File, the file updated, and a sales report is produced.

Customer Balance and Sales records are shown below, with the required sales report:

	FORTRAN	
Item Description	*Name*	*Field Definition*
Customer Balance Record (Direct access file, 1,000 records formatted, size indicated below, associated variable KEY1):		
Account number	ID	I5
Customer Name	N1,N2,N3,N4,N5	5A4
Unpaid balance (must allow for decimal and sign	BAL	F9.2
Sales Record:		
Account number	NØ	I5
Location number	LØC	I4
Sales amount	SALE	F5.2
Sales Report:		
Account number	NØ	I5
Customer Name	N1,N2,N3,N4,N5	5A4
Sales amount	SALE	F5.2
New balance	BAL	F7.2

The logical flowchart for this problem is shown in Figure 6–5, and the program in Figure 6–6.

The problem requires that a sales record be read; then the balance record bearing the same number must be found and extracted from the direct-access file as quickly as possible. The sales report must be written, and the updated master record returned to its original location in the direct-access file.

Access time can best be minimized if the computer can be processing one record and at the same time searching for the next. To do this, first

FIGURE 6–5
Flowchart of Direct-Access Processing

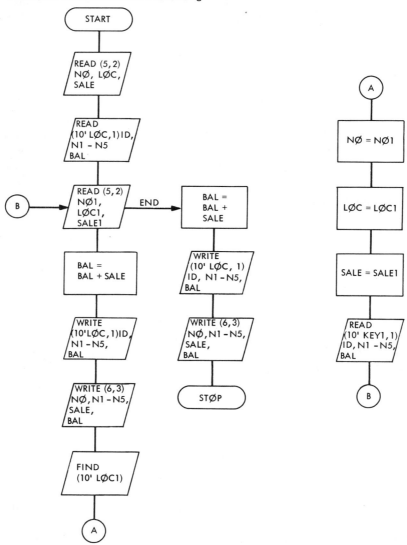

FIGURE 6–6

Direct-Access Program

IBM

FORTRAN CODING FORM

PROGRAM	SALES REPORT AND FILE MAINTENANCE		PUNCHING INSTRUCTIONS	GRAPHIC
PROGRAMMER	MC CAMERON	DATE		PUNCH

```
C      ILLUSTRATION OF DIRECT-ACCESS PROCESSING
1      FORMAT(I5,5A4,F9.2)
2      FORMAT(I5,I4,F5.2)
3      FORMAT(20X,I5,5X,5A4,5X,F7.2,5X,F9.2)
       DEFINE FILE 10(1000,34,E,KEY1)
       READ(5,2)NO,LOC,SALE
       READ(10'LOC,1)ID,N1,N2,N3,N4,N5,BAL
15     READ(5,2,END=50)NO1,LOC1,SALE1
       BAL = BAL + SALE
       WRITE(10'LOC,1)ID,N1,N2,N3,N4,N5,BAL
       WRITE(6,3)NO,N1,N2,N3,N4,N5,SALE,BAL
       FIND(10'LOC1)
       NO = NO1
       LOC = LOC1
       SALE = SALE1
       READ(10'KEY1,1)ID,N1,N2,N3,N4,N5,BAL
       GO TO 15
50     BAL = BAL + SALE
       WRITE(10'LOC,1)ID,N1,N2,N3,N4,N5,BAL
       WRITE(6,3)NO,N1,N2,N3,N4,N5,SALE,BAL
       STOP
       END
```

a sales record is read and its associated master record read from the direct-access file. Then, another sales record is immediately read and the computer instructed to find its related master. While the first record is being processed, the search for the next master is undertaken. After writing the output record, the computer is again instructed to read from the master file; this time, however, the necessary record has already been located and positioned for reading, and so input time is reduced to a minimum. Upon completion of a FIND operation the file's associated variable, KEY1, points to the proper master record. Therefore, the related READ command instructs the computer to read record number KEY1 from the file.

This sort of "look-ahead" processing optimizes computer operations, but does introduce certain complexities. Care must be taken to see that reading of the second sales record does not obliterate the first record's data, for it has not yet been processed. This is accomplished by assigning unique data names to items from the second record, and then moving the elements to the specified locations after completing the processing of the first.

Detection of processing termination is also complicated. An END= conditional in the sales file indicates that processing is almost complete, but it must be remembered that the last record has not been treated. Therefore, when no more input records are available, the last must be written in the report, and the updated master returned to the direct-access file.

CHAPTER SUMMARY

This chapter expands input-output methodology beyond the rather simple READ and WRITE statements of Chapter 3. First, additional FØRMAT specifications permitting alphanumeric data to be read and written are considered. The A FØRMAT allows for alphanumeric fields in input or output records—a capability essential in business data processing. The H, or Hollerith, notation permits the construction of messages in output records, as does the use of quotes to contain literal messages in output formats.

Chapter 2 introduced real numbers whose decimal lies to the left or right of the seven significant digits usually written, and explained that in these the decimal location is indicated by an exponent. Real numbers containing more than seven significant digits, called double-precision numbers, were also covered. The FØRMAT specifications for these numeric forms are covered in this chapter. Although they are seldom used in business data processing, they are found in related statistical and quantitative analysis.

The use of the slash in FØRMAT specifications, to denote multiline records, is not an essential part of the FORTRAN language. However, the slash is a convenient tool, and may permit the combination of several FØRMAT statements into a single command.

The use of format-free, or list-directed input and output can greatly simplify some programs, as can use of NAMELIST. These are usually found in short programs or programs processed through a low-speed terminal. While program simplification is achieved, this kind of input works only with records prepared in special ways, and output is not subject to the sophisticated control normally required.

Files containing records arranged in sequential order place severe restrictions on the use of the computer as a data-processing tool. On the other hand, the ability to process records directly against a file, without batching or sorting, brings to the system in-line and real-time capability. In business data processing, this is one of the most important extensions of programming capability since the creation of compiler languages.

Summary of FORTRAN Statements.   The following new statements are covered in this chapter:

1. FØRMAT Specifications:

A*w*	Used for input or output of alphanumeric data
*w*H	Used for transmission of alphanumeric messages
E*w.d*	Used to define fields containing E-notation data
D*w.d*	Used to define fields containing double precision data
/	Used to divide FØRMAT statements between records

2. Format-free input-output statements:

READ(*a*,*,END=*i*)*list*	Used to cause list-directed (format-free) reading, IBM G1 and H FORTRAN and WATFIV *a* = number of input unit *i* = statement number
READ *, *list*	Used to cause list-directed reading from systems input unit, IBM G1 and H FORTRAN
READ, *list*	Used to cause list-directed reading from systems input unit, WATFIV
WRITE(*a*,*)*list*	Used to cause list-directed writing, IBM G1 and H FORTRAN and WATFIV *a* = output unit number
PUNCH *, *list*	Used to cause list-directed output on card punch, IBM G1 and H FORTRAN
PUNCH, *list*	Used to cause list-directed output on card punch, WATFIV
PRINT *,*list*	Used to cause list-directed output on printer, IBM G1 and H FORTRAN
PRINT, *list*	Used to cause list-directed output on printer, WATFIV

3. NAMELIST /i_1/$list_1$/i_2/$list_2$/, ... ,/i_n/$list_n$
   i = NAMELIST name
   list = list of of data-names to be transmitted

4. Direct-access file processing instructions:

DEFINE FILE $a_1(m_1,r_1,f_1,v_1), \ldots, a_n(m_n,r_n,f_n,v_n)$

	Use: Define a direct-access file.
	a = file number
	m = number of records in file
	r = number of characters per record
	f = format status:
	L: to be processed with or without format
	E: to be processed with format
	U: to be processed without format
	v = name of associated variable
READ(a ' r,b)$list$	Use: Read a record from a direct-access file.
	a = file number
	r = location of record to be read
	b = format number, if necessary
FIND(a ' r)	Use: Find a record in a direct-access file prior to reading.
	a = file number
	r = location of record to be found
WRITE(a ' r,b)$list$	Use: Write a record onto a direct-access file.
	a = file number
	r = location into which record is to be written
	b = format number, if necessary

QUESTIONS

1. What kind of data may be contained in fields defined by the A specification?

2. What is the maximum size of fields defined by the A specification?

3. What is the difference between the A and the H notation?

4. What is the difference between the H notation and FØRMAT data enclosed in quotes?

5. What is the use of the E FØRMAT notation?

6. What is the use of the D FØRMAT notation?

7. How is the decimal location indicated in the output of an E-notation field?

8. How many blank records will the presence of two slashes (//) at the beginning of a FØRMAT specification produce?

9. How many blank records will the presence of two slashes (//) between two other FØRMAT specifications produce?

10. What is the meaning of a 0, written as the first character of an output line and transmitted to the printer?

11. What is the meaning of a +, written as the first character of an output line and transmitted to the printer?

12. What are the differences between IBM FORTRAN and WATFIV list-directed input commands?

13. What is the function of the asterisk (*) in the IBM list-directed READ statement?

14. How are real values written in list-directed IBM FORTRAN? In WATFIV?

15. How are fields separated from one another in list-directed input?

16. How are fields separated from one another in list-directed output?

17. How is the file indicated in the DEFINE FILE statement?

18. What are the essential components of the DEFINE FILE statement?

19. How can the computer "tell" whether a READ instruction relates to a sequential-access device (card reader, tape unit, etc.), or a direct-access file?

20. What is the "associated variable"?

21. Assume that a file's associated variable has a value of 27. What will be its value after reading a single record from the file?

22. Assume that a file's associated variable has a value of 15. What will be the variable's value after executing a FIND command on the file?

23. Can direct-access files be processed as though they were sequential? How?

24. May records in direct-access files be unformatted?

25. What is the advantage of a direct-access file over a sequentially-ordered-access file?

EXERCISES

1. Given below are input values as they exist in input records, the format specifications by which they are read, and the format specifications by which they are written. For each, indicate (a) the appearance of the item in storage, and (b) the appearance of the item in output (b = blank).

Input Value	FØRMAT Specification	
	Used in Reading	*Used in Writing*
a. ABCD	A4	A4
b. ABCD	A4	A6

Input	FØRMAT Specification	
Value	Used in Reading	Used in Writing
c. ABCD	A4	A2
d. ABCDE	A5	A5
e. ABCDE	A5	A2
f. ABC	A3	A3
g. ABC	A3	A5
h. ABCbb	A5	A5
i. ABCbb	A5	A1
j. bABCb	A5	A4

2. Given below are input values as they exist in input records, the format specifications by which they are read, and the format specifications by which they are written. For each, indicate (a) the appearance of the item in storage, and (b) the appearance of the item in output (b = blank).

Input	FØRMAT Specification	
Value	Used in Reading	Used in Writing
a. WXYƵ	A4	A2
b. WXYƵ	A4	A5
c. WXYƵ	A4	A4
d. bbYƵ	A4	A2
e. bbbXYƵ	A6	A4
f. XYƵbbb	A6	A6
g. XYƵbbb	A6	A8
h. XY	A2	A4
i. XY	A2	A1
j. bXYƵb	A5	A4

3. Each input record contains customer name, street address, and city and state, each recorded in a 20-place alphanumeric area. This is followed immediately by a five-place integer field containing the zip code.

   Write a program that will write name, street, and city and state on three lines. Zip code should be written on the line with city and state. Use a single format and write statement. Any data names may be used.

4. Prepare a program to read a single value from an input record, format F7.2. Write out the value, preceded by a dollar mark ($), and with a comma between the second and third integer positions, reading from the left.

5. Using the H notation, prepare a format statement that will skip one line, then write SALES = $ a AND EXPENSES = $ b

   THE PROFIT IS $ c

where a, b, and c are 7-place real numbers having 2 places to the right of the decimal.

6. Given below are sets of input records, FØRMAT statements, and READ commands. Give the values assigned to each input data element.

   1. Input record contents: 123456789TF
      1   FØRMAT(3F3.0,2L1)
          READ(5,1)A,B,C,D,E
   2. Input record contents: 1234567890TF
      1   FØRMAT(2(I2,F3.0),L2)
          READ(5,1)I,X,J,Y,A
   3. Input record contents: 12345678
      1   FØRMAT(5X,F3.3)
          READ(5,1)D
   4. Input record contents: 12345678912TRUEFALSE
      1   FØRMAT(2X,I3,3X,F3.4,L4,L5)
          READ(5,1)K,X,Y,Z
   5. Input record contents: AA1.12345bbbbb1
      1   FØRMAT(2X,F7.2,3X,I3)
          READ(5,1)X,L
   6. Input record contents: ABCDEF$1,000.12345
      1   FØRMAT(4A4,A2)
          READ(5,1)I,J,K,L,M
   7. Input record contents: JACK JØNES
      1   FØRMAT(2A4,A2)
          READ(5,1)X,Y,Z
   8. Input record contents: 1162 CANAL STREET
      1   FØRMAT(4A4,A1)
          READ(5,1)A1,A2,A3,A4,A5
   9. Input record contents: ABCDEFGH345
      1   FØRMAT(A6,A2,F3.0)
          READ(5,1)I,X,Y
   10. Input record contents: THE AMØUNT IS $25,648.13
       1   FØRMAT(3A4,A3,I2,A1,I3,A1,I2)
           READ(5,1)I1,I2,I3,I4,I5,I6,I7,I8,I9

7. Refer to Exercise 6 above. Given below are output FØRMAT and WRITE statements for each part of Exercise 5. For each input set, give the output line that will result from the indicated FØRMAT.

   1.   2 FØRMAT(5X,F7.2,5X,L1)
               WRITE(6,2)B,E
   2.   2 FØRMAT(2(2X,F5.0,2X,I3),2X,L2)
               WRITE(6,2)X,J,Y,I,A

3.   2   FØRMAT(19HbTHEbVALUEbØFbDbISb,F5.3)
            WRITE(6,2)D
4.   2   FØRMAT(1X,I7,L4,L5)
            WRITE(6,1)K,Y,Z̵
5.   2   FØRMAT(19HbTHISbISbEXERCISEb5)
            WRITE(6,2)
6.   2   FØRMAT(1X,A3,A4,A5,A2,A2)
            WRITE(6,2)M,I,J,K,L
7.   2   FØRMAT(1X,2A4,A2)
            WRITE(6,2)X,Y,Z̵
8.   2   FØRMAT(16HbTHEbADDRESSbISb,5A4,A2)
            WRITE(6,2)A1,A2,A3,A4,A5
9.   2   FØRMAT(1X,F3.0,A6,A2)
            WRITE(6,2)Y,I,X
10.   2   FØRMAT(1X,3A4,A3,I2,A1,I3,A1,I2)
            WRITE(6,2)I1,I2,I3,I4,I5,I6,I7,I8,I9

8. Assume an input record to contain the following:

CHARLES K. SMITH1162 WESTØVER DRIVE

In the situations below, indicate the appearance of the values in storage
and the output record when read and written by the FØRMATS given:

1.   1   FØRMAT(8A4,A3)
       2   FØRMAT(1X,4A4,1X,4A4,A3)
           READ(5,1)X1,X2,X3,X4,I1,I2,I3,I4,I5
           WRITE(6,2)X1,X2,X3,X4,I1,I2,I3,I4,I5
2.   1   FØRMAT(8A4,A3)
       2   FØRMAT(1X,4A4/1X,4A4,A3)
           READ(5,1)X1,X2,X3,X4,I1,I2,I3,I4,I5
           WRITE(6,2)X1,X2,X3,X4,I1,I2,I3,I4,I5
3.   1   FØRMAT(4A4,3A6,A1)
       2   FØRMAT(1X,4A6,3A8,A6)
           READ(5,1)X1,X2,X3,X4,I1,I2,I3,I4
           WRITE(6,2)X1,X2,X3,X4,I1,I2,I3,I4
4.   1   FØRMAT(4A4,I4,3A6)
       2   FØRMAT(1X,4A4,I6,3A6)
           READ(5,1)X1,X2,X3,X4,I1,I2,I3,I4
           WRITE(6,2)X1,X2,X3,X4,I1,I2,I3,I4
5.   1   FØRMAT(4A4,3A6,A1)
       2   FØRMAT(1X,3A4,A5,3A6,A1)
           READ(5,1)X1,X2,X3,X4,I1,I2,I3,I4
           WRITE(6,2)X1,X2,X3,X4,I1,I2,I3,I4

9. Given below are input values, the format specification used in reading

the values, and the format specification used in writing them. For each, show how the value will appear in an output record.

		FØRMAT Specifications	
	Value	*Input*	*Output*
a.	12345E3	E7.3	E14.7
b.	1.2345E−3	E9.3	E15.7
c.	−12345E5	E8.3	E12.5
d.	12345E−3	E8.0	E8.0
e.	12345E−3	E8.5	E12.5
f.	12345E3	E7.2	E10.3
g.	123456789D+3	D12.0	D16.9
h.	123456789D3	D11.3	D14.7
i.	1D−5	D4.0	D8.1
j.	123456789D4	D11.0	D16.9

10. Given below are input values, the format specifications used in reading the values, and the format specifications used in writing them. For each, show how the value will appear in an output record.

		FØRMAT Specifications	
	Value	*Input*	*Output*
a.	12345E0	E7.0	E14.7
b.	123456E0	E8.3	E17.7
c.	12345E5	E7.0	E12.5
d.	12345E−5	E8.0	E13.5
e.	12345E3	E7.2	E10.3
f.	12345.E3	E8.2	E11.3
g.	123456789D0	D11.0	D16.9
h.	123456789D2	D11.0	D16.9
i.	123456789D3	D11.2	D14.7
j.	123456789D−3	D12.1	D14.7

11. *a.* Give a statement to define file 40, to contain 400 records of 50 characters each, formatted. The associated variable is KEY1.

   b. Give the command to find the twelfth record from file 40, defined above.

   c. Give the command to read the twelfth record, found in step "b" above, by format 2 (data items are A, B, and C).

   d. Give the commands necessary to write by format 2 (data items A, B, and C) the 25th through 29th records into file 40, defined above.

12. *a.* Give the statement to define file 50, to contain 100 records of 30 characters each, formatted. The associated variable is named KEY2.

   b. Give the instructions necessary to read 100 records containing variables X, Y, and Z (Format 2) from input unit 5 and write them into file 50 in sequential order, using the same format.

13. Refer to the direct-access file in exercise 12 above. Give instructions to read an input record from input unit 5 containing a variable, K (format I3). Then, read record K from the direct-access file and write its contents on output unit 6 by format 7.

PROBLEMS

1. *Instructions:* Write a program to read a single input record of the type indicated below, and write three output records, as follows:

	FORTRAN
Name	*Field Size*
Input record:	
X	A4
Y	A6
Z̶	A2
Output record 1:	
X	A4
X	A6
X	A3
Output record 2:	
Y	A6
Y	A8
Y	A3
Output record 3:	
Z̶	A2
Z̶	A1
Z̶	A5

Elements in output records are to be separated by 5 spaces.

2. *Instructions:* Write a program to read 2 input records of the type indicated below. For each, write three output records, as follows:

		FORTRAN	
Item Description		*Name*	*Field Size*
Input record:			
Integer value		I	xxxx
Integer value		J	xxx
Real value		A	xxxxx‸
Real value		B	xxxx‸xxx
Output record:			
Integer value		I	xxxxx
Integer value		J	xxxx
Real value		A	xxxxx.
Real value		B	xxxx.xxx

Instructions:

A.   Read the first input record by standard format, using I and F specifications. Then write out its contents three times in three different ways:

(1) In a format-free record
(2) Using I and F format specifications
(3) Writing A and B once under E format control, allowing for 7 places to the right of the decimal, and again under D format control, allowing 10 places to the right of the decimal.

B. Read the second record format-free (data items are separated by a space). Then, repeat steps 1–3 in requirement A above.

3. The Jones Maintenance Company prepares customer bills by computer. Repair records are received from the shop, containing the following information:

Customer name	20 alphanumeric positions
Street address	20 alphanumeric positions
City and State	20 alphanumeric positions
Zip code	5 integer positions
Parts charge	Real, xxxxx
Labor charge	Real, xxxxx

For each input record, a customer statement is to be prepared showing the parts charge, the labor charge, and a 20% overhead charge. A 6% sales tax is then to be assessed, and the statement totalled. One line is to be skipped between (a) the statement address and body; (b) body and tax; (c) tax and total. A sample statement is reproduced below. All words and dollar marks are to be included in the statement.

```
       JOHN  H  JONES
       1525  APPLETON  WAY
       BAYSIDE,  ILLINOIS    21702

       PARTS              $150.00
       LABOR               200.00
       OVERHEAD             70.00

       SALES  TAX         $ 25.20

       TOTAL             $445.20
```

4. Customer accounts are processed by computer at the Apex Company. Transaction records are grouped by account number in the input file. Input and output records appear as follows:

	FORTRAN	
Description	*Name*	*Field Size*

Input record:

Customer name	A1,A2,A3,A4,A5	20 pos., alphanumeric
Street address	S1,S2,S3,S4,S5	20 pos., alphanumeric
City-State	C1,C2,C3,C4,C5	20 pos., alphanumeric
Record type indicator . . .	K	x
Amount	AMT	xxxxx

Transaction records are grouped behind their related balance records. Balance records contain a 1 in the K field. Sales records, containing a 2 in the K field represent additions to the balance. Cash receipt records, indicated by a 3 in the K field, represent deductions from the balance, as do returns records, represented by K = 4. There may be no, one, or more than one transaction records behind a balance record for a particular account. Type 2, 3, and 4 records may be mixed behind their respective balance record.

Instructions: Prepare customer statements of the type indicated below. All wording shown in the example is to be reproduced in the statement. One line is to be skipped between the statement heading and body, and one line between the body and total line. The total should be double-printed for emphasis.

```
        JOHN H JONES
        1665 GRANVILLE DRIVE
        EVANS, IDAHO


        BALANCE       $225.00
        SALE           100.00
        RETURN         100.00
        COLLECTION     225.00
        SALE            75.00


        NEW  BALANCE   $ 75.00
```

5.   Input records are as shown below:

	FORTRAN	
Description	*Name*	*Field Size*
Account number	NØ	xxxxx
Item description	K1,K2,K3,K4,K5	20 pos., alphanumeric
Number of units	UNITS	xxxx
Account balance	BAL	xxxxxx

Instructions: Read the above records from punched cards. As they are read, the records should be written in secondary storage in a direct-access file. The file designation is 10. Eight records will be stored in the file. They are to be formatted, and of the length indicated above. INV is the name of the associated variable. (Note that the decimal is not punched in the BAL field.) After the eight input records have been read and stored, they should be read back from the direct-access file and written on the printer for accuracy verification.

6. Assume that a direct-access file, designated as 10, is maintained in secondary storage. As input records are processed against the file, a transaction register is written. Records in the direct-access file, the input file, and the required contents for the transaction register are shown below:

	FORTRAN	
Description	*Name*	*Field Size*
Direct-access file (designated no. 10; contents, 15 records; formatted; of the image shown below; associated variable, KINV):		
Account number	NØBAL	xxxxxx
Item description	D1,D2,D3,D4	16 pos., alphanumeric
Number of units on hand ...	UNITS	xxxxx
Average cost per unit	AVGCST	x.xxx
Cost of units on hand	CØST	xxxx.xx
Input record:		
Location of master record in direct-access file	LØC	xx
Transaction type indicator ..	K	x
Number of units	NØUNT	xxx
Cost	TCØST	xxx$\underset{\wedge}{x}$x
Transaction register:		
Item description	D1,D2,D3,D4	16 pos., alphanumeric
Message*		
Units on hand before transaction	UNITS	xxxx
Number of units in transaction	NØUNT	xxxx
Units on hand after transaction†	UNITS	xxxxx
Cost of units received or issued	TRANS	xxx.xx

* RECEIPTS or ISSUES, as appropriate
† Old balance, adjusted for units received or issued in this transaction.

Instructions: Input records are filed in the order of their occurrence. After reading a record, the following steps must be taken:

(1) Locate the related record in the direct-access file, and read its contents. This should be done in the most efficient way possible.

(2) Receipts records are indicated by K = 1. For such records, the number of units is to be added to the number of units on hand,

and the transaction cost to the cost of units on hand. Also, a new average cost per unit must be computed, by dividing Cost by Number of Units. The direct-access record must be returned to the file, and a transaction register line written.

(3)   Issues are indicated by K = 2. The TCØST field is not used in these records. Instead, issues cost must be determined by multiplication of number of units issued by average cost per unit. The number of units on hand and cost of units on hand must be reduced, the master record returned to the direct-access file, and a transaction register line written.

(4)   After all transaction records have been processed, one line is to be skipped below the transaction register. Then, the contents of the direct-access file are to be written out.

7.   The XYZ Company maintains master employee data on a direct-access file. Each week, the hours worked by each employee are determined and recorded. This record, with necessary data from the direct-access file, is used to compute payroll amounts.

Details of input and output are as follows:

	FORTRAN	
Item Description	*Name*	*Field Size*
Personnel master file (maintained on direct-access unit 10, 8 records, formatted, contents as shown below. Associated variable, MSTR) record contents:		
Employee Social Security no.	SØCSEC	xxxxxxxxx
Employee name	N1,N2,N3,N4,N5	18 pos., alphanumeric
Hourly pay rate	RATE	xx.xx
Year-to-date earnings ...	YTD	xxxxx.xx
Employee hours record:		
Employee Social Security no.	NØ	xxxxxxxxx
Hours worked	HRS	xxx
Location of master record	LØC	xx
Output record:		
Employee name	N1,N2,N3,N4,N5	18 pos., alphanumeric
Year-to-date earnings prior to current period .	YTD	xxxxx.xx
Current earnings	EARN	xxxx.xx
Year-to-date earnings, including current period	YTDN	xxxxx.xx

Processing details:

(1)   After reading an Employee hours record, the corresponding master record should be read. Then, Social Security number

should be compared. If they agree, processing should continue; if not, the master record should be written out with the notation RECØRD IMPRØPERLY LØCATED. Processing should then continue with the reading of the next employee hours record.

(2) If the Social Security numbers agree, current pay should be calculated. The master record should be updated by addition of this amount to year-to-date earnings, and the master record returned to its proper place. The output record should be written, as shown.

8. The ABC Supermarket has connected its cash registers in the checkout line to its data processor, which also maintains a master file of sales information in direct-access mode. As items are checked out, the clerk indicates on the cash register the file location and number of units of the item sold. This is transmitted automatically to the computer, which looks up the item in its direct-access file, finds the unit price and extends the item charge, and accumulates the customer bill. When all items have been similarly rung up for a customer, a 6% sales tax is computed and the total furnished. Next, the clerk indicates the amount of payment; billed amount is deducted from this and the amount of change to be returned, if any, is written.

Assume that the card reader serves as input and the printer as output. Input and output records appear as below, which also shows the appearance of records in the direct-access file.

FORTRAN

Item Description	*Name*	*Field Size*
Direct-access file: (File designation, 10; 12 records; formatted; size as indicated below; associated variable, KEY)		
Item	N1,N2,N3	10 pos., alphanumeric
Unit Price	PR	x.xxx
Transaction record:		
File location number	NØ	xx
Number of units	UNITS	xxx
Customer-complete indicator . .	K	x
Output record:		
Item name	N1,N2,N3	10 pos., alphanumeric
Unit price	PR	x.xxx
Item price	ITEM	xxx.xx
Tax-total record:		
Message*		
Amount	AMT	xxxxx.xx

* TAX or TØTAL or CHANGE, as appropriate

The file location number in the transaction record is to be used to locate the master record in the direct-access file. Unit prices are obtained from the master record, as is the item name. An output line is to be prepared for each transaction record. Then, when a given customer's check-out is complete, as indicated by K $= 1$, the total of his charges is to be written, followed by a skipped line, sales tax, and the total. The next input record contains the amount of customer payment (PAY, format xxxxxx). Total charges are to be deducted from this, and the amount of change owed written at the bottom of the output record with the caption CHANGE. This step should be deleted if the amount of payment is exactly the same as the amount owed.

9. Superite Discount Stores maintain inventory data in a computer direct-access file. Computer terminals are located at customer check-out stations. As a customer is checked out, the clerk keys the file location of each item purchased and the number of units sold. This is transmitted to the computer which locates the appropriate record in the direct-access file, and extracts the per-unit price and item description. The per-unit price is multiplied by the number of units sold to determine the sales amount, which is written with the item description.

Item sales are accumulated until all sales to the customer have been processed (indicated by K $= 1$); then a 6% sales tax is computed and written, and the total sales and tax printed.

Sales data are also accumulated by item in another direct-access file. When all records have been processed, these are written out in the form of a sales journal. Details of input, direct-access, and output records are shown below:

	FORTRAN	
Item Description	*Name*	*Field Size*
Direct-access file, inventory data: (File no. 10; contents, 15 records; formatted; size as indicated below, associated variable, INV).		
Item description	N1,N2,N3	10 pos., alphanumeric
Price per unit	PR	xxxx
Record location in sales data file	LØC	xx
Direct-access file, sales data: (File no. 11; contents, 15 records; formatted; size as indicated below, associated variable, KSAL)		
Item description	N1,N2,N3	10 pos., alphanumeric
Number of units sold	UNITS	xxxx
Sales amount	AMØUNT	xxxxx.xx
Input record:		
Location of master record in inventory data file	LØCX	xx
Number of units sold	NØ	xxx
End-of-sale-indicator	k	x

FORTRAN

Item Description	Name	Field Size
Output record:		
Item description	N1,N2,N3	10 pos., alphanumeric
Number of units sold	UNITS	xxxx
Sales amount	AMT	xxxxx.xx

Processing Instructions:

(1) The card reader is to be used to represent the check-out unit input, and the printer the unit output. As each input record is read, the proper master record must be found in direct-access file 10 and an output record created.

(2) Also, sales data are to be accumulated by inventory item (denoted by LØC) in direct-access file 11. The item amount from the sale being processed should be added to similar amounts from previous sales of the same item in file 11.

(3) The completion of a customer check-out is indicated by $K = 1$. At this time his sales slip (the output record) should be completed by assessing a 6% sales tax and writing the total of sales and tax.

(4) After all input records have been processed, the records in direct-access file 11 should be written out on the printer in sequential order.

10. The Apex Company manufactures many different items. For each, a standard bill of materials record is maintained on a direct-access file. This shows the raw materials required per finished unit for every item the company manufactures regularly.

The company also maintains its raw materials inventory on a direct-access file. This file contains a record for every raw material carried in stock. Records for scheduled manufacturing orders are prepared, each showing the location of the associated bill of materials and the number of units to be made. Once a Manufacturing Schedule record is read, the related Bill of Materials record is found and extracted from the direct-access Bill of Materials file. Multiplication of the materials requirements by the number of units to be manufactured determines the Raw Materials Requirements for the job. This is to be written out as the Materials Requirement Report.

In addition, as raw materials requirements are determined they are to be added to the Requirements field of Raw Materials Inventory records in the Raw Materials Inventory file. After all Manufacturing Schedule records have been processed, this file should be scanned. The raw material part number and standard order quantity of any part having requirements exceeding the sum of units on hand plus those on order is to be written out as a Reorder Report. Three lines are to be skipped between the Raw Materials Requirement report and the Reorder Report.

Input and output records, and direct-access records, appear as follows:

Item Description	FORTRAN Name	Field Size
Bill of Materials direct-access file (No. 10: 8 records, formatted, size as indicated below, associated variable KBILL.) Record contents:*		
Material #1 raw material number	NØNE	xxxxx
Material #1 number of units required ...	ØNUNIT	xxx
Material #1 record location in inventory file	LØC1	xxx
Material #2 raw material number	NTWØ	xxxxx
Material #2 number of units required ...	TWUNIT	xxx
Material #2 record location in inventory file	LØC2	xxx
Material #3 raw material number	NTHRE	xxxxx
Material #3 number of units required ...	THUNIT	xxx
Material #3 record location in inventory file	LØC3	xxx
Raw Materials direct-access file (No. 11: 10 records, formatted, size as indicated below, associated variable KMAT.) Record contents:		
Raw material number	NØ	xxxxx
Number of units on hand	UNITS	xxxx
Number of units on order	ØRD	xxx
Number of units required	REQ	xxx
Standard order quantity	QTY	xxx
Input record (Manufacturing Schedule)		
Production job number	NØPR	xxxx
Location of Bill of Materials record	LØCREC	xxx
Number of units to be produced	PRØD	xxx
Output record (Raw Materials Requirements)		
Production job number	NØPR	xxxx
No. units raw material required—material 1	REQØN	xxxx
No. units raw material required—material 2	REQTW	xxxx
No. units raw material required—material 3	REQTR	xxx
Output record (Reorder report)		
Raw material number	NØ	xxxx
Number of units to be ordered	QTY	xxxxx

* No unit manufactured requires more than three different raw materials.

7 Advanced Control—The DØ Statement

Any problem suitable to computer solution may be programmed by using the instructions introduced in previous chapters. The resultant program might be rather awkward, however, especially if it involved complex iterative processes and masses of data.

This chapter discusses methods of computer control that are designed to simplify programming in certain often-encountered situations. It treats the DØ statement, a combined arithmetic-control command.

THE DØ STATEMENT

This command causes program segments to be repeated. As such, it is very useful in programs containing iterative procedures.

Command Nature

The DØ statement is of the general nature

$$\text{DØ } k\ i = n_1, n_2, n_3$$

where k is a statement number, i the name of an integer variable, and n_1, n_2, and n_3 the variable's "parameter values." Punctuation is required as shown, although spacing is optional. Like all other executable commands, the statement may be assigned its own statement number.

In effect, the DØ statement says: "Perform all the instructions after this, through the one numbered k. Repeat these as many times as required for variable i, assigned an initial value of n_1, to reach the terminal value n_2, being incremented by n_3 with each repetition."

Thus, a statement such as the following might be appropriate:

$$DØ \ 25 \ I = 1, \ M, \ 2$$

This indicates that the program segment following, through statement 25, is to be executed. It is to be repeated until index I, assigned an initial value of 1, and increased by 2 with each iteration, reaches the value M.

The technical requirements of the DØ statement are discussed below.

Statement Range. The FORTRAN statements following the DØ, including statement k, are known as the DØ command's *range*. Statement k must logically follow the DØ command, although it need not necessarily follow it physically in the program.

Statement Index. An integer data name must be specified as i, and this is called the statement index. Inclusion of the name in the DØ command defines the variable; it may be used in computation as a data item or written out, just as any other variable.

Index Parameters. The values to be assumed by the index are controlled by the "index parameters"—the items following the index name. These must be unsigned integer constants or variables; if variables, they must be positive and must have been defined before citation in the DØ statement.

The first parameter, called n_1 in the general form above, sets the initial value of the index, which will retain this value through the first iteration. Thus, in the example above, the index I is assigned an initial value of 1.

The second parameter, called n_2, sets the index's terminal value. The program segment will be repeated until the index is about to exceed this value. In the above illustration, M is cited as the terminal value; the range of the DØ statement will be repeated so long as I does not exceed M.

The third parameter sets the amount by which the index is increased with each iteration. It is an optional member of the command. If the amount of the increment is one, n_3 need not be specified and 1 is assumed. Thus, n_3 will be written only if the increment in some value other than 1. If n_3 is omitted, the comma preceding it is also omitted, and the command appears as follows:

$$DØ \ k \ i = n_1, n_2$$

Example of the DØ Statement

While the DØ statement has many characteristics that have not been introduced, the command is somewhat obscure when discussed abstractly. The following example is presented to show the instruction's basic nature.

Problem. A table showing the amount of 1 at 6% compound interest is to be prepared for five periods. The equation $I = (1+r)^n$ will be used, where r represents the interest rate, and n the number of periods for which interest is earned.

Analysis. The program might be written as in Figure 7–1. Its results are shown in Figure 7–2.

FIGURE 7–1
The Basic DØ Statement

```
C          INTEREST TABLE PREPARATIØN
     1     FØRMAT(10X,I2,5X,F7.4)
           DØ 10 I = 1, 5
           XINT = 1.06**I
    10     WRITE(6,1)I,XINT
           STØP
           END
```

FIGURE 7–2
Table of Amount of 1

Period	Amount
1	1.0600
2	1.1236
3	1.1910
4	1.2625
5	1.3382

In Figure 7–1, the range of the DØ loop may be seen to contain two statements, including the statement 10. The DØ statement commands the computer to repeat this loop until a variable named I, assigned an initial value of one and increasing by one with each iteration, is about to exceed five. Then, having satisfied the DØ command, the computer will execute the next instruction—STØP—and the program will be terminated.

A transfer command, such as the GØ TØ, is not required to cause a repetition of the commands in the DØ range. Both the return and the number of iterations are completely controlled by the DØ statement, and the program automatically transfers to the command following the range when the requirements of the DØ are satisfied.

The example in Figure 7–1 also points out the possible uses that may be made of the DØ index. It is used as a data element in the computation of the amount of compound interest; and in printing, it serves as the period indicator. The DØ index is frequently used as an operand or a member of the output list, although its use is restricted somewhat by the rules set out below.

The program displayed in Figure 7–1 is satisfactory for preparing an interest table of the stipulated rate and number of periods, but the constants built into it restrict its scope. A more useful, general-purpose program might be written by using a parameter record to enter the interest rate and number of periods and by using a variable as the terminal index value. Such a program is shown in Figure 7–3.

FIGURE 7–3
DØ Statement with a Variable Parameter

```
C        INTEREST COMPUTATION - GENERAL FORM
    1    FORMAT(F2.2,I2)
    2    FORMAT(10X,I3,5X,F7.4)
         READ(5,1)R,N
         DØ 10 I = 1,N
         XINT = (1.+R)**I
   10    WRITE(6,2)I,XINT
         STOP
         END
```

In this version of the program, the interest rate is read as R and the number of calculation periods as N. After reading this record, the computer enters the range of the DØ statement and is commanded to repeat the loop until I is about to exceed N. The use of a variable as an index parameter value is thus demonstrated; it may be recalled that an integer variable can be used as the initial value, increment, or final value of the index. This assumes, of course, that the variable has been previously defined.

Rules for Using the DØ Statement

In the course of introducing the DØ statement and its basic nature, its primary characteristics and formation requirements were set out. Other rules concerned with activities in the DØ range must also be observed in most FORTRAN systems if the instruction is to perform properly.

Rule 1. The first statement in the range must be executable. This requires that the statement immediately following the DØ command be such an executable statement as an input-output, arithmetic, or control command. It must not be a specification statement such as the FØRMAT, LØGICAL, DIMENSIØN, or the EQUIVALENCE, or CØMMØN statement discussed in Chapter 9. DØ examples in Figures 7–1 and 7–3 comply with this requirement.

Rule 2. The DØ index may or may not be used as a data element. In the DØ examples cited in Figures 7–1 and 7–3, the index value was used as a data element. Whether or not it is so used depends entirely on the program's logic.

As an example of a situation not requiring the index as a data item, assume that a group of records is to be read, and each 10th record written out as a file sample. Assuming appropriate formats, this might be coded as in Figure 7–4. It may be seen that J, the DØ index, is not required as a data element in computation or output.

FIGURE 7–4
Reentering a DØ Loop

STATEMENT NUMBER		FORTRAN STATEMENT
C		PRINTING FILE SAMPLES.
1		FØRMAT(4F10.0)
100		DØ 12 J = 1, 10
12		READ(5,1,END=50)A, B, C, D
		WRITE(6,1)A, B, C, D
		GØ TØ 100
50		STØP
		END

Rule 3. Each entry into the DØ range redefines the index. Figure 7–4 illustrates one other rule governing the DØ statement's execution. Each time the DØ statement is encountered from outside its range, the

index is reassigned its initial value. Thus, in Figure 7–4, the range is entered and nine records read without writing. Upon reading the 10th record, the DØ statement is satisfied, control transfers outside its range, and the record is printed. After printing, the GØ TØ command transfers control back to the DØ statement, the index is assigned an initial value of one, and the process is repeated.

Rule 4. The index must not be redefined in the DØ range. The DØ statement assigns a value to its index. This must not be changed in the DØ range by assigning the index any other value. The following commands provide an example of this error:

$$DØ\ 10I = 1,6$$
$$10 \qquad I = J + K$$

This does not mean that the DØ index cannot be used as an *operand* in computation, for this in no way affects its value. Such a use may be seen in Figures 7–1 and 7–3, where the index is used as an exponent.

Rule 5. DØ loops may be nested. A very powerful program may be created by writing one DØ loop inside another. This is called a "nest" of DØ ranges. Any number of DØ ranges may be nested. When DØ statements are nested, the inner is satisfied with each iteration of the outer.

Thus, if the following nest were written—

$$DØ\ 10I = 1,4$$
$$DØ\ 8J = 1,5$$
$$8 \qquad . \ . \ . \ . \ .$$
$$10 \qquad . \ . \ . \ . \ .$$

the inner range through statement 8 would be executed five times with each iteration of the outer DØ statement. Statement 8 would be executed 20 times, while statement 10 would be executed only 4 times.

A complete example of nested DØ statements may be seen in Figure 7–5, where a table of compound interest amounts for five periods at rates 1 through 4 percent is prepared. First, the outer DØ controls the number of different interest rates used, and its index is used to calculate the rate, R. Then, the inner DØ controls the computation of interest for five periods at the computed rate. With the satisfaction of the inner loop, the outer DØ regains control and computes a new interest rate. The inner loop is reentered, its index is redefined, and the process is repeated. Only with the satisfaction of the outer DØ is the program released from the loop, and allowed to stop.

When nesting DØ loops, the inner range must lie entirely inside the outer. While the loops may share the same last command, as seen in Figure 7–5, the inner loop cannot extend beyond the end of the outer range.

Rule 6. The last statement in a DØ range must not be a transfer. The final statement in the range of a DØ statement must not be a branch command such as the IF, GØ TØ, or computed GØ TØ. These would conflict with the natural operation of the DØ statement, which is itself a transfer instruction.

This rule must be carefully applied, for it is easily broken in certain instances. For example, assume that a file of sales records is to be searched and sales of inventory number (NØ) 123 are to be written and all others ignored. The number of records in the file, J, is furnished by a parameter card.

A program to accomplish the file search, assuming record contents and formats, is shown in Part A, Figure 7–6. However, this program is incorrect. After testing for the desired inventory number in statement 25, the false branch transfers back to the DØ instruction. Thus, for this branch of the program, the IF statement is the last command, and the rule cited above has been broken. It must be stressed that *no branch within a DØ range may terminate with a transfer instruction.* The statement described next is used to avoid this error.

The CØNTINUE Statement. A special FORTRAN statement is provided to serve as a terminal command when a DØ range would otherwise end with a transfer. This instruction is of the nature

$$k \qquad \text{CØNTINUE}$$

FIGURE 7–5
Nested DØ Loops

COMM.	STATEMENT NUMBER	CONT.	FORTRAN STATEMENT
C			INTEREST TABLE PREPARATION
	1		FORMAT(10X,I1,F7.4)
			DØ 10 I = 1, 4
			XI = I
			R = XI/100.
			DØ 10 J = 1, 5
			XINT = (1.+R)**J
	10		WRITE(6,1)J,XINT
			STØP
			END

FIGURE 7–6

Loop Termination

C	STATEMENT NUMBER	C	FORTRAN STATEMENT
C			PART A. IMPROPER LOOP TERMINATION.
			READ(5,1)J
	10		DO 30 I = 1, J
			READ (5,2)NO,A,B,C,D
	25		IF(NO .NE. 123) GO TO 10
	30		WRITE(6,3)NO A,B,C,D
			STOP
			END
C			PART B. PROPER LOOP TERMINATION.
			READ(5,1)J
			DO 30 I = 1, J
			READ (5,2)NO,A,B,C,D
	25		IF(NO .NE. 123)GO TO 30
			WRITE(6,3)NO,A,B,C,D
	30		CONTINUE
			STOP
			END

where k is a statement number. The instruction serves as a "no-op," or nonoperating, command. To it will be assigned the statement number terminating the DO range.

The statement's use and the proper termination of alternative IF branches may be seen in part B of Figure 7–6. The true branch of the IF statement transfers to the end of the loop, statement 30, where the CONTINUE command appears. This being the terminal command in the DO range, control automatically returns to the DO statement, and the loop is again executed (or the program ended, as appropriate). A false conclusion causes the record to be written, and the CONTINUE statement is encountered with the same results. Thus, the CONTINUE statement is employed to avoid the improper use of a transfer statement as a DO's terminal command.

Rule 7. The DO range may be left normally or by transfer. If the DO statement's index is satisfied, the program transfers to the command following the range in a "normal" exit. When desired, the statement range may be left by a transfer. The mode of exit has some bearing on the program's execution, for in some FORTRAN versions, the value of the index is lost with a normal exit, but not if a transfer is made. The loss upon normal exit is not serious because the terminal parameter represents the index value in the last iteration.

As an example of a transfer from the DØ range, assume that employee personnel records are to be searched and the record for employee number (NØ) 1234 is to be written with its file order number. After writing, the program is to stop. The number of input records is indicated by value K in a parameter card.

A program for making the required file search may be seen in Figure 7–7 (formats and record contents are assumed). After reading

FIGURE 7–7
Transferring from a DØ Range

```
C        TRANSFER FROM A DØ RANGE
   1     FORMAT(I4)
   2     FORMAT(I4,3F10.0)
   3     FORMAT(1X,2(I4,5X),3(F10.0,5X))
   4     FORMAT(19H RECORD NOT IN FILE)
         READ(5,1)K
  10     DØ 25 I = 1, K
         READ(5,2)NØ,A,B,C
         IF (NØ .EQ. 1234)GØ TO 30
  25     CØNTINUE
         WRITE(6,4)
         GØ TO 40
  30     WRITE(6,3)NØ,I,A,B,C
  40     STØP
         END
```

a personnel record, the employee number is compared with 1234. If it does not equal 1234, the searching loop is continued. When the proper record is found, the program transfers out of the loop, the record is printed with its file order number, and execution ceases.

In programs of this nature, the possibility of a missing record or incorrect key number must be considered. Such a condition must exist if the DØ loop is left normally, for this would mean that the matching record was not located. Therefore, the program in Figure 7–7 causes an error message to be written in the event of normal exit, after which the program is terminated.

Consideration should be given to error detection in all programs, and techniques of the sort demonstrated here used to indicate improper processing conditions.

Rule 8. Transfers into a DØ range are not permitted.   While it is possible to transfer from a DØ range, the reverse is not allowed. One exception to this is the transfer from an inner to an outer DØ in a nested set; in this, the transfer is treated as being entirely within the range of the outer DØ, and is permitted.

Summary of Rules.   While some FORTRAN versions are not subject to all, these eight rules govern the proper use of the DØ statement in minimum systems. Summarized for convenience, they are as follows:

1. The first statement in the range must be executable.
2. The DØ index may or may not be used as a data element.
3. Each entry into the DØ range redefines the index.
4. The index must not be redefined in the DØ range.
5. DØ loops may be nested.
6. The last statement in a DØ range must not be a transfer.
7. The DØ range may be left normally or by transfer.
8. Transfers into a DØ range are not permitted.

Flowcharting the DØ Statement

The flowchart treatment of the DØ statement is not as standard as the representation of other commands. The flowchart must show the DØ statement and the commands in its range, and the conditions necessary for making a normal exit. An acceptable technique is displayed in Figure 7–8, containing the flowchart for the program in Figure 7–7.

The DØ statement is represented by a diamond, indicating that it is a decision command. Commands in the statement's range are written from one point of the diamond. The state of the index within the range is indicated beside the flowchart path. This is shown as $I \leqslant K$ in Figure 7–8, indicating that the range will be repeated so long as I is less than or equal to K.

The routine to be followed upon the DØ statement's satisfaction is drawn from another point on the diamond, and the condition of the index is again indicated. In Figure 7–8 this is shown as $I > K$, meaning that the normal exit will occur when I is greater than K.

FIGURE 7–8
Flowcharting the DØ Statement

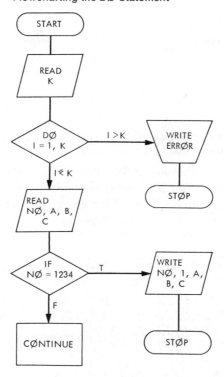

Illustrations of the DØ Statement

The discussion above contains a number of DØ statement illustrations. The four examples to follow point up certain other operative characteristics of the command.

In each instance, the program is iterative in nature—repeating some set of instructions a number of times but with some change in each iteration. Parameter values in the DØ statement may be fixed, although a more general program form is created when these are represented by variables, and their values are read in or calculated. This technique is used in most of the illustrations.

Illustration 1. Preparation of Depreciation Schedule. A program is to be written for the preparation of depreciation schedules by the straight-line method. No depreciation is to be taken in 1975, the year of acquisition. Input and output requirements are as follows:

	FORTRAN	
Item Description	*Name*	*Field Size*
Input record:		
Asset number	NØ	xxxx
Estimated use-life	LIFE	xx
Cost	CØST	xxxxxxx
Scrap value	SCRAP	xxxxxx
Output record:		
Asset number	NØ	xxxx
Year	KYR	xxxx
Depreciation for year	DEP	xxxxx.xx
Accumulated depreciation	ACCUM	xxxxx.xx
Undepreciated balance	BAL	xxxxx.xx

The program for preparing the schedule is shown in Figure 7–9. LIFE is used as the limit parameter in the DØ statement and is therefore read in integer mode. It must be floated before it can be used in computing the annual depreciation amount.

FIGURE 7–9
Preparing a Depreciation Schedule

```
C        DEPRECIATIØN STATEMENT PREPARATIØN
1        FØRMAT(I4,I2,F7.2,F6.2)
2        FØRMAT(1X,2(I5,5X),3(F9.2,5X))
         ACCUM = 0.
         READ(5,1)NØ,LIFE,CØST,SCRAP
         XL = LIFE
         DEP = (CØST-SCRAP)/XL
         DØ 10 K = 1, LIFE
         KYR = 1975 + K
         ACCUM = ACCUM+DEP
         BAL = CØST - ACCUM
10       WRITE(6,2)NØ,KYR,DEP,ACCUM BAL
         STØP
         END
```

This program is designed to read data pertaining to an asset, prepare its depreciation schedule, then stop. With slight modification, it could be written to prepare the schedules of any number of assets.

Illustration 2. Computing a Mean. In this illustration, the mean of a set of values is to be computed. The number of values is indicated by N

(FØRMAT xxx), punched in a parameter card preceding the data records. The values, called X, are of FØRMAT xxxx. The mean, XBAR, is to be written by FØRMAT xxxx.xx.

A program for this computation may be seen in Figure 7–10. The

FIGURE 7–10
Computing the Mean

```
C          COMPUTING THE MEAN
    1      FORMAT(I3)
    2      FORMAT(F4.0)
    3      FORMAT(F8.2)
           SUMX = 0.
           READ(5,1)N
           AN = N
           DO 5 I = 1, N
           READ(5,2)X
    5      SUMX = X + SUMX
           XBAR = SUMX/AN
           WRITE(6,3)XBAR
           STOP
           END
```

DØ statement substantially simplifies the programming of this sort of problem, for it defines the variable, increments it, and tests it—steps requiring three instructions when the IF statement is used for iteration-control purposes.

Illustration 3. Modifying an Index Value. Sometimes the index of a DØ statement may not be of the form necessary to use as a data element, but it can be modified to make it useful. This may be seen in the following situation:

Assume that the equation $Y = 40X - X^2$ is given. Find the approximate maximum value which may be assumed by Y in the interval $X = 1$, $X = 30$ using incremental X values of 2.

A program for finding this value may be seen in Figure 7–11. K, the DØ index, is in the wrong mode for use in computing Y. Therefore, it is floated to become X.

This program also illustrates a DØ statement with some increment other than 1. In this instance, the DØ execution is controlled in such a

FIGURE 7–11
Modifying an Index Value

COMM	STATEMENT NUMBER	CONT.	FORTRAN STATEMENT
	1		FØRMAT(F7.1)
			DATA Y1/0./
			DØ 10 K = 1, 30, 2
			X = K
			Y = 40.*X - X**2
			IF(Y - Y1)15,15,10
	10		Y1 = Y
	15		WRITE(6,1)Y1
			STØP
			END

way that the index value may be converted into X; therefore, K is incremented by 2 with each iteration.

Illustration 4. Computing a Factorial. The DØ statement permits easy computation of factorials. For example, the following program computes 10 factorial:

$$
\begin{aligned}
&\text{FACT} = 1. \\
&\text{DØ } 5\text{I} = 2,10 \\
&\text{X} = \text{I} \\
5\quad &\text{FACT} = \text{FACT*X}
\end{aligned}
$$

The index is floated, permitting the computation of large amounts, and used as the multiplier.

A more general program could be written to compute N! by reading N as a parameter value. Computations would be substantially the same as for the above.

CHAPTER SUMMARY

The DØ statement is not an essential FORTRAN command; any program using it could be written without it. However, it is very convenient to use in writing iterative programs.

The DØ statement is often compared with the IF command. Of

course, the latter is of much more general utility because it controls evaluation and branching in many noniterative situations. It must also be used in program loops if the DØ statement is not employed, however, and so they do merit contrasting.

Use of the IF statement as an iteration control requires that two other commands be written also: one to define an index and another to increment it. It is very easy to make a logical error in incrementing or testing the index, causing the iteration to be repeated once too often or not often enough.

On the other hand, use of the DØ statement requires that the number of iterations be known or determinable before entering the loop; a transfer number is of no value in setting up the DØ instruction. Therefore, when the number of iterations is known, the DØ statement is quite simple to use, but when termination may occur unexpectedly, the IF instruction must be employed.

QUESTIONS

1. What is the "range" of a DØ statement? How is it indicated?
2. What are the DØ statement's "index parameters"? How are they indicated?
3. May any of the index parameters be omitted? If so, which one or ones?
4. Must a DØ statement contain a data name? If so, what is its mode?
5. What is the mode of the index parameters? Must they be constants?
6. May a DØ statement index be incremented by fractional amounts?
7. What kind of statement must appear first in a DØ command's range?
8. Are any restrictions placed on the last instruction in a DØ range? If so, what are they?
9. May the DØ statement index be used as a data element?
10. May the DØ statement index appear on the left side of an arithmetic command?
11. When the DØ statement has control of a program segment, what changes the value of its index?
12. What are nested DØ statements?
13. What is the function of the CØNTINUE statement?
14. When a DØ range is left normally, what statement is first executed after departure?
15. May a program transfer from a DØ range? If so, what is the value of the DØ index after transfer?

16. Assume that a program must enter a DØ range more than once. How may this be done?

17. When DØ statements are nested, which range is executed the most times?

18. What is the difference between the DØ and IF statements?

19. Is a transfer into a DØ range permitted?

20. May nested DØ statements use the same last statement?

EXERCISES

1. Write the instructions necessary to print the numbers 1 through 5 in increments of ½.

2. Write the instructions necessary to print the integers 1 through 20 in reverse order: 20, 19, 18, etc.

3. Write the instructions necessary to print every third integer between 1 and 30: 1, 4, 7, etc.

4. Write instructions necessary to print the set of numbers in the series 1, 2, 4, 7, 11, 16, ... until 211 is reached.

5. Write the instructions necessary to read 10 X values, each from a different input record. The following is to be done while reading:
   (a)   The X values are to be summed, as SUMX.
   (b)   Y values are to be computed, as follows:

$$Y_1 = \frac{X_1 + X_2}{2}, \ Y_2 = \frac{X_2 + X_3}{2}, \ \ldots, \ Y_9 = \frac{X_9 + X_{10}}{2}$$

   The Y values should be printed as they are calculated.
   (c)   The average of the 10 X values should be written.

6. Input data records contain A, B, and C (FØRMAT 3F5.0). These records are to be assigned batch numbers. Write a program to read them and write records containing A, B, C, and the batch number, I. I is to be 1 for the first 100 records, 2 for the next 100, etc. I will never exceed 99.

7. Assume the equation $Y = 2 + 4X - X^2$. Compute and print values of Y for $X = 1, 20$, with X increasing in increments of ½.

8. Write a program to read a set of N records, each record containing a variable, X. As records are read, print out those whose X value is equal to its order number in the set.

9. "Hash totals" are totals of data which are not ordinarily summed, such as account numbers, employee numbers, or weights. Write a program to read records containing the number of units of inventory sold, UNITS by FØRMAT 2 (other record contents are immaterial). Sum the units for records in batches of 100. Write the sum by FØRMAT 3.

PROBLEMS

Follow the instructions to problems in Chapter 3 in preparing programs for these problems.

1. You are to write a program to prepare asset depreciation schedules using the sum-of-years' digits or declining balance methods. A full year's depreciation is to be taken in 1975, the first year.

    Input and output records are as follows:

| | *FORTRAN* | |
Item Description	Name	Field Size
Input record:		
Asset name	*	*
Depreciation indicator†	K	x
Estimated use-life	LIFE	xxx
Cost	CØST	xxxxxxx
Estimated scrap value	SCRAP	xxxxxxx
Output record:		
Asset name	*	*
Depreciation method	**	**
Year	YR	xxxx
Depreciation for year	DEP	xxxxx.xx
Accumulated depreciation	ACUM	xxxxx.xx
Undepreciated balance	BAL	xxxxx.xx

   * A 20-place alphanumeric field.
   † Indicates depreciation method to be used, where 1 = sum-of-years' digits, 2 = declining balance.
   ** Should contain "SUM OF YEARS" or "DECLINING BALANCE," as appropriate.

Instructions:

(a) The program is to process more than one input record, continuing until an end-of-file state is encountered.

(b) The method of depreciation is to be determined by testing the K field. Each type of schedule is to be prepared in a different DØ loop.

(c) Computational instructions may be found in Chapter 5, Illustration 3, and Problem 16.

2. The discounted value (*D*) of 1 may be found by the following equation:

$$D = \frac{1}{(1 + r)^n}$$

where r represents the discount rate and n the number of discount periods.

Instructions: Prepare a table showing the amount of 1 discounted for 1 through 10 periods at discount rates of .07, .075, .08, and .085. The table should appear as follows (the first line is furnished as guide):

	Discount Amount			
Period	.07	.075	.08	.085
1	.9346	.9302	.9259	.9217

3. A parameter record containing N (FØRMAT I3) precedes a set of n data records, each containing one value of X (FØRMAT F4.0). The X values are arranged in ascending sequences. These X records are to be read in a DØ loop, and the following computations made:

    (a) The middle value in the set of X values is to be printed. Should N be even, there will not be a middle value; instead, the average of the two middle values should be printed.

    (b) The following accumulations should be made:

    SUMX, the sum of the X values
    SUMXS, the sum of the squares of the X values.

    After all X records have been read, the following should be computed:

    (a) The mean, calculated as $\dfrac{\Sigma X}{N}$

    (b) The standard deviation, calculated as $\sqrt{\dfrac{\Sigma X^2 - \dfrac{(\Sigma X)^2}{N}}{N - 1}}$

4. The least squares method of fitting a straight line to data requires that the following equations be solved for a and b:

$$\Sigma Y = Na + b\Sigma X$$
$$\Sigma XY = a\Sigma X + b\Sigma X^2$$

A parameter record, containing N (FØRMAT I3) precedes a set of n data records, each of which contains one value of X and one of Y (FØRMAT 2F2.0). Write a program that will accumulate the following values as data records are read:

$$SUMX = \text{sum of } X \text{ values}$$
$$SUMY = \text{sum of } Y \text{ values}$$
$$SUMXY = \text{sum of } (X \text{ times } Y) \text{ values}$$
$$SUMXS = \text{sum of } X^2 \text{ values}$$

After reading, the program should solve the equations for (a) and (b) above and print them by F10.2 formats.

5. A company sells $100,000 face amount of five-year bonds, paying interest of 6% per year semiannually. The bonds sell for $104,376.03, at which price they yield interest at the effective rate of 5%.

    Instructions: Prepare an amortization table, containing the following. (Headings are to be programmed, but not column numbers. The opening balance and first lines are included as guides):

Interest Payment Number (1)	Amount of Interest Paid (2)	Amount of Effective Interest (3)	Premium Amortization (4)	Bond Carrying Value (5)
				104,376.03
1	3,000.00	2,609.40	390.60	103,985.43

Explanation of columns:
(1)   The interest payment number, 1 through 10.
(2)   Interest paid. This will remain at $3,000 for each period.
(3)   Effective interest. This is computed as 2½% (½ the annual effective rate of 5%) times column 5, the bond carrying value.
(4)   Premium amortization. The difference between the amount of interest paid, and the amount of effective interest (column 2 — column 3).
(5)   Bond carrying value. The bonds' sale price, less the premium amortization.

6.   Federal income tax is currently withheld from married persons paid once each month on the following basis:
(a)   First, $62.50 per exemption is subtracted from gross income.
(b)   Then, tax is based on the remainder according to the graduated table below:

Wages Less Exemptions		Income Tax to Be Withheld	
Not over $46.00		0	
Over	But Not Over		Of Excess Over
$ 46	$ 171	14%	$ 46
171	725	$ 17.50 plus 16%	171
725	896	106.14 plus 20%	725
896	1,404	140.34 plus 24%	896
1,404	1,771	262.26 plus 28%	1,404
1,771	2,104	365.02 plus 32%	1,771
2,104		471.58 plus 36%	2,104

For example, assume that a married taxpayer with four exemptions earns $1,000 per month. His tax withholding would be computed as follows:

Gross income $1,000.00
Less: Exemptions (4 × $62.50) 250.00
Subject to withholding .... $ 750.00

Amount withheld: $106.14, plus (.2 × (750 − 725) or $111.14

Instructions: Prepare a tax withholding table for married persons paid on a monthly basis. Columns should show the amount withheld for 0, 1, 2, and 3 exemptions. The table should show withholdings on salaries of from $500 to $1,500 per month, with entries in increments of $25. Table layout with a sample entry is shown below:

Gross Income	Number of Exemptions			
	0	1	2	3
$775	. . .	. . .	. . .	. . .
800	121.14	108.64	98.14	88.14
825	. . .	. . .	. . .	. . .

7. On January 1, 1975, Jones pays $8,110.90 for an annuity that will pay him $1,000 on December 31, 1975, and on the same date in the nine following years—10 payments in all. His payment represents the present value of an annuity at 4%. A portion of each payment he receives—4% on the unreturned principal—is interest. The balance represents a return of principal.

Instructions: Prepare a table showing, by year, the following (headings are not to be programmed):

Year	Annuity Payment	Interest	Return of Principal	Unreturned Principal
				8,110.90
1975	1,000	324.44	675.56	7,434.34

The first year is provided as a guide.

8. On January 1, 1975, Smith borrows $20,000. This, with interest at 6% per year (.5% per month) is to be repaid in 20 years in monthly payments of $143.29.

Instructions: Prepare a loan repayment schedule as follows (headings are not to be programmed):

Year	Month in Yr.	Payment Amount	Interest Charge	Amount of Principal Reduction	Unpaid Balance
					20,000.00
1975	1	143.29	100.00	43.29	19,956.71

The first line is provided as a guide. Note that the year and *month number* are to be shown; therefore, the program must contain provision for writing a new year and restarting the month number after every 12 entries.

9. The formula for computing the binominal probability is

$$P_b(r) = C_r^n \, p^r q^{n-r}, \text{ where } C_r^n = \frac{n!}{r! \, (n-r)!}$$

This indicates the probability of r successes in n trials where the probability of a success is p on any trial and $q = 1 - p$.

Instructions: Write a program that will compute and print the probability of producing two defective units in a run of seven units on a machine that has a record of 10% defectives. (In other words, $r = 2; n = 7;$ and $p = .1$). Print your answer by FØRMAT F7.4.

10. A firm has four departments: A, B, C, and D. Each department incurs direct expenses and is also charged with a part of each other department's expenses. A table showing the direct expenses and per-cents of each department's expense charged to other departments appears below.

Instructions: Write a program that will compute and print in a single output record the final expenses charged to each department.

		% Charged to			
Department	Direct Costs	A	B	C	D
A	$50,000		5	8	2
B	37,500	10		6	6
C	75,000	15	7		10
D	40,000	5	10	10	

Hint: This problem may be approached by setting up the following equations tentatively representing each department's costs:

$$A = 50,000 + .05B + .08C + .02D$$
$$B = 37,500 + .10A + .06C + .06D$$
$$C = 75,000 + .15A + .07B + .10D$$
$$D = 40,000 + .05A + .10B + .10C$$

As each equation is solved, it yields a new departmental cost amount to be used in subsequent equations. For example, $A = 50,000 + 1,875 + 6,000 + 800$, or $58,675. Therefore, B will be calculated as

$$B = 37,500 + .1(58,675) + .06(75,000) + .06(40,000)$$

The new values of A and B will be used in solving for C, etc. The first solution of the equations will not produce the correct answers. Instead, the new departmental cost amounts must be used, and the program must be carried through another iteration. The total costs for the departments will gradually converge with continued iterations. When an iteration produces total costs which vary little (less than $1) from those of its predecessor, the iterative process may be terminated. Sub-traction from a department's costs of that percent allocated to other departments will leave the proper charge. For example, assume that the final iteration reflects Department A costs as $80,000. Of this, 30% is allocated to other departments, leaving 70%, or $56,000 as the cost of Department A.

8 Processing Data Arrays

Some computer problems require that large amounts of related data be stored in the computer's memory. The data elements might be account balances to be updated, the location of records in direct-access storage, tables from which values are to be read, or any other kind of information. In these situations, the data group consists of more than one data element and the identity of each item must be retained in computer storage.

A *data array* is used to contain such masses of data. The data group is given a name, and each element is referenced by citation of the name with a subscript. Subscripts can easily be modified in the program, permitting a general-purpose program referring to any data element to be written. If each element had a unique name, this could not be done,

THE NATURE OF AN ARRAY

Assume that the following list of real numbers represents expense account balances:

Expense Account	*Amount*
1	100.00
2	25.13
3	406.25
4	521.11
5	288.97
6	788.90

This is an array. Because the values are of real mode, it should be assigned some floating-point name, such as ACCT. The set of values would then be called the ACCT array.

Array Elements

Each item in the array is called an *array element*. The elements do not have unique names as in previous chapters; instead, each is referred to by citing the array name and its relative position in the table. Thus, $ACCT_1$ refers to the first value, 100.00; $ACCT_5$ refers to the fifth item, 288.97. A general item reference can be made by citing $ACCT_n$; this can refer to any array element, and the one chosen depends on the value of n when the selection is made.

Subscripts

The reference to the position of an item in an array is called a *subscript*. In the citations of the previous paragraph—$ACCT_1$, $ACCT_5$, and $ACCT_n$—the symbols 1, 5, and n written at the foot of the array name are subscripts.

Of course, it is not possible to write subscripts below the line or in small letters in FORTRAN; therefore, letters are capitalized and letters and numbers are written in parentheses following the array name. The citations above would be written as follows: ACCT(1), ACCT(5), ACCT(N).

Subscripts must be *unsigned nonzero integer* constants or variables referring to unsigned nonzero integer values. Combinations of constants and variables may also be used. The exact subscript construction requirements vary somewhat among computers.

The difference between a constant and variable subscript is the same as that between any other constant and variable. If a constant subscript, such as ACCT(1) is used, the citation can never refer to any element other than the first. A citation such as ACCT(N) may refer to any element; the one chosen at a particular time depends on the value then assigned N. Of course, N must have been defined prior to its use as a subscript and its value should not exceed the number of elements in the array.

Array Dimensions

An array may consist of a single row or column of elements, such as did the ACCT array above. This is referred to as a *one-dimensional* array. Its elements are cited by single subscripts, as in the previous examples.

Arrays may also consist of more than one column or row, in which case they are called *two-dimensional*. For example, assume that the set of account balances depicted earlier was for one month and the balances for three months appear as follows:

Expense Account	Month 1	Month 2	Month 3
1	100.00	125.13	140.27
2	25.13	55.96	45.00
3	406.25	450.33	475.98
4	521.11	525.25	275.99
5	288.97	304.55	327.73
6	788.90	804.34	827.75

Each row, running across, represents a different expense. Each column, running down, represents a different month.

A two-dimensional array is also called a *matrix*.

The elements of a two-dimensional array are referenced by citing the array name followed by a double subscript, for example, ACCT(I,J). The subscripts, enclosed in parentheses, are separated by a comma. Either or both may be constants or variables, as described above; they must both be or refer to unsigned nonzero integers.

The first subscript refers to the *row* on which the element lies, and the second to its *column*. For example, ACCT(2,3), the element in the second row, third column, is 45.00.

Three-dimensional matrices are also permitted in FORTRAN IV. These may be thought of as rectangular and as having depth as well as surface dimensions. These are assigned three subscripts, such as ACCT(I,J,K), where I and J are row and column references, respectively, and K indicates depth. Because these are seldom used in business processing, they are not discussed in this text.

The DIMENSIØN Statement

Arrays occupy blocks of computer storage. These storage blocks must be reserved when the program is compiled, otherwise instructions or other data might be assigned storage locations in the array area. This space reservation is accomplished by the DIMENSIØN statement.

This, a specification statement, is of the nature

$$\text{DIMENSIØN} \quad A(s_1), B(s_2), \ldots, X(s_n)$$

This statement indicates to the computer that the assigned variable names refer to entire arrays, not data items. It must precede any other reference to the array.

The specification also sets out the array size. It may contain one unsigned nonzero integer constant, indicating the number of elements in a one-dimensional array; or two such constants, separated by a comma, which indicate the shape of a two-dimensional matrix.

As an example of the DIMENSIØN statement, assume that the following arrays are needed in a program:

X, a one-dimensional array to contain 25 or fewer floating-point values

Y, a two-dimensional floating-point array with 10 rows and 5 columns (this could also be called a 10×5 matrix)

I, a 4×3 integer matrix

The statement identifying these and specifying their size would appear as follows:

$$\text{DIMENSIØN} \quad X(25), Y(10,5), I(4,3)$$

Any number of arrays may be dimensioned in a single statement. The specifications are separated by commas. In the definition of a two-dimensional array, the first integer sets the number of rows and the second the number of columns.

Note that the array size descriptor must be a *constant*. Variable citation is not permitted, for the dimension statement must reserve memory space before the program is executed and before variables could be assigned values. Thus, a statement such as DIMENSIØN AJAX(I,J) is not a valid instruction.

Whenever an array may be used to contain a variable number of elements, it should be dimensioned at its largest possible size. While smaller arrays can be fitted into the larger space, to attempt storage of an array in a space too small for it is to encourage the misuse of computer memory space. Thus, in the above example, X was assigned a dimension of 25, the largest number of elements it might contain.

The dimension statement, like other specification statements, cannot be assigned a statement number.

As mentioned above the DIMENSIØN statement must appear in the program prior to any reference to an array element. When possible, it is usually written near the first of the program with other specification statements.

Using Other Type Statements to Establish Array Dimensions

The REAL, INTEGER, and LØGICAL explicit specification statements may also be used to define the size of an array in addition to establishing its mode. For example, the statement

$$\text{REAL } K(10,5)$$

defines K as a floating-point array of size 10×5. This is an adequate array definition, and the dimension statement is not required.

Type statements can, in fact, do more than establish array size and mode. They can also assign initial values to the array elements. For example, in the statement

$$\text{REAL } K(4,5)/20*1.0/$$

the array K is defined as being of real mode, of 4×5 size, and each array element is assigned an initial value of 1.

Assigning a Value to Array Elements

Ordinarily, array elements are assigned values by reading or calculating. Sometimes, however, it is desired to assign values when neither of these techniques is particularly appropriate. This situation arises, for example, when array elements must be defined by the assignment of some initial value before processing begins.

Values may be associated with array elements under these circumstances through the use of either of two kinds of commands. The REAL, INTEGER, or LØGICAL type statement may be used to associate a value with the array elements, as discussed above. Or, the DATA statement, described in Chapter 4, may be used to assign initial values.

To illustrate the use of the DATA statement, assume that each element of a 6×8 array, X, is to be assigned an initial value of zero. This might be done by the following statement:

$$\text{DATA } X/48*0.0/$$

When placed after the DIMENSIØN statement establishing the array, this statement assigns a value of zero to each element.

Processing Data Arrays

With one exception, the array name must always be subscripted. This exception occurs when reading or writing arrays under certain circumstances and is discussed below. In other instances, the form of the subscripts must agree with the dimensions of the array, single-dimension arrays having one subscript and two-dimensional matrices, two.

Array Input and Output. It is not practical to read or write array elements by citing each element separately. Instead, the DØ statement may be used to facilitate input and output, or one of two special input-output instructions may be employed.

1. Using a DØ Statement. The input or output command may be written inside a DØ loop, and the DØ statement index used as a subscript referring to array elements.

For example, assume that a one-dimensional array, X, is to contain 25 or fewer elements. Each element is punched in a different card, and the data deck is preceded by a parameter card containing N, the number of elements to be read. The following program could be used to read these elements, then write them out (formats assumed):

```
        DIMENSIØN X(25)
        READ(5,1)N
        DØ 5 I = 1, N
5       READ(5,2)X(I)
        DØ 6 K = 1, N
6       WRITE(6,3)X(K)
        STØP
        END
```

Controlled by the first DØ statement, N values will be read in from different records. As I ranges from 1 to N, the X elements will be stored in adjoining positions of the X array. In output, as K ranges from 1 to N, the same elements will be extracted from the array locations and written on different records.

Different DØ indices were used in the input and output loops above. This is acceptable, or the same index names could have been employed. The name of the subscript is not significant once the loop is ended; what matters is that the subscript is acting in the desired manner.

Two-dimensional arrays may be handled in a similar fashion by nesting two DØ loops. For example, assume that elements of the two-dimensional Y array (known to be 8 × 10 or smaller) are punched in different input records. The data deck is preceded by a parameter card containing M and N, the number of rows and columns of the Y matrix. Elements are to be stored row-wise; that is, the first row is to be filled with the first N elements, then the second row with the next N elements, and so on, until all M rows are stored.

This program can be written as follows (formats assumed):

```
          DIMENSIØN Y(8,10)
          READ(5,1)M, N
          DØ 5 I = 1, M
          DØ 5 J = 1, N
     5    READ(5,2)Y(I,J)
          STØP
          END
```

The program enters the outer loop, varying I from 1 to M. It then enters the inner loop, varying J from 1 to N. The inner loop must be satisfied for each iteration of the outer; therefore, it will cause N records to be read, varying J by one with each until $J = N$. The inner loop will be satisfied for each value of I. Thus, the READ command will be interpreted as follows:

```
          READ(5,2)Y(1,1)
          READ(5,2)Y(1,2)
          READ(5,2)Y(1,3)

          . . . . . .
          READ(5,2)Y(1,N)
          READ(5,2)Y(2,1)

          . . . . . .
          READ(5,2)Y(M,N)
```

Output would be similar to input.

The above input method has one major disadvantage. It assumes that each array element occupies a different record or that the input-output command cites by name all elements on the record. Input or output is rather complicated if this is not the case.

For example, if input records each contain six elements to be loaded by rows in a two-dimensional array, the input command would be written as follows:

READ(5,1) A(I,1), A(I,2), A(I,3), A(I,4), A(I,5), A(I,6)

The DØ statement controlling I and other indexing instructions would become somewhat complex, especially if there were more than six columns in the array.

A simpler form of array input-output is available. The one described above is useful only if processing steps, such as element summation, are to be executed while reading or writing.

2. Combined I/Ø-DØ Statements.   Where arrays are to be read or written, an instruction combining certain features of the input-output command and the DØ statement may be used. This is of the following general form for a one-dimensional array:

$$READ(j,k) \ (X(i), \ i = n_1, n_2, n_3)$$
$$WRITE(j,k) \ (X(i), \ i = n_1, n_2, n_3)$$

j is the input unit, and k is some format number. X represents the array name, and i a variable serving as a subscript. n_1, n_2, and n_3 serve as the subscript's parameters; n_1 setting the initial value, n_2 the terminal value and n_3 (omitted if 1), the increment. The parameters must be unsigned nonzero integer constants or variables referring to such values. The statement must be punctuated as shown.

The statement works much like a combined DØ and input or output statement.

In the READ instruction, reading occurs, and the ranging of the index from its starting value through its terminal value causes array elements to be stored in proper locations. If there is only one element per record, this instruction is comparable to the ones described above. For example, the following load routines do the same thing:

1	FØRMAT(F4.0)	1	FØRMAT(F4.0)
	DØ 5, I = 1,15		READ(5,1)(X(I), I = 1,15)
5	READ(5,1)X(I)		

Each statement causes 15 records to be read and a value to be extracted from each and stored in the X array.

The combined I/Ø-DØ form does much more than the simple input-output loops shown above, however. It works directly with the FØRMAT statement and automatically extracts from (or writes in) a record as many elements as specified by the FØRMAT statement. For example, assume the following:

An array may contain 30 or fewer elements. Six elements are recorded in an input record, and the number of elements to be read is indicated in a parameter card as N. Read and store the elements.

```
          DIMENSIØN X(30)
  1       FØRMAT(I 2)
  2       FØRMAT(6F8.0)
          READ(5,1) N
          READ(5,2)(X(I), I = 1, N)
          STØP
          END
```

The READ command, working with FØRMAT 2, extracts six data elements from each record. I advances by 1 for each *element*, until N elements have been extracted from the record. Thus, when the READ command is executed, $(N - 1)/6 + 1$ data records are read.

The output command works in the same way as the READ statement.

Two-dimensional arrays can be read or written by a modification of the same command. For these, the input and output instructions are as follows:

$$\text{READ}(k,l) \quad ((X(i,j), i = n_1,n_2,n_3),j = m_1,m_2,m_3)$$
$$\text{WRITE}(k,l) \quad ((X(i,j), i = n_1,n_2,n_3),j = m_1,m_2,m_3)$$

i is the row subscript and j the column subscript. This command will cause i to range from n_1 by n_3 (which may be omitted, if 1) until it equals n_2, and j to range from m_1 by m_3 (which may also be omitted) until it equals m_2. The inner subscript, i, will vary faster than j, going through its entire range with each increment of j. Thus, values read by the above statement are stored by columns. Exchanging subscripts i and j (as $X(j,i)$) would cause row-wise storage.

These instructions work closely with their related FØRMAT and extract or write as many variables from each input (or output) record as the format specification requires. As an example of the command's execution, assume the following:

The A array has a maximum size of 6×7 elements. Elements are to be read and stored by rows. A parameter card containing M and N indicates the number of rows and columns to be filled. Each input record contains five A elements.

The following program reads and stores the values as required.

```
          DIMENSIØN A(6,7)
  1       FØRMAT(2I1)
  2       FØRMAT(5F6.2)
          READ(5,1)M, N
          READ(5,2) ((A(I,J), J = 1,N), I = 1,M)
```

J, varying rapidly, will cause each row to be filled. I, varying slowly, will vary the row subscript only after J has moved through its range. Thus, the values will be stored as follows:

$$A(1,1)A(1,2)A(1,3) \ldots A(1,N)$$
$$A(2,1)A(2,2)A(2,3) \ldots A(2,N)$$
$$A(M,1)A(M,2)A(M,3) \ldots A(M,N)$$

Values are written in a similar way, using the WRITE command.

3. Reading or Writing Entire Arrays. Where an entire array is to be read or written, the following instruction may be used:

$$READ(5,1)X$$
$$WRITE(6,1)X$$

where X is the array name. This is the only time when an array can be referred to by name without subscripts (except in the DATA statement).

This command works with the FØRMAT and DIMENSIØN statements, reading or printing as many elements as indicated by the latter in the design of the former. For example, the following instructions

$$DIMENSIØN\ X(10)$$
5     $FØRMAT(2F6.0)$
$$READ(5,5)X$$

would cause the reading and storage in a one-dimensional array of 10 values, 2 from each input record.

Two-dimension arrays can also be transmitted by citation of the array name in READ or WRITE statements. They are handled in a column-by-column manner. For example, the program below would cause writing in the indicated sequence:

$$DIMENSIØN\ X(3,4)$$
5     $FØRMAT\ (2F8.0)$
$$WRITE(6,5)X$$

Output:

Record 1	X(1,1)	X(2,1)
Record 2	X(3,1)	X(1,2)
Record 3	X(2,2)	X(3,2)
Record 4	X(1,3)	X(2,3)
Record 5	X(3,3)	X(1,4)
Record 6	X(2,4)	X(3,4)

This input-output instruction is satisfactory only when entire arrays are processed and when the column-by-column transfer mode is satisfactory. Otherwise, the combined statements discussed above are proper for reading and writing arrays.

Using Data Arrays

Arrays should be used whenever homogeneous data elements are to be stored in the computer's memory. Several situations are discussed below; others may be found in the broad scope of business data processing.

1. Transmitting Alphanumeric Data. The ability to read and write the contents of an entire array can be used in a very interesting way—to process alphanumeric messages.

As explained in Chapter 6, alphanumeric words have a maximum storage size of four characters. To read or write a message containing more characters requires that sets of words be used. In Chapter 6 each word was assigned a unique data-name, leading to rather tedious processing. The same data can be read or written as an array, and the entire message string transmitted with a single citation.

For example, assume that input records contain an 18-character field used to record customer names, and sales amount. Using processing methods outlined in Chapter 6, this is defined and processed as follows:

```
1      FØRMAT(4A4,A2,F6.2)
2      FØRMAT(1X,4A4,A2,5X,F8.2)
       READ(5,1)N1,N2,N3,N4,N5,SALE
          . . .
          . . .
       WRITE(6,2)N1,N2,N3,N4,N5,SALE
```

An array can be used to contain the alphanumeric data, and the same records processed in the following manner:

```
       DIMENSIØN  NME(5)
1      FØRMAT(4A4,A2,F6.2)
2      FØRMAT(1X,4A4,A2,5X,F8.2)
       READ(5,1)NME,SALE
          . . .
          . . .
       WRITE(6,2)NME,SALE
```

Format statements are exactly the same in each example. However, in the second instance a four-element array, NME, is used to receive the first five alphanumeric words. Citation of the array name causes all five elements to be read or written, eliminating the necessity of specifying each element by name.

The DIMENSIØN statement must specify the number of alphanumeric words to be stored.

2. Object-time FØRMAT. The ability to store alphanumeric data in an array includes the storage of format specifications, and the READ and WRITE statements have been modified to access such a specification set. This is an especially valuable processing capability when standard processing routines are to be applied to record sets having different formats.

To use object-time formatting, an alphanumeric array large enough to contain a format specification list must be dimensioned. It will hold the list only; FØRMAT and the format statement number are not stored. As a step preliminary to actual data processing, the format specification is read from an external source and stored in the array. Then, in execution, the array name is cited in the appropriate input or output statement in lieu of a format number.

To illustrate this technique, assume that a set of records containing the indicated data is available:

	FØRMAT	
Item Description	*Name*	*Specification*
Transaction number	NØ	I4
Salesman number	NSMAN	I3
Customer number	NØCST	I4
Transaction cost	CØST	F5.2
Transaction revenue	AMT	F5.2
Transaction margin	TMAR	F4.2

These records contain information to be used in several different reports. It is possible, of course, to prepare a different program for each. If the processing structure of each program is the same, however, object-time formatting can be used to select the desired data for each report. Change of the records containing the input and output format specification required will arrange for reading and writing the desired data.

Assume that three reports are required: The first is to contain transaction number, cost, and revenue. The second is to contain customer number, revenue, and margin. The third is to contain the salesman number, revenue, and cost.

These can all be prepared by the following program:

```
        DIMENSIØN FMT1(18),FMT2(18)
        READ(5,1)FMT1
        READ(5,1) FMT2
  1     FØRMAT(18A4)
  10    READ(5,FMT1,END=50)I,B,C
        WRITE(6,FMT2)A,B,C
        GØ TØ 10
  50    STØP
        END
```

Two one-dimensional arrays are prepared, FMT1 and FMT2. Each is assigned 18 elements, sufficient to store a 72-character format specification. Then, the input format specifications are read into FMT1. To meet the requirements of the first report, this report contains the following:

$$(I4,7X,2F5.2)$$

The required output format is then read into FMT2. It appears as:

$$(5X,I5,2(5X,F7.2))$$

Statement 10 refers to FMT1, instead of a statement number, in citing the location of controlling format specifications. Input records will be read by the specifications stored in the array. Output records are written in a similar fashion, using the specifications stored at FMT2.

Data records follow the two format records in the input stream, and are processed by the program in normal fashion.

To prepare other reports, appropriate format specifications would be entered in the first two records, in front of actual data.

3. Table Look-Up. Data that must be retrieved in a random fashion is frequently stored in an array, or table, in which entries are found by search.

For example, assume that a company prepares two sets of data pertaining to accounts receivable—account numbers and unpaid balances. No more than 1,000 accounts are ever active at one time; the number in use is indicated by M, in a parameter card.

The account numbers and balances are to be stored in two arrays, called NØ and BAL, respectively, in such a way that an account's number and balance occupy the same position in each data set. Then, as inquiry records are read containing an account number, that number's balance is to be found and written. Details of input and output records are shown below.

		FORTRAN	
Item Description		Name	Field Size
Balance records:			
Account number		NØ*	xxxxx
Account balance		BAL*	xxxxx.xx
Inquiry record:			
Account number		NUM	xxxxx
Parameter record:			
Number of active accounts		M	xxxx
Output record:			
Account number		NØ*	xxxxx
Account balance		BAL*	xxxxx.xx

* An array name.

The program for loading the account data, then searching the array and printing balances, appears in Figure 8–1. Statement 101, loading the two arrays, is somewhat different from the input commands illustrated previously because the same index is used as a subscript on

FIGURE 8–1
Table Look-Up Program

```
C        TABLE LOOK-UP.
         DIMENSION NØ(1000),BAL(1000)
1        FØRMAT(I5,F7.2)
2        FØRMAT(I5)
3        FØRMAT(I4)
4        FØRMAT(1X,I6,5X,F9.2)
5        FØRMAT(12H RECØRD NØ. ,I6,12H NØT IN FILE)
         READ(5,3)M
101      READ(5,1)(NØ(I),BAL(I),I=1,M)
10       READ(5,2,END=50)NUM
102      DØ 6 K=1,M
         IF(NUM .EQ. NØ(K))GØ TO 7
6        CØNTINUE
         WRITE(6,5)NUM
         GØ TO 10
7        WRITE(6,4)NØ(K),BAL(K)
         GØ TO 10
50       STØP
         END
```

both input values. This is quite acceptable; any number of data items, subscripted or not, may be referenced in the input statement.

The search routine is to be found in statements 102 through 6. K, the DØ index, is used as a subscript and causes each account number in the array to be compared with the control number, NUM. Mismatching numbers are ignored, and the search process continues.

The program branches from the DØ range when matching values are found, and the account number and balance are printed. It may be recalled that a transfer from the DØ range does not destroy the DØ index; therefore, it may be used as a subscript in the output statement.

The search program in Figure 8–1 contains commands for signaling an error when the account number is not discovered in the table. This is typical of the many verification routines that should be used in programs of this nature.

4. Retrieving Records from Direct-Access Files. It is usually impractical to include a direct-access record location in transaction data, because of the processing difficulties it entails. Instead, reference data such as account number is used in transactions to identify the data sets involved. A contents table is also maintained in computer-sensible form. This includes the reference data and the location of each item's related record in the direct-access file. The location of appropriate direct-access records is determined by using the table look-up process described in Example 3 above.

As an example, assume that employee master records are maintained in a direct-access file. Each record contains an employee number, name, address, and pay rate. Transaction records containing an employee number and hours worked are randomly positioned in the input file. For each, the associated master record must be located and read, gross pay calculated, and a pay statement written.

A contents table showing the direct-access file location of each employee master record is also maintained on a direct-access file. This must be moved to the computer's primary memory before processing can begin.

Record contents are shown below:

	FORTRAN	
Item Description	*Name*	*Field Size*
Employee master record (in direct-access file 10, 1,000 records, formatted, size as indicated below; associated variable KBAL):		

	FORTRAN	
Item Description	*Name*	*Field Size*
Employee number	NØBAL	xxxxxxxxx
Employee name	NME	20 characters, alphanumeric
Street address	STR	20 characters, alphanumeric
City–State	CITY	20 characters, alphanumeric
Pay rate	RATE	xx.xx
Table of contents		
(in direct-access file 11,		
1,000 records, formatted,		
size as indicated below;		
associated variable KTABL):		
Employee number	NØTBL	xxxxxxxxx
Address of master record	KADR	xxxx
Detail record:		
Employee number	NØ	xxxxxxxxx
Hours worked	HRS	xxx
Pay statement:		
Employee name and address ..	20 characters alphanumeric per line	
Pay rate	RATE	xx.xx
Hours worked	HRS	xx.x
Pay earned	PAY	xxx.xx

THE FORTRAN program is presented in Figure 8–2.

In the DIMENSIØN statement, space is reserved for two 1,000-element arrays. One, named NØTBL, is to contain employee numbers. The other, called KADR, is to contain the direct-access file location of the employee master record. Data elements pertaining to a given employee occupy similar locations in the arrays; for example, if an employee's number is in the 14th location in NØTBL, the direct-access address of his master record is in the 14th location in KADR.

Dimensions are provided for three other arrays. These are to contain the alphanumeric data pertaining to name, street, and city.

Two direct-access files are defined. The first, designated file 10, is to contain the employee master records. The second, file 11, contains the table of contents data when not needed in the computer's primary memory.

The table of contents is read and stored in statement 040. The READ command instructs that 1,000 values of NØTBL and KADR be read and stored array-fashion.

Once the table of contents has been loaded, processing of transaction records can begin. First, a transaction record is read. Next, the corresponding employee number is sought in the NØTBL array; failure to find a matching number is signalled as an error. Once a matching number is found, the direct-access location of the appropriate master record

FIGURE 8-2 Direct-Access File Processing

IBM

FORTRAN CODING FORM

X28-7327-6 U/M 050
Printed in U.S.A.

| PROGRAM | | PUNCHING INSTRUCTIONS | GRAPHIC | | PAGE | OF |
| PROGRAMMER | DATE | | PUNCH | | CARD ELECTRO NUMBER* | |

```
C     RETRIEVING DIRECT-ACCESS RECORDS                                          010
      DIMENSION NOTBL(1000),KADR(1000),NME(5),STR(5),CITY(5)                    020
      DEFINE FILE 10(1000,74,E,KBAL),11(1000,13,E,KTABL)                        030
      DO 8 I = 1,1000                                                           040
8     READ(11'I,1)NOTBL(I),KADR(I)                                             050
1     FORMAT(I9,I4)                                                            060
10    READ(5,2,END=50)NO,HRS                                                   070
2     FORMAT(I9,F3.1)                                                          080
      DO 12 I = 1,1000                                                         090
12    IF(NO.EQ.NOTBL(I))GO TO 20                                              100
      WRITE(6,6)NO                                                            110
6     FORMAT(' RECORD NO',I10,'NOT IN FILE')                                 120
      GO TO 10                                                               130
20    READ(10'KADR(I),3)NOBAL,NME,STR,CITY,RATE                              140
3     FORMAT(I9,15A4,F5.2)                                                   150
      PAY = HRS * RATE                                                       160
4     FORMAT(40X,5A4)                                                        170
      WRITE(6,4)NME                                                          180
      WRITE(6,4)STR                                                          190
      WRITE(6,4)CITY                                                         200
      WRITE(6,5)RATE,HRS,PAY                                                 210
5     FORMAT(40X,F5.2,5X,F4.1,5X,F7.2)                                      220
      GO TO 10                                                               230
50    STOP                                                                   240
      END                                                                    250
```

is known to be at the position indicated by the corresponding KADR element. Thus, the direct-access READ statement shown on line 120 cites KADR(I) as the address of the record to be retrieved.

Other processing is routine. Attention is directed again to the ease with which alphanumeric data can be read and written when the elements have been consolidated into array form.

5. Maintaining a Waiting Line.   In many business situations, such as inventory accounting and production simulation, it is necessary to create a waiting line, or "queue." These are arrays of values, and when element one is removed, the others' positions must be shifted. If the first item is chosen and the others moved up, the array of values is called a "push-up list"; the reverse is a "push-down list."

To demonstrate this type of array processing, assume that a properly dimensioned array, X, contains M elements and is stored in the computer's memory.

(*a*)   First, assume that the first value is to be printed, and the other elements moved up.

A program for accomplishing this is found below.

$$\text{WRITE}(6,1)\ X(1)$$
$$\text{D}\emptyset\ 5\ I = 2,\ M$$
$$5\qquad X(I-1) = X(I)$$

This shows the use of subscripts slightly more complex than employed previously. The program is quite simple, however, because the D$\emptyset$ index properly indicates the movement of data.

(*b*)   Assume the same problem, except that the Mth value is to be printed, and the array pushed down.

This program might be written in the following manner:

$$\text{WRITE}(6,1)\ X(M)$$
$$\text{D}\emptyset\ 5\ I = 2,M$$
$$K = M + 1 - I$$
$$5\qquad X(K+1) = X(K)$$

In this instance, a subscript is required that is decreasing in value. One may be created by subtracting I from $(M + 1)$. As I increases, the subscript decreases.

6. Sorting.   Business reporting frequently requires that data stored in one sequence be rearranged. This process is called sorting, and is one of the major manipulatoins performed on arrayed data.

Several sorting methods are used. If voluminous records are to be sorted, a process is generally employed that requires several input-output devices such as tape units or disks. This is called an *external sort*. Because the process is very important to most data-processing operations, although rather complicated, most computer manufacturers provide a generalized sort program for their processing systems.

Simple sorts of short data sets are performed in the computer's primary storage unit; these are called *internal sorts*. These are frequently incorporated in data processing programs. They can be designed to place data items in ascending or decending sequence.

Several internal sorting algorithms have been defined. One, called the "exchange process," requires that the first item in the list be compared with succeeding items. If items are to be sorted into descending sequence, the largest value is placed in the first position. Then, the second item is compared with others in the array below it and the largest value in this set selected and placed in the second position. The list is completely sorted when it is determined that each item has a larger value than any other falling below it in the array.

As an example of this process, assume that a set of records is to be read, each containing an account number and balance. Account numbers are to be stored as elements of the NØ array and account balances in corresponding locations in an array named BAL. There are no more than 200 records in the file; a count of the actual number of records is to be taken while reading.

After reading, account balances are to be sorted into descending order; that is, the largest balance is to be in the first position of the array, followed by the next largest, etc. Account numbers are to be rearranged accordingly. Account balances and numbers are to be written out after sorting.

A flowchart for this process is shown in Figure 8–3 and its related program in Figure 8–4.

Records are counted as they are read. The counter, I, is used as a subscript in storing account numbers and associated balances. After all records have been read, I must be reduced by one, because the reading process leaves it with a value that is one greater than the number of records processed. Next, M is set at $I - 1$. This will be used to control the number of sorting passes, which is always one less than the number of items to be rearranged. Then the sorting process begins.

This is accomplished in a nest of 2 DØ statements. The first controls the number of sorting passes. Within each pass, the second DØ statement causes the element being tested to be compared with all beneath

FIGURE 8–3
Flowchart of Internal Sort

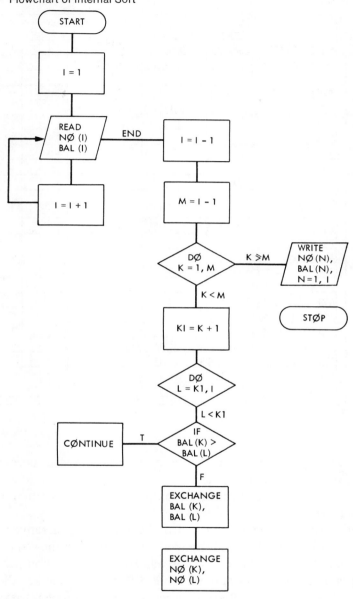

FIGURE 8–4
Sorting Arrayed Data

```
C          SORTING ARRAYED DATA
           DIMENSION NØ(200),BAL(200)
           I=1
    1      FORMAT(I4,F6.2)
    5      READ(5,1,END=10)NØ(I),BAL(I)
           I=I+1
           GØ TØ 5
   10      I=I-1
           M=I-1
           DØ 20 K=1,M
           K1=K+1
           DØ 20 L=K1,I
           IF(BAL(K).GT.BAL(L))GØ TØ 20
           TEMP=BAL(K)
           BAL(K)=BAL(L)
           BAL(L)=TEMP
           TEMP=NØ(K)
           NØ(K)=NØ(L)
           NØ(L)=TEMP
   20      CONTINUE
           WRITE(6,2)(NØ(N),BAL(N),N=1,I)
    2      FORMAT(5X,I4,5X,F8.2)
           STØP
           END
```

it in the array. If the element is larger no rearrangement is necessary; if not, the two values change places.

After all items have been sorted, output records are written and the program terminated.

Internal sorts can be used to control the writing of rearranged direct-access records. Key data can be loaded into an array in the same way as the account balances above, and the related record location put in the corresponding position of another table. After sorting the key data and related location indicator, the direct-access records can be retrieved and written in the desired sequence.

7. Matrix Addition and Multiplication. While a complete discussion of matrix arithmetic is not appropriate in this text, brief mention of addition and multiplication is made because computer arrays afford a simple way to handle the computations.

Matrix Addition. In matrix addition, the elements of two or more arrays are added to form a new array. The arrays to be added must have the same dimensions.

For example, assume the following:

$$[X]=\begin{bmatrix} X_{1,1}\ X_{1,2}\ X_{1,3},\ \ldots,\ X_{1,N} \\ X_{2,1}\ X_{2,2}\ X_{2,3},\ \ldots,\ X_{2,N} \\ \cdots\cdots\cdots\cdots \\ \cdots\cdots\cdots\cdots \\ X_{M,1}\ X_{M,2}\ X_{M,3},\ \ldots,\ X_{M,N} \end{bmatrix} \quad [Y]=\begin{bmatrix} Y_{1,1}\ Y_{1,2}\ Y_{1,3},\ \ldots,\ Y_{1,N} \\ Y_{2,1}\ Y_{2,2}\ Y_{2,3},\ \ldots,\ Y_{2,N} \\ \cdots\cdots\cdots\cdots \\ \cdots\cdots\cdots\cdots \\ Y_{M,1}\ Y_{M,2}\ Y_{M,3},\ \ldots,\ Y_{M,N} \end{bmatrix}$$

Thus, both X and Y are M $\times$ N matrices. When added, they create another M $\times$ N matrix, Z, where $Z(I,J) = X(I,J) + Y(I,J) \left\} \begin{array}{l} I = 1,M \\ J = 1,N \end{array}\right.$

To illustrate the process of matrix addition, assume that Store A and Store B have reported monthly expenses for a three-month period, as follows:

	Store A Months				Store B Months		
Expenses	1	2	3	Expenses	1	2	3
1	200.00	450.00	275.00	1	850.00	975.00	400.00
2	215.00	225.00	275.00	2	455.00	650.00	720.00
3	100.00	115.00	125.00	3	275.00	255.00	280.00
4	125.00	125.00	125.00	4	250.00	250.00	250.00

The three months' expenses for each store is represented by a 4 X 3 matrix. The SUM matrix, representing the sum of the stores' expenses by months and accounts, appears as follows:

	Expense Sums Months		
Expenses	1	2	3
1	1050.00	1425.00	675.00
2	670.00	875.00	995.00
3	375.00	370.00	405.00
4	375.00	375.00	375.00

A program for reading, computing, and writing these arrays appears in Figure 8–5.

FIGURE 8–5
Matrix Addition

COMM	STATEMENT NUMBER	CONT	FORTRAN STATEMENT
C			EXAMPLE ØF MATRIX ADDITIØN
			DIMENSIØN A(4,3),B(4,3),SUM(4,3)
	1		FØRMAT(4F5.2)
	2		FØRMAT(1X,3(F9.2,5X))
			READ(5,1)A
			READ(5,1)B
			DØ 10 I-1,4
			DØ 10 J-1,3
	10		SUM(I,J) - A(I,J) + B(I,J)
			WRITE(6,2) ((SUM(K,L),L-1,3),K-1,4)
			STØP
			END

Each input record contains one month's expense balances. Because these are to be stored as columns, the "READ array name" version of matrix input can be used.

Addition occurs in a nest of two DØ statements, each controlling one subscript. Because the outer DØ controls the row subscript, each row is prepared before going to the next.

The combined output-DØ statement must be used in printing the solution matrix, for each row should occupy a different record. The SUM matrix is written out in this manner.

Matrix Multiplication. Matrix multiplication requires that the left-hand matrix have as many columns as the right-hand matrix has rows. Multiplication can be executed only if this condition is met. Other matrix dimensions are irrelevant.

Assume the multiplication of the X matrix times the Y matrix to produce the Z matrix. Matrices appear as follows:

$$[X] = \begin{bmatrix} X_{1,1} & X_{1,2} & X_{1,3}, & \dots, & X_{1,K} \\ X_{2,1} & X_{2,2} & X_{2,3}, & \dots, & X_{2,K} \\ \dots & \dots & \dots & \dots & \dots \\ \dots & \dots & \dots & \dots & \dots \\ X_{J,1} & X_{J,2} & X_{J,3}, & \dots, & X_{J,K} \end{bmatrix} \quad [Y] = \begin{bmatrix} Y_{1,1} & Y_{1,2} & Y_{1,3}, & \dots, & Y_{1,L} \\ Y_{2,1} & Y_{2,2} & Y_{2,3}, & \dots, & Y_{2,L} \\ \dots & \dots & \dots & \dots & \dots \\ \dots & \dots & \dots & \dots & \dots \\ Y_{K,J} & Y_{K,2} & Y_{K,3}, & \dots, & Y_{K,L} \end{bmatrix}$$

The product matrix will have as many rows as the left-hand matrix and as many columns as the matrix on the right. Therefore, when the X and Y matrices above are multiplied, the Z matrix will have J rows and L columns.

An element $Z_{M,N}$ in the product matrix will be the sum of products of row M elements times column N elements. More explicitly:

$$Z_{m,n} = \sum_{i=1}^{k} X_{m,i}Y_{i,n} \quad \begin{cases} m = 1, \ldots, J \\ n = 1, \ldots, L \end{cases}$$

A simple case of matrix multiplication is the development of the product of a one-dimensional array times a two-dimensional array. To demonstrate this, assume that a firm manufactures four different products. Production volume for the coming month is fixed for these and is shown below in the X array.

In disposing of next month's production, the company may use one of five different marketing schemes. These are represented by a two-dimensional array containing four rows and five columns, the rows representing the four different products and the columns the different marketing strategies. This is known as the Y array.

X Array				Y Array					
Production Schedule				Gross Profit Yielded on Each Product					
Products				Product	Market Scheme				
1	2	3	4		1	2	3	4	5
20	20	30	30	1	1	2	0	3	4
				2	1	1	2	1	1
				3	1	2	1	2	0
				4	1	2	3	1	2

In other words, next month's production will consist of 20 units of products 1 and 2, and 30 units of products 3 and 4. If marketed by scheme 1, each product yields a gross profit of $1. Marketing plan 3 fails to yield a gross profit for product 1, but $2 per unit is earned on product 2, $1 per unit on product 3, and $3 per unit on product 4.

Problem. Prepare a gross profit matrix (Z) which reflects the gross profit earned by each marketing strategy.

Solution. The Z matrix will be a 1 X 5 array, having as many rows as the X matrix and as many columns as the Y matrix. Each element in the Z matrix will represent the sum of row elements times column elements; for example,

$$Z_{1,1} = X_{1,1} Y_{1,1} + X_{1,2} Y_{2,1} + X_{1,3} Y_{3,1} + X_{1,4} Y_{4,1}.$$

Of course, the row subscripts are unnecessary because the product matrix only has one row. They are included here only for completeness.

Using the X and Y values above, the Ƶ matrix would appear as follows:

Ƶ *Matrix*
Gross Profit
Market Scheme

1	2	3	4	5
100	180	160	170	160

To illustrate the multiplication of two two-dimensional matrices, assume that three production schedules are possible rather than just one. These (the new X matrix) are as follows:

Alternative Production
Schedules
(X Matrix)

Production Plan	Product			
	1	2	3	4
1	20	20	30	30
2	40	30	20	10
3	25	25	25	25

The product array will now be a 3 × 5 matrix, as follows:

Ƶ *Matrix*
Gross Profit
Marketing Schemes

Production Plan	1	2	3	4	5
1	100	180	160	170	160
2	100	170	110	200	210
3	100	175	150	175	175

Each element is the sum of the products of row and column elements. For example,

$$Ƶ_{2,4} = (40 \times 3) + (30 \times 1) + (20 \times 2) + (10 \times 1)$$

The program for producing and printing the two-dimensional Ƶ matrix is shown in Figure 8–6.

It is assumed that the X and Y matrices are entered by rows.

Ƶ matrix elements are to be used to contain sums of several multiplications. Before they are used in the manner shown in statement 6, they must be defined. Therefore, statement 101 contains a DATA statement setting all Ƶ elements to zero.

Actual matrix multiplication occurs in statement 6. Three DØ statements are required to control this command—one for selection of the multiplier row, another for selection of multiplicand column, and a third for selection of row and column elements. These may be seen as statements 102, 103, and 104.

FIGURE 8–6
Illustration of Matrix Multiplication

COMM.	STATEMENT NUMBER	CONT.	FORTRAN STATEMENT
C			ILLUSTRATION OF MATRIX MULTIPLICATION.
			DIMENSION X(3,4),Y(4,5),Z(3,5)
	101		DATA Z/15*0.0/
	1		FORMAT(4F2.0)
	2		FORMAT(5F1.0)
	3		FORMAT(1X,5(F5.0,5X))
			READ(5,1)((X(I,J),J=1,4),I=1,3)
			READ(5,2)((Y(I,J),J=1,5),I=1,4)
	102		DO 6 M = 1,3
	103		DO 6 N = 1,5
	104		DO 6 I = 1,4
	6		Z(M,N) = Z(M,N) + X(M,I)*Y(I,N)
			WRITE(6,3)((Z(I,J),J=1,5),I=1,3)
			STOP
			END

The Z matrix is printed by the combined output-DO statement after its computation.

CHAPTER SUMMARY

Array notation is somewhat new in business data processing. However, much business information has always been in array form. For example, accountants' work sheets are two-dimensional arrays, and ledgers may be viewed as matrices as well.

The FORTRAN language brings several very powerful commands to matrix manipulation. First, through the identification of a data-set as an array, the use of iterative processes is facilitated. Second, data input and output is simplified through the use of combined input-output and DO statements. Finally, the nature of iterative processing itself greatly simplifies programming, for it permits the programmer to write a generalized routine and apply it to various array elements by subscripts.

Persons concerned with business data processing are just becoming aware of the great power array processing methods offer, and computers have only recently had primary memories large enough to permit the storage of extremely large arrays. Progress to date makes apparent the fact that the processing method is very useful, however, and one may expect to soon find many applications to problems of business information processing.

Summary of New FORTRAN Statements.   One new and two amended statements were introduced in this chapter. They are:

1. DIMENSIØN A(s_1),B(s_2,), . . . , X(s_n)
    A, B, and X = names of one, two, or three-dimensional arrays
    s = unsigned nonzero integer constants representing the dimensions
        of the array
2. READ(j,k)(X(i),i=n_1,n_2,n_3)
    WRITE(j,k)(X(i),i=n_1,n_2,n_3)
    Purpose: To read or write the elements of a one-dimensional array
    X = name of array element
    i = subscript
    n_1,n_2,n_3 = initial, terminal, and incremental values of i. n_3 is optional.
3. READ(k,l) ((X(i,j),i=n_1,n_2,n_3),j=m_1,m_2,m_3)
    WRITE(k,l)((X(i,j),i=n_1,n_2,n_3),j=m_1,m_2,m_3)
    Purpose: To read and write the elements of a two-dimensional array
    X = name of array element
    i = row subscript
    j = column subscript
    n_1,n_2,n_3 = initial, terminal, and incremental value of i. n_3 is optional
    m_1,m_2,m_3 = initial, terminal, and incremental value of j. m_3 is optional

QUESTIONS

1. What is a data array?
2. Why are data arrays stored in the computer's memory?
3. What is the difference between a one- and two-dimensional array?
4. What is the relation between arrays and DØ statements?
5. In the array notation X(I,J), what is X? What is I? What is J?
6. What is the function of the DIMENSIØN statement?
7. Where must the DIMENSIØN statement appear in the program?
8. May more than one array be described in a single DIMENSIØN statement?

9. May the array dimensions set out in a DIMENSIØN statement be represented by variables?
10. May subscripts consist of floating point variables? Of integer variables?
11. May constant subscripts be negative?
12. In the command READ(5,1) ((X(I,J),I=1,5),J=1,10) which subscript varies most rapidly?
13. What is wrong with the following instruction:
    DIMENSIØN X(I,J) Y(4,2) Z(A,3)
14. Assume that in the input statement READ(5,1)A, A represents an array. How is the computer informed of this? How are the array's dimensions made known to the computer?
15. Assume that an array, Y, is to be written. When can the command WRITE(6,1)Y be used? When must a command such as

    $$\text{WRITE(6,1)((Y(I,J),J=1,N),I=1,M)}$$

    be used?
16. How, other than by reading or calculating, may values be assigned to array elements?

EXERCISES

1. Write FORTRAN instructions for the following: A 6 X 8 matrix, called X, is to be read. Each record contains a row of 8 elements, FØRMAT F4.0. After reading, each row is to be totaled and the resultant sum written.
2. Assume the same matrix as in 1 above. After reading, each column is to be totaled and the resultant sum printed.
3. Refer to Exercise 1 above. After reading the X array, find its largest and smallest elements and write their values and subscripts.
4. Write FORTRAN instructions for the following: An 8 X 8 matrix, called Y, is to be read, where each input record contains a row of 8 elements, FØRMAT F4.0. After reading, the diagonal of the matrix

    $$Y_{1,1} Y_{2,2}, \ldots, Y_{8,8}$$

    is to be totaled and the sum written.
5. Each record in a set contains one value of X, FØRMAT F4.0. There are fewer than 200 records in the set. Write a program to read the records and store their contents in the X array. A count of records should be kept. Then, the mid-value of the array should be found and written. If the array contains an even number of elements, the average of the two middle values should be computed and written.

6. Refer to exercise 5 above. After reading the X values, sort them in ascending order. Write out the results, 6 values to a record.

7. Refer to exercise 5 above. After reading the X values, sort them in descending order. Write out the results, 6 values to a record.

8. Input records contain four data items: A, FØRMAT F5.0; B, FØR-MAT F3.2; I, FØRMAT I4; and J, FØRMAT I5.

    Prepare a program that will read and write any one of the above data items, using object-time format. Input FØRMAT specifications should be stored in FMT1, and output specifications in FMT2.

9. Input records contain the same items as described in Exercise 8 above. Prepare a program that will read and write any two of the data items, using object-time FØRMAT. Input FØRMAT specifications should be stored in FMT1, and output specifications in FMT2.

10. A one-dimensional array, B, and the number of array elements, N, are stored in the computer's memory. Some B elements are zero. Write a program to create the C array, consisting of the nonzero B elements in order of their appearance in B.

11. The T array and the number of array positions, N, are stored in the computer's memory. Write a program that will find the first zero position in T, and store A in the location.

12. The one-dimensional R array and the number of array elements, J, are stored in the computer's memory. Write a program to move all the R elements up one position in the array (R_2 becomes R_1, R_3 becomes R_2, etc.)

13. The one-dimensional X array and the number of array elements, K, are stored in the computer's memory. Write a program to reverse the array elements (A_1 becomes A_k, etc.)

14. X is a 6 X 5 real array. Assign its elements a value of 5.4 each in 2 different ways. Can you think of a third way, other than reading?

PROBLEMS

Problems should be written in accordance with the instructions given in the problem section of Chapter 3.

1. The X Company has fewer than 200 expense accounts. Data on each account is maintained in a record, as described below. Prepare a program for the following:

    (a) Read the expense records, storing their contents in the account number (NØ) and balance (BAL) arrays, respectively.

(*b*) Sort account numbers into ascending order, rearranging balances accordingly.

(*c*) Write out the sorted arrays, showing each balance with its account number.

(*d*) Resort the balance array in descending sequence, and write out the largest 25% of the balances with their associated account numbers.

Details of input and output are shown below:

	FORTRAN	
Item Description	*Name*	*Field Size*
Input record:		
Account number	NØ	xxxx
Account balance	BAL	xxxx$\underset{\wedge}{x}$x
Output record:		
Account number	NØ	xxxx
Account balance	BAL	xxxx.xx

2. Input records contain the following data:

	FORTRAN	
Item Description	*Name*	*Field Size*
Account number	NØ	xxxxx
Account name	NME	20 places, alphanumeric

There are less than 100 records of the type indicated above.

After reading the records and storing their contents, account numbers are to be sorted into ascending sequence. Then, the sorted numbers and related account names are to be written. (Hint: It may be recalled that alphanumeric data can be stored in arrays. Accordingly, account names can be processed in a 2-dimensional matrix.)

3. Write a program to prepare a transaction register and update master records. The master file is maintained as direct-access file 10. It contains 20 formatted records as described below; the associated variable is KBAL.

A formatted contents table is maintained as direct-access file 11. It contains the account number and file location of every record in the master file. Its associated variable is KNØ.

Transaction records are read in random sequence. When a record is read, the location of its master record should be determined. Then, the master record should be updated by adding the amount from the transaction record to the master balance. The updated record should then be returned to the master file and the transaction register written. Record contents appear as follows:

	FORTRAN	
Item Description	*Name*	*Field Size*
Master record:		
Account number	MSTRNØ	xxxx
Master balance	BAL	xxxx.xx
Contents table record:		
Account number	KØNT	xxxx
Record location	LØC	xx
Transaction record:		
Account number	NØTRAN	xxxx
Transaction amount	AMT	xxxₓx
Transaction register:		
Account number	NØTRAN	xxxx
Transaction amount	AMT	xxx.xx
Updated master balance	BAL	xxxx.xx

After all transaction records have been processed, the updated master file should be written out, suitably formatted.

4. A contents table indicating the location of records in a direct-access file is maintained on punched cards. Periodically, the table must be purged of accounts no longer active and new accounts put in the vacant spaces.

Contents table records of 200 or fewer are in the file. At the end of the record set is a transfer record containing 9999 in the NØ field. Purge and addition records follow this transfer record. These contain the data indicated below.

A purge record indicates that the cited item should be removed from the contents table by setting the account number field to zero.

An addition record indicates an addition to the contents table and direct-access file. The first zero location in the account number table should be found. The new account number should be inserted, and the new master record written in the corresponding direct-access file location.

After all purge and addition records have been processed, the master file should be written out. Any purged records (indicated by 0 in the contents table) should be skipped in the write-out.

Record contents are as follows:

	FORTRAN	
Item Description	*Name*	*Field Size*
Contents table records:		
Account number	KNØ	xxxxx
Direct-access file location	LØC	xx
Purge-addition records:		
Account number	NØ	xxxxx
Action indicator*	K	x
Account amount (blank if purge)	AMT	xxxxₓx

<u>FORTRAN</u>

Item Description	*Name*	*Field Size*
Master file records (associated variable KVAR):		
Account number	MSTNØ	xxxxx
Account amount	AMTMST	xxxx.xx

  * 1 = purge
   2 = addition

5. Write a program to update account balances by the following method.

 A set of records contains all account numbers, their related balances, and the totals of all debits and credits made to the account. Records appear as shown below.

 These records and their balances are to be read and stored in four one-dimensional arrays, called NØ, BAL, DEBIT, and CREDIT. There are never more than 200 account balances, and there may be fewer.

 A transfer record containing -1 in the NØ field is placed at the back of the balance records. When this is encountered, it may be assumed that all balance records have been read and their contents stored.

 Transactions records follow the balance records. These are read in random sequence. When a record is read, the account to be posted must be found by scanning the NØ array and finding a matching account number. Absence of a matching number constitutes an error.

 Once a matching account is found, its balance and the total of debits or credits is to be updated. The following scheme is to be followed in updating:

Account Number	*Type of Account*	*Treatment of Debits*	*Treatment of Credits*
1000–1999	Asset	Added	Subtracted
2000–2999	Liability	Subtracted	Added
3000–3999	Net Worth	Subtracted	Added
4000–4999	Revenue	Subtracted	Added
5000–5999	Expense	Added	Subtracted

 Transaction amounts are to be added to the account's sum of either debits or credits and added to or subtracted from the account balance according to the table above. In addition, the totals of all debits and all credits posted is to be maintained and printed when processing is complete.

 After all transactions have been posted, records containing updated account balances are to be written and the program terminated.

 Input and output records appear as follows:

	FORTRAN	
Item Description	*Name*	*Field Size*
Balance record		
(use for both input and output*):		
Blank space	—	x
Account number	NØ	xxxx
Account balance†	BAL	xxxxxx.xx
Debits posted to account†	DEBIT	xxxxxx.xx
Credits posted to account†	CREDIT	xxxxxx.xx
Transaction record:		
Account number	NUM	xxxx
Transaction type‡	K	x
Transaction amount	AMT	xxxxx̬xx
Total of all debits posted	TØTDR	xxxxxx.xx
Total of all credits posted	TØTCR	xxxxxx.xx

* Data fields are separated by five blank spaces.
† Decimal is punched in field.
‡ Debit = 1; credit = 2

6. Write a program to prepare a frequency distribution for as many as 40 questions. Each question may have up to 10 different answers, which are coded as numbers 0 through 9. Responses are punched into cards in adjacent columns, and one card is used for each response.

   Input records are preceded by a parameter record containing K, the number of questions to be tabulated, and L, the number of response records. Its format is I2,I3.

   Input records should be assigned a format of 40I1 and read in as elements of the I array. In this manner, each question's response is stored as an array element.

   Tabulations are to be accumulated in the KTAB array, a 10 X 40 matrix. The matrix positions are used to tabulate the number of times a particular response is given to each question; KTAB(1,1) indicating the number of zero responses to question 1, KTAB(2,1) the number of "1" responses to question 1, KTAB(4,8) the number of "3" responses to question 8, etc.

   When all questionnaires have been tabulated, the KTAB matrix should be listed, with the responses to each question written on a different line.

7. This problem's input consists of two types of records. There is a single record of the first type, and 50 or less of the second type. Card contents are as follows:

	FORTRAN	
Item Description	*Name*	*Field Size*
Card 1: Number of data		
cards following	N	xx
Card 2: Data value	X	xxxx̬

Instructions:

(*a*)   The exact number of X-value cards is indicated by the value punched as N in the first card.

(*b*)   The X cards are to be read, and their values stored as elements of the X array.

(*c*)   As X values are read, the following are to be computed:

> SUMX, the sum of the X values
>
> SUMXS, the sum of the squares of the X values

For the purpose of accumulation, these data fields should be defined as zero before beginning to read in the X values.

(*d*)   The arithmetic mean of the X values is to be computed, as XBAR.

(*e*)   The standard deviation of the X values is to be computed, as STD. Use the formula

$$STD = \sqrt{\frac{\Sigma X^2 - \dfrac{(\Sigma X)^2}{N}}{N - 1}}$$

(*f*)   XBAR and STD are to be printed, using FØRMAT F10.4 for each.

(*g*)   The X array is then to be scanned, and any values falling greater than one standard deviation (+ or −) from the mean are to be printed.

8. This problem's input consists of two types of cards. There is a single card of the first type, and 50 or less of the second type. Card contents are as follows:

Item Description	FORTRAN Name	Field Size
Card 1: Number of data cards following	N	xx
Card 2: Data value	X	xxxx$_\wedge$

Instructions:

(*a*)   The exact number of X-value cards is indicated by the value punched as N in the first card.

(*b*)   The X cards are to be read, and their values stored as elements of the X array.

(*c*)   Elements of the X array are to be sorted into ascending order; thus X(1) should be the smallest value, and X(N) the largest.

(*d*)   The value at the midpoint should be stored in the array as

$X(N+1)$. If the X array contains an even number of elements, this value should be the average of the two mid-values.

(*e*)   The elements of the X array should be written out, one to a record. Use appropriate format.

9.   Two branch stores use the same 10 expense accounts. Each month they submit an expense report to the home office, and this is punched into a card by the format shown below.

   The expense cards are accumulated for six-month periods, the cards of store B being filed behind those of store A. When the sixth expense report is received and punched from both stores, the following processing is undertaken:

(*a*)   The expense records of store A are read and stored in the A array, the months arranged by columns and the expense accounts by rows (in other words, a 10 X 6 array is to be used for each store). Store B records are read and stored in similar fashion in the B array. When this has been done, a new array called C (also a 10 X 6 matrix) is to be created by adding matrices A and B. The C matrix is to be written by rows.

(*b*)   The one-dimensional array, D, is then to be formed by summing the rows of C. This, a 10-element array, will reflect the expenses by account. It is to be printed in a single output record.

(*c*)   Finally, the one-dimensional array, E, is to be formed by summing the columns of C. This, a 6-element array, will reflect the expenses by month. It is to be printed in a single output record, and the program is to stop.

   Input and output records and their contents are as follows:

Item Description	FORTRAN Name	Field Size
Input record:		
Month number (1,2,3,etc.)	MØ	x
Account amounts*	AMT	xxxxxxx
Output record 1 (for writing C and E):		
Account number (1,2,3,etc.)(C only) . . .	NØ	xx
Amount†	SUMAMT	xxxxx.xx
Output record 2 (for writing D):		
Amount‡	SUMEXP	xxxxx.xx

   * A 10-element array.
   † A six-element array.
   ‡ A 10-element array.

10.   The present value (*P*) of an annuity of 1 dollar payable annually for *n* years, beginning a year hence, drawing interest at rate (*r*), with interest compounded annually, is:

$$P = \frac{(1 + r)^n - 1}{r(1 + r)^n}$$

Instructions: Prepare a table showing the present value of an annuity of 1 for periods 1 through 10 at interest rates of 1%, 2%, 3%, 4%, and 5%. The table should show different periods as rows and different rates as columns. Use format xx.xxxx for each output element and xx for the period number.

Hint: Prepare an output record containing I, the period number, and a five-element array for a period's amounts at the stipulated rates. Use an inner loop to compute the five amounts, and an outer loop to control the writing of the 10 lines of output.

11. In cash flow analysis the present investment amount and amounts of returns are sometimes known with acceptable certainty. In these instances, the discount rate equating present investment with future yields may be determined through trial and error, using the formula

$$P = \frac{F}{(1 + r)^n}$$

where

P = present value
F = future value
r = discount rate
n = number of periods

To find the appropriate discount rate, a possible rate is arbitrarily chosen. All future yields are discounted by this rate, and their sum is compared with the actual investment cost. A sum larger than the true cost indicates a discount rate too small, and vice versa. Should a rate too low be chosen first, it will then be increased and the process of computation repeated. Gradually, the discounted sum of future yields will approach the investment cost. It is often impractical to search for the exact discount rate equating yields and cost; instead, the cost is straddled with computed present values above and below it.

Instructions: Write a program for the followings:
1. Read cash amounts from input records, and store them in the 1-dimension array AMT. The first value represents the cost of an investment. Other amounts are cash flow values, by years. There are never more than 25 cash flow amounts. The actual number must be counted while reading and storing.
2. Find the discount rates that compute present values above and below the investment amount. Start trials with a discount rate of 1%, and increase the rate by .1% with each trial.

Input and output records appear as follows:

	FORTRAN	
Item Description	*Name*	*Field Size*
Input record:		
Amount of current investment,		
or future cash flow	AMT	xxxxxxx$_\wedge$
Output record:		
Rate giving larger discounted		
value	R1	.xx
Rate giving smaller discounted		
value	R2	.xx
Value computed using R1	AMT1	xxxxx.xx
Value computed using R2	AMT2	xxxxx.xx

R1 is the rate yielding a present value just larger than the investment cost, and AMT1 is the amount of the present value. R2 is the rate yielding a present value just smaller than the investment cost, and AMT2 is its present value.

12. Write a program to compute a six-month moving average of X for N months. Input and output records appear as follows:

	FORTRAN	
Item Description	*Name*	*Field Size*
Input records:		
Parameter record:		
Number of months	N	xx
Data record:		
Amount of X	X	xxxx$_\wedge$
Output record:		
Amount of moving average	AVG	xxxx.xx

Computations are to be made as follows:

(*a*)   An average is computed as the sum of six X values divided by 6. Then, to compute the next average, the oldest X value is dropped and a new one added. Thus, for N elements will be computed N − 5 averages.

(*b*)   Therefore, the first six X values should be arrayed and summed as they are read. The first average may then be computed and written. The first X value should then be subtracted from the sum of Xs, and the last five values in the array pushed up into the first five positions. A new X may be read, stored in the sixth array position and added to the sum of Xs, and a new average calculated.

(*c*)   The process described in (*b*) should be continued until all data records have been treated.

13. The ABC Company can schedule its weekly production in one of five ways, with each resulting in the production quantities indicated below:

Production Quantity
Units of Inventory Number

		1	2	3	4	5
Production Method	1	100	100	100	100	100
	2	50	50	200	75	125
	3	150	150	75	75	50
	4	75	125	75	125	100
	5	25	25	25	200	200

Four distribution schemes are available for shipping production to the market outlet. The cost per unit of each of these is as follows:

Unit Distribution Costs
Distribution Method

		1	2	3	4
Inventory Item	1	$10	$15	$ 8	$12
	2	10	15	8	12
	3	10	7	9	15
	4	10	12	9	10
	5	10	8	10	5

Instructions: Read and store the Production and Distribution matrices. Elements are recorded by rows. The Production matrix is to be called PRDCT, and its input format is 5F3.0. The Distribution matrix is to be called DIST, and its input format is 4F2.0.

After reading, prepare CØST, a new matrix, by multiplication of the PRDCT and DIST matrices. Write out CØST. Then, find the production-distribution combination producing the lowest cost and write the cost sum for the five products as a single data item.

14. Two main methods are used for assigning cost to inventory when purchases are made at different prices. One is called first-in, first-out, or FIFO. In this, the inventory sold is assigned the oldest recorded costs. Remaining inventory is assigned the newest costs.

The other is called the last-in, first-out, or LIFO, in which the inventory sold is assigned the newest recorded costs. When this method is used, the inventory still on hand is assigned the oldest recorded costs.

As an example of the methods, assume the following:
Inventory on hand and purchased:

Purchase	Number of Units	Cost per Unit
Beginning inventory	1,000	1.00
1	500	1.10
2	500	1.15
3	800	1.20

At the end of the accounting period, 1,300 units remain unsold.
By the FIFO method these would be assigned costs as follows:

$$800 \text{ @ } \$1.20 \ldots\ldots \quad \$960.00$$
$$500 \text{ @ } \quad 1.15 \ldots\ldots \quad 575.00$$
$$\text{Total} \ldots\ldots\ldots \quad \$1,535.00$$

The cost of units sold would be $(1,000 \times 1.00 + 500 \times 1.10)$, or $1,550.

The LIFO method would assign the following costs to unsold inventory:

$$1,000 \text{ @ } \$1.00 \ldots\ldots\ldots \quad \$1,000.00$$
$$300 \text{ @ } \quad 1.10 \ldots\ldots\ldots \quad 330.00$$
$$\text{Total} \ldots\ldots\ldots\ldots \quad \$1,330.00$$

The cost of units sold would be:

$$200 \text{ @ } \$1.10 \ldots\ldots\ldots \quad \$220.00$$
$$500 \text{ @ } \quad 1.15 \ldots\ldots\ldots \quad 575.00$$
$$800 \text{ @ } \quad 1.20 \ldots\ldots\ldots \quad 960.00$$
$$\text{Total} \ldots\ldots\ldots\ldots \quad \$1,755.00$$

Instructions: The X Company uses the FIFO inventory method for some inventory items and the LIFO method for others. Beginning inventory balances and receipts are maintained in records which appear as follows:

	FORTRAN	
Item Description	*Name*	*Field Size*
Item Number	NØ	xxxx
Inventory method indicator*	K	x
Number of units	UNITS	xxxx˄
Cost per unit†	CØST	x.xx

  * FIFO = 1,
   LIFO=2
   Ending-balance record = 3 (see below).
  † Decimal is punched.

The records are grouped by item number, and an inventory item may be represented by more than one input record.

The last record in an item's set does not contain balance or receipt information, but the number of units still on hand. This is prepared by the same format as balance and receipt records and shows the number of units remaining in the UNITS field. The CØST field contains zeros.

Unit quantity and cost data are to be arrayed from the beginning balance and receipt records. Ten-element arrays are large enough to contain any inventory item's data.

When the ending-balance record is read, the cost of units sold and units remaining is to be determined. It must be recalled that the ending inventory may consist of more than one cost group, as in the illustration of the LIFO inventory above. In this event, the ending inventory should be assigned a weighted-average value, determined by dividing the number of units on hand into the sum of the units' costs. When the unit cost of the ending inventory has been determined, it should be written out by the same format used in reading.

9 Subprograms

As pointed out in an earlier chapter, computers can only execute such simple arithmetic operations as addition and subtraction. These abilities are supplemented in FORTRAN by certain "functions," such as that for computing the square root, which are actually subprograms built into the language.

If available functions are not suitable, it is possible for a programmer to create his own. These may be produced by a single statement in the main program, or longer subprograms can be written separately and tied to the main program by a calling routine.

The first is called a *Statement Function*. It is written as a single command in the main program.

Subprograms, written outside the main program, are divided into two types. The first, called a *Function Subprogram,* always returns at least one value to the main program. The second, called a *Subroutine Subprogram,* may return a value, although this is not necessary. It can perform data input, manipulation, and output before returning computer control to the main program.

STATEMENT FUNCTION

A statement function is so named because it must be created by a single, assignment-like command. While it can take the place of either arithmetic or logical manipulation, it is customarily used to substitute a function name for an arithmetic computation that occurs frequently in a program.

Calling the Function

A statement function is "called," or used, by citing its name and argument or arguments in an arithmetic or logical expression, as appropriate. This is the same means used to call a basic FORTRAN function.

For example, assume that a function named PAY has been created previously in a payroll processing program and that it has two arguments, RATE and HØURS. The PAY function is to compute gross pay.

In the computation of Social Security tax, this function might be called by an arithmetic statement such as the following:

$$SSTAX = PAY(RATE,HØURS)*.054$$

This would call the arithmetic statement function named PAY, which must have been previously defined in the program by the procedure described below. The values assigned the variables RATE and HØURS would be transmitted to the function and used according to its dictates. The result, returned to the calling command and multiplied by .054, would be stored at the location SSTAX.

The function's arguments must be inclosed in parentheses. If more than one argument is cited, commas must be used as separators.

Defining the Function

The statement function must be "defined," or created before it may be called and used. This is done in a single statement similar to the standard arithmetic or logical assignment command. It appears as follows:

Function name (argument list) = Expression

Function Name. The function name must be the same as that used later in the calling instruction. For example, if a function is to be known as PAY, this will be written in the defining statement as "function name."

The function name must meet the same requirements as a data name. It must consist of from one to six letters or numbers (the first character must be alphabetic). The mode of the function is determined by the name's first character, unless overridden by a type statement.

Argument List.   The set of variables appearing in parentheses after the function name is called the "argument list." These are the variables to be used in the statement expression. The list must contain only non-subscripted variables. The variables cited must agree in *number, order,* and *mode* with the arguments in the calling command, although they need not be assigned the same names. As in the calling command, commas are to separate multiple arguments.

For example, it may be recalled that in calling **PAY** above, the following citation was used: **PAY(RATE,HØURS)**. Therefore, in defining the arithmetic statement function, two floating-point variables must be cited as arguments. These might appear as follows:

$$PAY(A,B)$$

Expression.   In defining the statement function, "expression" may be any set of operands and operators meeting the requirements of an expression. It will include as operands the variables cited in the function argument; otherwise, they would not have been included in the argument list. The expression may also contain variables not in the argument list if they have been defined in the main program prior to the statement function's use.

To illustrate the function's creation, assume that gross pay is computed by the multiplication of rate and hours. The arithmetic statement function **PAY** might therefore appear as follows:

$$PAY(A,B) = A * B$$

Of course, the data names A and B are not used in the calling statement, which was written as

$$SSTAX = PAY(RATE,HØURS)*.054$$

However, when the program is executed, RATE is substituted in the function for A, and HØURS for B, the association being indicated by the order in which the arguments are written. Values of RATE and HØURS are transmitted to the statement function, computation is made, and the result returned as **PAY**.

Example of Statement Function

As a further example of this function, assume that a firm pays its salesmen a bonus as well as a salary, called SAL. The bonus is 15% of sales, excluding a 10% excise tax. Sales, including tax, are reported as SALES.

A statement function might be constructed as follows:

$$B\emptyset NUS(X) = (X/1.1)*.15$$

Then when gross pay is to be computed, the following statement could be used:

$$PAY = SAL + B\emptyset NUS(SALES)$$

When this command is executed, SALES replaces the variable X in the function definition and the bonus amount is calculated.

Significance of the Statement Function

The statement function permits the programmer to write a computation once and assign it a name. Then, wherever this computation appears in the program, it may be represented by name, even though the variables may change from one use to another. The statement function, while not essential, is a convenient way to avoid repetitious coding.

SUBPROGRAMS

The statement function is always written as a single command in the main program. It can compute only one value.

Functions are sometimes required that use several statements in calculation, or produce many results, or which do not return a value to the main program at all. These are all handled in "subprograms"— statement sets that look almost like regular programs, but which are in reality under the control of another FORTRAN program. Two subprogram types are available; the *function* and the *subroutine*.

FUNCTION SUBPROGRAM

This eliminates one restriction inherent in the statement function— it can consist of any number of FORTRAN instructions. It can also return more than one value to the main program, although it normally is used to return only one.

The function subprogram is written and compiled as a separate program. Its linkage to the main program is described below.

Calling the Function Subprogram

Statement functions and function subprograms are used in exactly the same way. The function is cited by name and argument in an arithmetic or logical expression. This transmits the argument values to the subprogram, where they are manipulated according to the commands of that routine. The results of manipulation are returned to the calling statement.

Arguments in the Calling Statement.   The real arguments in the assignment statement calling the function subprogram may be of the following nature:

1.   An alphanumeric literal.
2.   Arithmetic or logical constant.
3.   Any type of variable or array element.
4.   Any type of array name.
5.   Any type of arithmetic or logical expression.
6.   The name of a FUNCTIØN or SUBRØUTINE subprogram.

Structure of the Function Subprogram

The function subprogram is a separate program, its unique nature being indicated by its first statement. This must be unnumbered and must be of the following nature:

Type FUNCTIØN function-name(argument list)

Type.   If the first letter of the function name appropriately indicates the function's mode, this may be omitted. Otherwise, the type specification DØUBLE PRECISIØN, LØGICAL, INTEGER, or REAL should be given here. For example, if a function named UNIT is to return an integer value to the main program, its mode would be specified as

INTEGER FUNCTIØN UNIT(A,B,C)

Function-name.   This provides the link between the function subprogram and the main program. It is formed by standard data-name rules. The first character sets the mode of the function, unless the "type" prefix is used.

Linkage is actually established by the citation of the function name in the main and subprograms. For example, if a subprogram is named UNITS, its main program connection would appear as follows:

Main Program	Subprogram
X = A + UNITS(I,J,K)	FUNCTIØN UNITS(L,M,N)
	. . .
	UNITS = L+M−N
	RETURN
	END

Argument List. The argument list is a set of dummy variables. They are used to establish the logic of the subprogram. When the main program is executed and calls the subprogram, actual values are passed from it to the subprogram through the argument list and used in data manipulation. In the example above, the values assigned I, J, and K in the main program will be passed to the subprogram and used whenever L, M, and N are cited.

Dummy arguments must agree in *number, order,* and *mode* with actual arguments in the calling statement. They can cite data elements or arrays.

An array name in the dummy argument list is signalled by the presence of a DIMENSIØN or explicit type statement in the subprogram. Of course, this must coincide with the citation of an array name in the argument list of the calling statement in the main program.

Subprogram array dimensions must be equal to or smaller than those of the main program, and the array shapes must agree. Actual array dimensions need not be specified in the subprogram, although they may be if desired.

Single-dimension arrays are frequently dimensioned with a single element in the subprogram. This establishes the data name as that of an array, rather than an element, and it sets necessary linkage with the main program. Of course, proper array dimensions will be given in the main program.

Multi-dimensional arrays can be assigned specific dimensions in the subprogram, or their size may be given in the dimension or type statements by variables representing values that must be supplied from the main program. They must not exceed the size of the array given in the main program.

For example, consider the following:

1. Main program	Subprogram
DIMENSIØN X(25)	FUNCTIØN CALC(Y)
A = CALC(X)	DIMENSIØN X(1)

Actual dimensions are supplied in the main program. In the subprogram, the dimension statement with its single element merely establishes X as an array, rather than a data element.

<table>
<tr><td>2.   *Main program*</td><td>*Subprogram*</td></tr>
<tr><td>DIMENSIØN X(5,4)</td><td>FUNCTIØN CALC(Y)</td></tr>
<tr><td>A = CALC(X)</td><td>DIMENSIØN Y(5,4)</td></tr>
</table>

In this instance, array dimensions are explicitly stated in both the main and subprograms.

<table>
<tr><td>3.   *Main program*</td><td>*Subprogram*</td></tr>
<tr><td>DIMENSIØN X(5,4)</td><td>FUNCTIØN CALC(Y,I,J)</td></tr>
<tr><td>A = CALC(X,5,4)</td><td>DIMENSIØN Y(I,J)</td></tr>
</table>

Array dimensions are explicitly given in the main program, and the dimensions passed to the subprogram as integer constants. In the subprogram, array dimensions are given as variables that are assigned values from the main program. This permits an array processing routine to be used with arrays of different dimensions.

<table>
<tr><td>4.   *Main program*</td><td>*Subprogram*</td></tr>
<tr><td>DIMENSIØN X(5,4)</td><td>FUNCTION CALC(Y,K,L)</td></tr>
<tr><td>. . .</td><td>DIMENSIØN Y(K,L)</td></tr>
<tr><td>I = 3</td><td></td></tr>
<tr><td>. . .</td><td></td></tr>
<tr><td>J = 2</td><td></td></tr>
<tr><td>A = CALC(X,I,J)</td><td></td></tr>
</table>

This is very similar to example 3, except that array dimensions are passed to the subprogram as variables that have been assigned values, rather than as constants. In both 3 and 4, subprogram array dimensions are received from the main program. This is called "object-time dimensioning," and permits subprograms to be used on different-sized arrays.

The Subprogram.   The function subprogram can contain any set of commands and be of any length. Eventually, it must assign a value to a variable given the name of the function, for this stores the subprogram's results in a computer location accessible to the main program. For example, if a function subprogram is named in the following manner:

$$\text{FUNCTIØN   CØMP(A,B)}$$

the program must contain an arithmetic statement defining CØMP, such as

$$\text{CØMP} = \text{A+B}$$

After the "function name" variable has been defined, the function subprogram may be ended whenever logically appropriate. This is accomplished by a statement of the following nature:

RETURN

This need not appear immediately following the statement defining "function name," although it may. There may be more than one RETURN in a function subprogram.

The subprogram is terminated by an END command.

Examples of Function Subprograms

The following examples showing function subprograms and their related main programs are quite short, and in each the function could have easily been coded as a part of the main routine. Brief examples are used because they stress the function's nature and its linkage with the main program without numerous extraneous commands. In practice, the main programs and functions may be very long.

1. Assume that sales records of the following nature are to be processed and the indicated output prepared:

		FORTRAN	
Item Description		*Name*	*Field Size*
Input record:			
Customer number		K	xxxx
Number of units sold		UNITS	xxxxₐ
Unit sales price		SPR	xxxₐ
Freight charge		FRT	xxxxxₐ
Output record:			
Customer number		K	xxxx
Sales price		PRICE	xxxxx.xx
Discount		DISC	xxx.xx
Net price		PRNET	xxxxx.xx

Quantity sales discounts are granted as follows:

Sales Amount	*Discount Rate*
0 –$ 500.00	0%
$ 500.01–$1,000.00	2
$1,000.01–$2,500.00	3
Over $2,500.00	5

The amount of discount is to be computed in an external function subprogram called DCØMP.

The main program and subprogram are shown in Figures 9–1 and

FIGURE 9–1

Main Program

C	MAIN PROGRAM
1	FORMAT(I4,F4.0,F3.2,F5.2)
2	FORMAT(1X,I5,5X,F9.2,5X,F8.2,5X,F9.2)
10	READ(5,1,END=20)K,UNITS,SPR,FRT
	PRICE = UNITS * SPR
	PRNET = PRICE - DCOMP(PRICE) + FRT
	DISC = DCOMP(PRICE)
	WRITE(6,2)K,PRICE,DISC,PRNET
	GO TO 10
20	STOP
	END

FIGURE 9–2

Function Subprogram

	FUNCTION DCOMP(X)
	IF(X .GT. 500.)GO TO 1
	DCOMP = 0
	RETURN
1	IF(X .GT. 1000.) GO TO 2
	DCOMP = .02 * X
	RETURN
2	IF(X .GT. 2500.) GO TO 3
	DCOMP = .03 * X
	RETURN
3	DCOMP = .05 * X
	RETURN
	END

9–2. The main program may be seen to call DCØMP twice: once to calculate PRNET and again to define DISC for output. Of course, this program could have been designed to call DCØMP only once, but this illustrates the fact that a subprogram may be called as many times as necessary.

In the subprogram, DCØMP is computed in several different commands, the branch to be executed depending on the sales amount. After each computation appears the RETURN command, returning control to the main program. As mentioned above, a subprogram may have as many returns as are logically appropriate.

The argument in the calling function is designated as PRICE, consistent with the data names of the main program. In the subprogram, however, the function argument (really a dummy variable) is simply referred to as X. This is a typical use of data names. It should be recalled that the argument names used in the subprogram and in the calling command must agree in *number, order,* and *mode,* but they do not have to be the same. When the function subprogram is executed, the value PRICE is transmitted from the main program and used each time X is cited.

2.   Assume that a matrix, 6×8 or smaller, is to be read in the main program. It is preceded by a parameter card, in which I indicates the number of rows, and J the number of columns, in the following array.

A subprogram called BIGEL is to be written to find the largest element in the array. The main program is then to print the value of the element.

Main and subprograms may be seen in Figures 9–3 and 9–4. Again, function argument of the calling command and the FUNCTIØN statement agree in order, mode, and number, although they do not have the same names. The size of the array, called X in the main program and A in the subprogram, is assigned the same dimension in both.

Significance of the Function Subprogram

The function subprogram offers one distinct advantage over the assignment statement function—it may contain more than one command. In fact, it may be of any desired length and consist of any instructions in the language.

Many programs require the same complex computation at several different points. This function allows the routine to be written only once. Then, its entire instruction set can be brought into the main program merely by citing its name and argument list, even though the variables to be manipulated are different in each instance. This can greatly reduce the length of the main program.

FIGURE 9–3
Main Program

```
      DIMENSION X(6,8)
1     FORMAT(8F5.0)
2     FORMAT(2I2)
3     FORMAT(F8.0)
      READ(5,2)I,J
      READ(5,1)((X(K,L),L=1,J),K=1,I)
      BIG = BIGEL(X,I,J)
      WRITE(6,3)BIG
      STOP
      END
```

FIGURE 9–4
Subprogram

```
      FUNCTION BIGEL(A,I1,I2)
      DIMENSION A(6,8)
      BIGEL = A(1,1)
      DO5 K = 1,I1
      DO5 L = 1,I2
      IF(A(K,L)-BIGEL)5,5,2
2     BIGEL = A(K,L)
5     CONTINUE
      RETURN
      END
```

SUBROUTINE SUBPROGRAMS

Subroutine subprograms are very similar to function subprograms. They are written externally to the main program, and linked by a calling statement. They are captioned by a unique statement indicating their beginning, and provide for return to the main program by one or more RETURN commands.

However, they provide much more flexibility than do their function counterparts. Linkage between main and subprograms is set through a unique command, rather than in an assignment statement. The subroutine may return one or more than one value to the main program, or it may not return any at all.

Calling Subroutines

Subroutine subprograms are called into the main program by a unique command of the nature

CALL subroutine-name(argument list)

Subroutine-name. This is assigned by the programmer. It can be any valid FORTRAN name. The first character in the name is not limited to any particular letter because it does not indicate the mode of subroutine results.

Argument list. This is a list of constants or variables. The items serve as communications channels between the main and subprograms. They may transmit data to the subroutine or return values to the main program. Items in the list may be of the following nature:

1. An alphanumeric literal.
2. Arithmetic or logical constant.
3. Any type of variable or array element.
4. Any type of array name.
5. Any type of arithmetic or logical expression.
6. The name of a FUNCTIØN or SUBRØUTINE subprogram.

Identifying Subroutines

Programs to serve as subroutines are identified by their first statement, which is of the following form:

SUBRØUTINE subroutine-name(argument list)

Subroutine-name. This must be the same as the name used in the calling statement in the main program.

Argument List. This is used to transmit data-items to and from the main program, otherwise arguments are the same as those described in the FUNCTIØN subprogram on page 283 above.

Examples of Subroutines

The following simple examples display the subroutine's nature more vividly than may be done by simple description. From these may be determined the relationship between the subprogram and main program.

1. As a simple example of subroutines and their relation to the main program, assume that two values, A and B, are to be read from an input record. They are to be added in a subroutine where A is also to be squared. The sum and A^2 are to be printed in the main program.

The main program and subroutine appear as follows:

	Main Program		Subroutine
1	FØRMAT(2F5.0)		SUBRØUTINE SUMSUB(X,Y,TØT)
2	FØRMAT(2F8.0)		TØT = X + Y
	READ(5,1)A,B		X = X∗X
	CALL SUMSUB(A,B,SUM)		RETURN
	WRITE(6,2)A,SUM		END
	STØP		
	END		

Note that the subroutine arguments are used in a more versatile manner than with function subprograms. They serve in two ways: They may *transmit data to the subprogram* or they may *receive results from the subprogram*. A given variable may be used in either or both of these ways.

In the above program, for example, A is transmitted to the subroutine as a data value and returned as A^2, a result. B is transmitted to the subroutine but not returned.

SUM represents a value generated by the subroutine that is returned to the main program. Undefined earlier in the main program, it receives its definition in the subroutine argument.

2. Two single-dimension arrays, one of account numbers and the other account balances, are to be stored in the computer's memory. Each input record contains an account number and its related balance; the set of input records is preceded by a parameter card containing N, the number of accounts. There are never more than 1,000 accounts.

After the accounts have been stored in memory, a subroutine is to be used to scan them and print out the number and balance of any accounts having a balance of $1,000 or more.

The main program and subroutine may be seen in Figures 9–5 and 9–6. This example illustrates two new points. First, all scanning and

FIGURE 9–5

Main Program

```
      DIMENSIØN NØ(1000),BAL(1000)
   1  FØRMAT(I4)
   2  FØRMAT(I4,F7.2)
      READ(5,1)N
      READ(5,2)(NØ(I),BAL(I),I=1,N)
      CALL SELECT(NØ,BAL,N)
      STØP
      END
```

FIGURE 9–6

Subprogram

```
      SUBRØUTINE SELECT(N,AMT,I)
      DIMENSIØN N(1),AMT(1)
   1  FØRMAT(1X,I5,5X,F9.2)
      DØ 10 K = 1,I
      IF(AMT(K) .LE. 1000.) GØ TØ 10
      WRITE(6,1)N(K),AMT(K)
  10  CØNTINUE
      RETURN
      END
```

printing is conducted in the subroutine; after its execution, the project is completed. Second, the array dimensions in the subroutine are quite different from those of the main program. Because N and BAL are one-dimensional arrays in the main program, the dimension statement in the subroutine serves merely to identify array names. Array sizes in the subprogram are immaterial.

3. Data analysis frequently requires that data be sorted into a certain sequence for reporting. The same data may be sorted by different criteria, permitting the same basic set of facts to be viewed in different ways.

For example, consider the following set of input records:

	FORTRAN	
Item Description	Name	Field Size
Item code number	UNIT	xxxx$_\wedge$
Transaction date	DATE	xxxxxx$_\wedge$
Salesman's number	SMNØ	xxxx$_\wedge$
Sales amount	AMT	xxx$_\wedge$xx

Assume that records of the above type never number more than 1,000. They are to be read, and their components stored in data arrays. Then, certain data-sorts are to be made. First, item code numbers are to be sorted into descending order and the code and its related sales amount written. Next, a sort of salesman number is to be made in descending sequence, and salesman number and related sales amount written. Finally, sales amounts are to be rearranged in ascending sequence and written with the date of sale.

Without the availability of subroutines, the above would require that three sort programs be written. However, it is quite easy to prepare a single sort subroutine, pass the data array to be sorted to it, and execute the sort and data output as needed.

The required main and subprograms are shown in Figures 9–7 and

FIGURE 9–7
Main Program

IBM　　　　　　　　　　　　　　　　　　　　　　FORTRAN CODING FORM

| PROGRAM | SØRT WITH SUBRØUTINE | PUNCHING INSTRUCTIONS |
| PROGRAMMER | MC CAMERØN　　　　　　　DATE | |

```
C        MAIN PROGRAM
         DIMENSIØN X(1000,4)
   1     FØRMAT(F4.0,F6.0,F4.0,F5.2)
         I = 1
   5     READ(5,1,END=10)(X(I,J),J=1,4)
         I = I + 1
         GØ TØ 5
  10     I = I - 1
         CALL SØRT(X,I,4,1,4,1)
         CALL SØRT(X,I,4,3,4,1)
         CALL SØRT(X,I,4,4,1,2)
         STØP
         END
```

FIGURE 9–8
Subprogram

IBM   FORTRAN CODING FORM

PROGRAM **SØRT WITH SUBRØUTINE**   PUNCHING INSTRUCTIONS

PROGRAMMER **MC CAMERØN**   DATE

```
C        SØRT  SUBPRØGRAM
         SUBRØUTINE  SØRT(X,I,J,K,K1,N)
         DIMENSIØN  X(100,4)
         I1 = I - 1
         DØ 10 L =1,I1
         DØ 10 M =L,I
         IF(N.EQ.2)GØ TØ 5
         IF(X(L,K).GE.X(M,K))GØ TØ 10
    4    DØ 100 M1 =1,4
         TEMP = X(L,M1)
         X(L,M1) = X(M,M1)
  100    X(M,M1) = TEMP
         GØ TØ 10
    5    IF(X(L,K).GT.X(M,K))GØ TØ 4
   10    CØNTINUE
         WRITE(6,2)(X(L,K),X(L,K1),L=1,I)
    2    FØRMAT(2(10X,F9.2))
         RETURN
         END
```

9–8. Data are read and arrayed in the main program. Although the data items have different meanings—item number, data, salesman's number, and amount—they are stored in a single two-dimensional array for processing convenience. Each record occupies a different row, and the column entries contain related data elements.

The array, its dimensions, an indication of the column to be sorted, the column to be written out with the sorted data, and an indicator calling for either an ascending or descending sort must be transmitted to the subprogram. This transmission differs according to the columns to be manipulated and sort type. The first subprogram reference, designating a descending-order sort by item code, is contained in the main program as

CALL SØRT(X,I,4,1,4,1)

In this, X transmits the array to the subprogram, and I and 4 its dimensions. The column to be sorted is indicated as 1, the related column to be written as 4, and the final 1 in the calling statement designates a descending-order sort.

The subroutine, shown in Figure 9–8, is related to the main program through its initial statement, which is

SUBRØUTINE SØRT(X,I,J,K,K1,N)

Note that all the data indices are variables. They accept data, either constant or variable, from the main program. Control data from the main program designate the type of sort to be conducted and data to be written in output. Because output is controlled by the subroutine, no data is returned to the main program.

The SØRT subroutine is not limited in use to the program in Figure 9–7. It can be used in any program that requires application of its general features. In practice, sophisticated routines of this type are usually maintained in the computer's repertoire, ready to be called into any program.

4.   Simulation programs may also use subroutines to advantage. These simulations are programs designed to make the computer serve as a model of some real-world situation. They are unlike other computer applications in that they may simulate a situation affected by the passage of time and permit the introduction of uncertainty.

To illustrate the simulation process, assume that a program is to be written that simulates the effect of flipping a coin 50 times. The probability of the coin's landing heads or tails is the same.

To simulate the process of coin flipping and the concomitant 50–50 odds, a number will be chosen at random from the interval .0000–.9999. A value less than .5 will be taken to represent heads, while a number .5 or greater will represent tails. A value chosen in this way is known as a *random number*.

A computer subroutine will be used to generate the random number. This might be done by several methods. One, called the "power residue method," involves large numbers and retention of the least significant digits. The details of the process differ slightly for binary and decimal computers. The general nature of the computation is set out below.

(*a*) *Random number computation using a binary computer.*   The computer is assumed to have a word size of b-bits. The arithmetic assumes the binary point to be at the extreme right of the word. Thus, all of the numbers involved are integers—including the random numbers generated. Once the result is available, however, the binary point should be moved to the extreme left in order to obtain random numbers distributed over the interval .0000–.9999. The following procedures will produce 2^{b-2} terms before repeating.

1. Choose for a starting value any odd interger u_0.
2. Choose as a constant multiplier an integer x of the form

$$x = 8t \pm 3$$

where t is any integer. (A value of x close to $2^{b/2}$ is a good choice.)
3. Compute xu_0. This produces a product $2b$-bits long; the high-order b-bits are discarded and the b low-order bits are the value u_1.
4. Each successive random number u_{n+1} is obtained from the low-order bits of the product xu_n.

(*b*) *Random number computation using a decimal computer.* The same process is followed, except that different values are chosen for u and x. More specifically:

1. Choose for a starting value any integer u_0 not divisible by 2 or 5.
2. Choose as a constant multiplier an integer x of the form

$$x = 200t \pm r$$

where t is any integer and r is any of the values 3, 11, 13, 19, 21, 27, 29, 37, 53, 59, 61, 67, 69, 77, 83, or 91. (A value of x close to $10^{d/2}$ is a good choice.)
3. Compute xu_0. This produces a product $2d$-digits long; the high-order d-digits are discarded, and the d low-order digits are the value of u_1.
4. Each successive random number xu_{n+1} is obtained from the low-order digits of the product xu_n.

The above description of random number generation is necessarily brief and may be supplemented by study of a statistics text.[1]

The main program and subprogram for coding of a random number generator may be seen in Figures 9–9 and 9–10. The integer I is transmitted to subroutine RAND from the main program. This is multiplied by a constant, chosen to be (200*936783+13), and the product is floated and converted to a decimal fraction. This is the random number.

The main program, shown in Figure 9–9, supplies the initial value of

---

[1] As, for example, George S. Fishman, *Concepts and Methods of Discrete Event Digital Simulation* (New York: John Wiley & Sons, Inc., 1973).

FIGURE 9–9

Main Program

COMM.	STATEMENT NUMBER	CONT.	FORTRAN STATEMENT
	1		`FORMAT(6H HEADS)`
	2		`FORMAT(6H TAILS)`
			`IX = 131072`
			`DO 10 I=1,50`
			`CALL RAND(IX,X)`
			`IF(X .GE. .5) GO TO 7`
			`WRITE(6,1)`
			`GO TO 10`
	7		`WRITE(6,2)`
	10		`IX = X * .1E6`
			`STOP`
			`END`

FIGURE 9–10

Subprogram

COMM.	STATEMENT NUMBER	CONT.	FORTRAN STATEMENT
			`SUBROUTINE RAND(I,X)`
			`I = I*(200*936783+13)`
			`L = I/10000`
			`XL = IABS(L)`
			`X = XL/100000`
			`IF(X .LT. 1.)GO TO 15`
			`KZ = X`
			`AK = KZ`
			`X = X-AK`
	15		`RETURN`
			`END`

1 (called IX in the main program). This is transmitted to RAND, and the random number, X, received from the subroutine. This is tested, and if it is less than .5, the message HEADS is printed. A larger random number causes the computer to print TAILS; thus the coin-flipping simulation is complete.

Before returning for the next iteration, the X is converted to an integer. When transmitted to RAND in the next iteration, it provides the basis for computing the next random number.

Simulation of random occurrences is one of the most sophisticated accomplishments of the electronic computer. It may be used in constructing a model of a very complex, unpredictable, activity. If events do not occur in a purely random fashion, this may also be simulated. The type of model building depicted in the very simple situation above promises to be one of the computer's greatest contributions to business planning.

Returns to Different Main Program Locations.   Ordinarily, program control returns from the RETURN statement of a subroutine to the main program statement following the CALL instruction. However, in IBM 360–370 FORTRAN and WATFIV provision is made for return to other main program points as well.

Alternative return points are specified in the calling command by inclusion of an argument &i, where "i" represents a valid statement number. This specification is matched in the dummy argument set of the SUBRØUTINE statement by an asterisk ($*$).

For example, consider the following:

	Main Program		*Subprogram*
	CALL SUB(A,B,&10,&20)		SUBRØUTINE SUB(A,B,*,*)
	X = A −B		IF(A.GT.B)GØ TØ 15
	. . .		IF(A.EQ.B)GØ TØ 25
10	X = A + B		RETURN
	. . .	15	RETURN 1
20	X = A * B	25	RETURN 2
			END

The main program transmits variables A and B to the subroutine, and also provides for two return points alternative to the normal. The subroutine accepts the variables, and substitutes asterisks for the return statement numbers.

Based on tests of the relative values of A and B, the subroutine returns in the normal manner or to one of the alternatives. RETURN 1 signifies a return to the first designated alternative, statement 10. RETURN 2 designates a return to statement 20.

Alternative returns are specified by the RETURN i command, where "i" represents an unsigned nonzero integer constant specifying one of the statement numbers in the argument list. The number written as "i" must not exceed the number of optional statement numbers provided in the list.

Using Subroutines

External subroutines are the most sophisticated form of program subsection. They may consist of any set of FORTRAN statements. Unlike the function subprogram, they may return more than one result to the main program; on the other hand, they are not required to return any result at all.

Subroutines are written and compiled apart from their main program. This permits work segmentation and avoids the recompilation of a long program in the event of an error in one of its parts. It also permits a repetitious program segment to be written once, then called wherever it is needed.

ALTERNATIVE SUBPROGRAM ENTRY POINTS

As noted above, function and subroutine subprograms are linked to the main program by a calling command. In the function subprogram, this is normally in the form of the subprogram name's citation in an assignment statement. Subroutines are normally called by citation of their name in a CALL command.

When called in the manner above, execution of the subprogram normally begins with the statement following the FUNCTIØN or SUBRØUTINE initialization command.

However, IBM 360–370 FORTRAN and WATFIV provide for the designation of alternative subprogram entry points. These points are designated in the subprogram by the following command:

ENTRY name (argument list)

"Name" is the name assigned the entry point. It must be constructed in accordance with rules pertaining to function and subroutine names. "Argument list" is a set of dummy arguments, as in FUNCTIØN and SUBRØUTINE initialization statements.

Function and subroutine subprograms are entered at alternative entry points by substitution of the entry name for subprogram name in an assignment statement (for function subprograms) or CALL command. The following examples illustrate the use of multiple entry points:

1. Multiple Entry into a FUNCTIØN Subprogram. Assume the following:

Main Program	Subprogram
DATA A,B,C,D/5.,3.,2.,4./	FUNCTIØN CØMP1(A,B,C)
Y = CØMP1(A,B,C)*D	ENTRY CØMP2 (C)
Z̶ = CØMP2(Y)/D	CØMP1 = (A−B)*C
. . .	RETURN
	END

The function subprogram is entered twice, at two different points. First, values of A, B, and C are transmitted to the subprogram and CØMP1 is computed as 4. This value is returned to the main program, multiplied by D, and Y computed as 16.

The subprogram is entered again, at entry point CØMP2, and the value of Y transmitted to be used in computation. In the subprogram it is received as C; therefore CØMP1 is calculated to be 32, and Z̶ is 8.

This illustrates several points. First, variables defined in the subprogram can be used by subsequent executions when the subprogram is entered at a lower point. In this instance, the values of A and B were available in the second computation, even though they were not transmitted to the subprogram in the CØMP2 argument list.

Second, while the function computations must agree in mode if the same name is to be cited, items in the argument list do not have to agree in number, order, or mode in the FUNCTIØN and ENTRY statements. In the illustration above, the first argument list included A, B, and C, while the second contained C only.

Finally, calculation of the variable defined as "function-name" returns the appropriate value to "entry-name" as well, provided they are of the same mode. For example, the subprogram above computes only a value for CØMP1. However, this computation is used and returns a value for CØMP2 when that point is cited as entry to the subprogram.

2. Multiple Entry into a SUBRØUTINE Subprogram. Assume the following:

Main Program	Subprogram
READ(5,1)A,B,C	SUBRØUTINE SUB1(A,B,C)
CALL SUB1(A,B,C)	RETURN
10 READ(5,2,END=50)X	ENTRY SUB2(X,Y)
CALL SUB2(X,Y)	Y = (A+B)/(X−C)
WRITE(6,3)Y	RETURN
GØ TØ 10	END
50 STØP	
END	

Values A, B, and C are read from an input record, and transmitted to the subroutine once. Then, for multiple input records, X is read, transmitted to the subroutine, and used in computation with A, B, and C from the first record. Y is returned to the main program and written. This is the same multiple-entry structure used by the FUNCTIØN subroutine.

SPECIFICATION STATEMENTS

Specification statements provide the computer with information about the nature of data and the proper treatment to be accorded. These statements specify the special treatment to be given and the names of the data elements to be so considered. They must precede the first appearance of the data name in any other command.

Several specification statements have already been introduced. The INTEGER and REAL type statements, altering the mode of data names, were introduced in Chapter 2. In the same chapter the LØGICAL type statement was described as endowing named variables with logical characteristics, and the DØUBLE PRECISIØN statement as assigning extra significant positions to real variables. The nature and use of the DIMENSIØN and DATA statements was also discussed. Each of these is a specification statement.

Two other specification statements are found in fairly complex FORTRAN programs. They are quite similar. One, the EQUIVALENCE statement, causes more than one data name contained in a program to be assigned to the same computer storage location. The other, the CØMMØN statement, causes data names of main and subprograms to be assigned the same storage location. The nature of each is discussed below.

The EQUIVALANCE Statement

This instruction is of the general nature

$$\text{EQUIVALENCE}(a_1, a_2, \ldots, a_n), (b_1, b_2, \ldots, b_n), \ldots$$

where a and b are sets of variable names. Unlike those of the CØMMØN statement below, all the named variables must be in the same main or subprogram as the specification.

The statement specifies that all variable names enclosed in parentheses are to occupy the same computer memory location. Thus, if the statement EQUIVALENCE (A,B,C), (X,Y) were given, the variables A, B, and C will occupy the same storage positions, as will X and Y. Any number of variable sets may be specified after the command name by enclosure in parentheses; and any number of data names may be included in each set.

This statement can use usefully employed in two ways. It can save memory space, and it can make more than one data name refer to the same value.

Some computer programs are so long that they threaten to exhaust the computer's memory capacity. Assuming that two or more variables are never given values at the same time, the EQUIVALENCE may be used to assign them the same storage location.

For example, assume that in a very long program, the variable K is used only near the beginning, then some variable A is used, then some variable X4 is used. These will ordinarily occupy three different memory locations; however, inasmuch as they are never used in the program at the same time, they are never in the computer's memory at once. Therefore, two storage locations could be saved by making the variables equivalent to one another.

As a second use of the specification, two or more data names may be made to refer to the same data element. For example, assume that by mistake, the data names STAX and SALET are both used in a program to refer to sales tax. Of course, it would be possible to go through the program and change one of the data names wherever it appears. In a long program, it might be simpler to make the two reference the same item by inclusion of the command EQUIVALENCE (STAX, SALET).

Coding Requirements. The EQUIVALENCE instruction cannot have a statement number. The specification name must be followed by one or more sets of data names enclosed in parentheses. Data names in sets must be separated by commas, and sets must also be separated by commas. Any number of sets and any number of data names within sets may be specified.

The specification may appear anywhere in the program, prior to the END statement.

Illustration. The nature of the EQUIVALENCE is indicated by the following brief example:

$$\text{EQUIVALENCE (A,X)}$$
$$\text{A} = 5.$$
$$\text{Z} = \text{X} + 2.$$
$$\text{END}$$

Z would be computed as 7. While X has not been defined as such, it is specified as occupying the same memory location as A. Therefore, when the arithmetic statement is executed, the value, 5., is extracted from memory and used as X.

The CØMMØN Statement

Arguments enclosed in parentheses were used to establish data paths between main and external subprograms in the discussion above. This is the standard means of transmitting data to the subprogram and, with subroutines, of returning values to the main program.

Another data transmission channel is also available. This is provided by the CØMMØN statement. Data declared as common by the inclusion of this statement in main and subprograms is available to both.

Two types of common data specification are available, blank and labeled. They can be mixed in a single CØMMØN statement if necessary.

Blank CØMMØN.   Data fields are specified as blank common by the following statement:

$$\text{CØMMØN } s_1, s_2, s_3, \ldots, s_n$$

where "*s*" represents a data name. The instruction is written in both the main and any required subprograms. Data items in the main and subprogram must be of the same type, although they need not have the same name.

For example, consider the following commands:

> Main program: CØMMØN A,B,C,I,J
> Subprogram: CØMMØN X,Y,Z,L,M

When the main and subprograms are compiled, A and X will be assigned the same storage location, and any value written there will be available as A in the main program, and also in the subprogram as X. Other common data names set out in the above example are B and Y, C and Z, I and L, and J and M.

Fields designated as blank common are common according to their location in the specification list throughout the main program and all subprograms where the statement is used. Where this is not intended the labeled common statement, described below, is used.

Labeled CØMMØN.   Specification sets in this version are divided into named groups called blocks; only those variables appearing in the block are common.

The instruction is of the general form

$$\text{CØMMØN} \; /n_1/s_1,s_2,s_3, \; \ldots \; ,s_n/n_2/s_j,s_k,s_l, \; \ldots \; ,s_m \; \ldots$$

where n_1 and n_2 represent the names of common data blocks and s represents a block number. Only subprograms sharing a labeled block with the main program can share data items in common.

For example, consider the following:

Main program: CØMMØN/SET1/X,Y,I,J/SET2/A,B,K,L
Subprogram 1: CØMMØN/SET1/D,E,M1,M2
Subprogram 2: CØMMØN/SET2/F,G,I5,I6

Subprogram 1 will share the block named SET1 with the main program, and Subprogram 2 will share block SET2 in similar fashion. However, the sharing of common items will be restricted to these two instances.

CØMMØN data blocks are assigned names in keeping with regular FORTRAN data names. The name must be preceded and followed by a single slash, as in the example above.

Blank and Labeled Specifications in the Same CØMMØN Statement. A single CØMMØN command can specify both blank and labeled items. Blank common is distinguished from its labeled counterpart by placing two consecutive slashes before the blank specification list or, if it appears first in the statement, by the absence of a label name. For example, in the command

$$\text{CØMMØN} \; \text{A,B,/LIST/I,J,K//C,D,E}$$

elements A, B, C, D, and E are in blank common, while I, J, K are members of the data block named LIST.

CHAPTER SUMMARY

These three programming modifications—the assignment statement function, the function subprogram, and the subroutine—are not essential to the creation of a FORTRAN program. However, they simplify programming in instances where a given computation or other operation must be repeated many times in a program, or where several persons are working on the same program. They broaden the programmer's capabilities beyond those supplied by the basic commands of the language.

The characteristics of each function and subprogram are summarized below.

Assignment Statement Function.   This is created in the main program by a single assignment-like statement of the following nature:

$$\text{Function-name(argument list)} = \text{Expression}$$

The function name may then be used in any assignment expression. A complex computation may be reduced to a single function name in this manner. Only one value, that of the function name, is derived from this command.

Function Subprogram.   This is written in a subprogram, which is identified by the following first statement:

$$\text{FUNCTI\O N function-name (argument list)}$$

The argument list serves as a communications channel with the main program, through which data values are transmitted from the main program to the subprogram. The function name identifies the variable and serves as a channel for sending the results of subprogram computation back to the main program. Some command in the subprogram must assign a value to the function name, and the value will be returned to the main program in the mode of the function name.

The subprogram is terminated by the RETURN command.

The function is called in the main program by inclusion of the function name and its arguments in an arithmetic or logical assignment expression. Values represented by the data names in the argument are transmitted to the subprogram, evaluated, and the result returned in the value assigned to the function name.

Subroutine Subprogram.   This is also created in a subprogram, and is identified by the following first statement:

$$\text{SUBR\O UTINE subroutine-name (argument list)}$$

The subroutine name serves only to identify the subroutine, not as a data channel. The variables listed as arguments accept data from the main program and return results from the subroutine to the main program. If no data or results are transmitted, the argument list is omitted.

The subroutine can execute any FORTRAN command, including writing. Therefore, results need not be returned to the calling program unless they are to be used in that program.

Like the external function, the subroutine is terminated by a RETURN command. Control is then returned to the main program, and the command following the calling instruction is next executed.

Subroutines are referenced in the main program by the special instruction

CALL subroutine-name(argument list)

in which "subroutine-name" must agree with the name assigned the subprogram in its initial statement.

The arguments in the CALL statement serve two purposes: they transmit data to the subroutine, and return results to the main program. A data name in the argument list may serve either or both purposes. Arguments may be either variables or constants.

QUESTIONS

1. What is a statement function? What is it used for?
2. In a statement such as X = FUNC(A,B,C)*Y what is FUNC? What are A, B, and C?
3. What is the argument of a statement function?
4. Must the argument names in the calling statement of a statement function be the same as those in the function statement? If not, how can they differ?
5. What is a subprogram?
6. What is the difference between a statement function and a function subprogram?
7. How is the function subprogram called?
8. How is the mode of the function subprogram indicated?
9. What is the argument list of a function subprogram? What is its relation with the calling statement?
10. How must arguments in the calling statement agree with those of the FUNCTIØN statement?
11. What is a dummy argument? How is it related to a real argument?
12. Where is the dummy argument used?
13. May variable array dimensions be used in subprograms? If so, how are actual dimensions indicated?
14. How is computer control transferred from a subprogram back to the main program?
15. When control is transferred from a subprogram back to the main program, to what statement does it return?
16. What is the difference between a function subprogram and a subroutine subprogram?

17. Must the subroutine return data values to the main program? If not, how are the results of its data manipulations made available?

18. How are subroutine results returned to the main program?

19. Can a subroutine return to more than one place in the main program? If so, how?

20. What is the function of the RETURN i instruction?

21. In the argument list (A,B,&5,&10,&15), what is the purpose of the last three members?

22. How are alternative entry points provided in function and subroutine subprograms?

23. In the statement EQUIVALENCE (A,X),(B,C) what is the relation between A and X? Between A and B?

24. What is the function of the CØMMØN statement?

25. What is the difference between blank and labeled CØMMØN?

EXERCISES

1. Create a statement function CØMP with arguments X, Y, and Z̄ to compute $X/Y + Z̄^2$. Then, reference this in an arithmetic statement by using it as the multiplier of A to compute Z̄. Arguments in the arithmetic statement should be named E, F, and G.

2. Create a statement function AREA with arguments A and B to compute A * B. Then, reference this in an arithmetic statement by dividing it into CØST to produce PSF, the cost per square foot. Arguments in the arithmetic statement should be named DIM1 and DIM2.

3. Create a statement function BUD with arguments A, B, and C to compute A * B + C. Then, reference this in an arithmetic statement subtracting it from ACT to produce VARY. Arguments in the arithmetic statement should be named SALE, FACT, and CØNST.

4. Write the main program and function subprogram for the following, assuming appropriate formats. Array values are to be read and stored in 6 X 8 matrix named X. Then, in a function subprogram called SUM, the elements in the array are to be summed and the sum returned to the main program where it is to be divided by 48 to produce AVG. This should be written in the main program.

5. Write the main program and function subprogram for the following, assuming appropriate formats. Elements of the 25-entry A array are to be read and stored. Then, in the SRCH function subprogram, the largest value is to be found. This is to be returned to the main program, where it is to be added to the values of the first and twenty-fifth elements, the sum divided by three, and written.

6. The following data items exist in a main and two subprograms:

> Main program: A,B,C,D,E
> Subprogram 1:   A,B,E,X,Y
> Subprogram 2:   A,B,D,X

Prepare a CØMMØN statement to properly define the relationship indicated above.

7. A subroutine subprogram name CAC is to provide three returns to the main program—one regular and two alternates to statements 201 and 301. Data elements A and B are to be transmitted to the subroutine, and X returned. Prepare the appropriate CALL and SUBRØUTINE statements for the main and subprograms.

8. In a main program, write instructions to read and store the 25 elements of the A array. Then, in a subroutine subprogram, sort the elements into descending order. The subroutine should be written to handle one-dimensional arrays of any size.

   After sorting, the elements should be returned to the main program and written. Assume appropriate formats.

9. Write the main program and subroutine subprogram for the following, assuming appropriate formats: Space for a matrix of dimension 10 X 5 is to be provided. It is to be called the A array. Then, the program is to read an array of this size or smaller, the actual dimensions being entered by a preceding parameter record containing N (the number of array rows) and M (the number of array columns).

   In a subroutine, the sums of each row's elements are to be calculated and stored in the X array. Further, the sums of each column's elements are to be calculated as the Y array. These arrays are to be returned to the main program and written out.

10. Write the main program and subroutine subprogram for the following, assuming appropriate formats: Two one-dimensional arrays called A and B are to be created, each designed to contain 25 elements. Then, 25 data records are to be read, each containing one element of A and B in that order, and these elements are to be stored in their respective arrays.

    In a subroutine, every A value is to be compared with every B value. Amounts which are identical are to be written out, with the related subscripts in the A and B arrays.

11. Write the main program and subroutine for the following: Assume that two dice are to be thrown, each containing the numbers 1 through 6 on its six sides. The probability of any side's landing up is ⅙.

    Simulate the throwing of the pair of dice 25 times. Use a random-number generator to simulate the throw of the dice. Test the result, and write it by selecting among six output statements, one which contains the message ØNE, another TWØ, etc.

PROBLEMS

1. In a set of 200 or fewer records, each record contains the following:

		FORTRAN	
Item Description		*Name*	*Field Size*
Transaction date		DATE	xxxxxx_∧
Customer number		CUST	xxxx_∧
Transaction cost		CØST	xxxₓx
Transaction revenue		REV	xxxₓx

   Records are to be read, and their contents stored as elements of the 200 × 4 SALE array. Then, in a subroutine, a generalized sort routine capable of placing items in either ascending or descending order is to be written. Using the subroutine, the three following reports are to be prepared:
   (1) Ascending order, sorted by customer number, listing customer number and transaction revenue.
   (2) Descending order, sorted by transaction revenue, listing transaction revenue and transaction cost.
   (3) Ascending order, sorted by date, listing date, customer number, and transaction revenue.
   Output is to be handled in the main program.

2. In a data set of 200 or fewer records, each record contains the following:

		FORTRAN	
Item Description		*Name*	*Field Size*
Transaction date		DATE	xxxxxx
Customer number		CUST	xxxx
Sales amount		AMT	xxxₓx

The first two items are integer data; the third, real. Data records are to be read, and their contents stored in corresponding positions of three one-dimensional arrays. Then, elements in the three arrays should be sorted by customer number, into ascending order. Next, they should be sorted into ascending sequence by transaction date. Data records should then be written, and the program terminated.
   Use a subroutine for sorting.

3. In a data set of 100 or fewer records, each record contains the following:

		FORTRAN	
Item Description		*Name*	*Field Size*
Inventory number		NØ	xxxx_∧
Sales volume, units		UNIT	xxxxx_∧
Sales volume, dollars		AMT	xxxxxₓx

The above data set is preceded by a parameter record containing PCT, format F2.2, which serves as a control value.

The data set is to be read, and its contents stored in a single 100 × 3 array. Then, in a subroutine, the following is to be performed:

(1) Records are to be sorted into descending order by sales volume units. The first PCT of records are to be written in detail, and the sales volume, both in units and in dollars, of all other items summed and written as ØTHER.

For example, if PCT is .10, the first 10% of the sorted file should be written in detail, and all other records aggregated as ØTHER.

(2) Records are to be sorted into descending order by sales volume, dollars. The first PCT of records are to be written in detail, and sales volume, both in units and dollars, of all other items summed and written as ØTHER.

4. The XYZ Company timed the arrival of customers during five-minute intervals and found the following:

Frequency of Occurrence	Number of Customers
5	0
10	1
18	2
25	3
16	4
9	5
6	6
5	7
2	8

Instructions: Simulate the arrival of customers over 250 five-minute intervals. Write out answers 10-to-a-line. Prepare a random-number generator as described in this chapter in a subroutine. Output should be written in the main program.

5. When a student enters the tuition payment queue of a large university, one of the following things happen:

Event	Percent of Occurrence
Completion satisfactory, payment accepted	80
Completion unsatisfactory, because	
Registration cards filled out wrong	5
Line closes for lunch	4
Wrong line	6
Not enough money	2
Other reasons	3

Instructions: Simulate the arrival and disposition of 100 students, indicating their manner of discharge from the queue with appropriate messages.

6. Tommy Smith is a freshman at a university located in the college town of Nonesuch. Before sending him away from home, his mother analyzed the weather conditions at Nonesuch and set out attire regulations accordingly. Her analysis and clothing rules were as follows:

Kind of Weather	% of Time	Proper Attire
Hot—dry	40	Regular
Hot—raining	30	Carry umbrella
Cold—dry	10	Wear topcoat
Cold—raining	20	Topcoat and umbrella

Each day's weather in Nonesuch is completely unrelated to that of the previous day. In other words, it is possible for one day to be cold and raining, the next, hot and dry. However, the portion of days is as the percentage column indicates.

Tommy frequently sleeps late, and so never looks outside to see what the weather on a particular day is like. Further, he is rather forgetful. Therefore, he attires himself, without regard to the weather, as follows:

Attire	% of Time
Regular	50
Umbrella	20
Topcoat	20
Topcoat and umbrella	10

Tommy's dress of one day is totally unrelated to that of any other day, occurring in a purely random sequence.

You are to write a program that will simulate Tommy's wearing habits and the weather for a 100-day period. For each day, you are to write a statement stating the weather conditions and date number, and another indicating what Tommy is wearing on this particular day. To do this, you should set up eight FØRMATS, one for each weather condition and dress. A sample follows:

1 FØRMAT(' HØT—DRY')

Weather conditions and attire should be written on the same line. Use a subroutine to create random numbers.

7. A program for simulating inventory activity is to be prepared, using a random-number generator written as a subroutine. In the situation description, the following notation is used:

$$I \quad = \text{inventory on hand, units}$$
$$P \quad = \text{stock on order, units}$$
$$R \quad = \text{reorder level, units}$$
$$Q \quad = \text{reorder quantity, units}$$
$$D \quad = \text{daily demand, units}$$
$$T_L \quad = \text{lead time, days}$$

The reorder system works as follows: An inventory clerk examines the stock on hand (I) and the stock on order (P) at the beginning of each day. If $I + P < R$ (the reorder level) he places an order for Q units which will be delivered T_L days later, at the end of the day. You may assume that Q is large enough, and T_L short enough so that at any one time not more than one order will be outstanding.

The daily demand, D, is a random variable. A tabulation has been made for the past 100 days:

D (In Units)	No. of Days that D Occurred
0	5
1	15
2	25
3	35
4	13
5	7

The lead time, T_L, is also a random variable, and a tabulation has been made for 25 times:

T_L (In Days)	No. of Times that T_L Occurred
3	7
4	10
5	8

Cost information: Inventory on hand at the beginning of each day costs $.08/unit storage cost for that day. If demand is unfulfilled on any day, a cost of $1/unit is charged for each unit demanded but not available. Unfulfilled demand is lost forever.

Write a program to find the optimum reorder level (R). Initial inventory is $I = 20$, $Q = 35$, and no reorder is outstanding. Prepare your own input and output. Simulate operations with reorder points of from 5 through 30 units for 30 days each.

8. This problem requires the simulation of customers' arrivals and departures from a multiunit service location. A random-number generator

should be created in a subroutine and must be called at several points in the program. Details of the situation are as follows:

Company X has three processing facilities, each capable of processing several service requests in any single time frame. The processing capacities of these facilities are shown below:

Facility 1:4 service requests per time frame
Facility 2:6 service requests per time frame
Facility 3:10 service requests per time frame

If a service request is received, it must be channeled to a facility if one is available. If more than one is available, the requests are to be assigned on a rotational basis—first to facility 1, then to 2, then to 3, etc.

If no facility is available, the request must be maintained in a queue, which can never contain more than 30 requests. The most recent request must occupy the lowest queue position.

When a facility becomes available, requests in the queue will be processed in the order of their arrival, before any new request may be processed. An analysis of activities (which may be either a service request or a service completion) for 50 time frames indicates the following:

No. of Activities per Time Frame	Frequency of Occurrence
0	3
8	3
15	4
20	5
30	7
35	8
45	10
50	10

Each day consists of 25 time frames. Service requests made on one day do not carry over to the next day.

Fractional division of activities among service requests and service completions varies during the day's time frames. The distribution is as follows:

	Service Request	Service Completion
First 5 time frames	70%	30%
Next 18 frames	50	50
Last 2 frames	40	60

Within this distribution, requests and completions occur randomly.

Instructions: The activities of 100 time frames (4 days) are to be simulated. If a service request is received, the "requestor" is to be identified by the assignment of a request number, assigned consecutively through the simulation. Should a service completion be noted, the completion is to be associated with a service facility randomly over the following scale:

.0000–.1999	Facility 1
.2000–.4999	Facility 2
.5000–.9999	Facility 3

If this would assign a completion to an empty facility, the message "no customers in facility" is to be written and the program should continue.

Other completions are to be recognized by printing the facility number and the requestor number appearing first in the facility. Then, other requestors being serviced in the facility are to be moved up, and the process continued. The number of customers waiting at each service facility and in the queue is to be written with appropriate caption after each day's simulation.

Index

This book has been set in 11 point and 10 point Times Roman, leaded 2 points. Chapter numbers are set in 30 point Univers Bold Extended, and chapter titles are set in 24 point Univers Medium Extended. The size of the type page is 27 by 45 picas.